American Trails Series
XXIII

West from Salt Lake

Diaries from the Central Overland Trail

Edited by
Jesse G. Petersen

THE ARTHUR H. CLARK COMPANY
An imprint of the University of Oklahoma Press
Norman, Oklahoma
2012

Library of Congress Cataloging-in-Publication Data
West from Salt Lake : diaries from the central overland trail / edited by Jesse G. Petersen.
p. cm. — (American trails series ; v. 23)
Includes bibliographical references and index.
ISBN 978-0-87062-407-0 (hardcover : alk. paper) 1. Overland Trails—History—Sources. 2. Pioneers—West (U.S.)—Diaries. 3. Overland journeys to the Pacific—Sources. 4. Frontier and pioneer life—West (U.S.)—History—Sources. 5. West (U.S.)—Description and travel. I. Petersen, Jesse G. II. Title. III. Series.

F593.W46 2012
978.'02—dc23

2011035729

West from Salt Lake: Diaries from the Central Overland Trail is Volume 23 in the American Trails Series.

The paper in this book meets the guidelines for permanence and durability of the Committee on Production Guidelines for Book Longevity of the Council on Library Resources, Inc. ∞

1 2 3 4 5 6 7 8 9 10

This work is dedicated to the memory of
Gregory M. Franzwa.

Contents

Maps

Preface

I FIRST MET JAMES O. HALL in late 2003, when I was about halfway through a ten-year research project relating to the opening of the Central Overland Trail by Capt. James Simpson. At that time, Jim was developing a website that featured historical information about the early history of the Tooele County area. He had learned that I had done research on the Lincoln Highway, and he wanted to know if I could verify some information that he intended to post on his website. We soon became good friends. As time went by, Jim became quite interested in my Simpson project, and one day he asked me what I had learned about the use of the central route by emigrants. I told him that I had not been looking for this type of information, but as far as I knew, the central route had not been used by emigrants. In retrospect, I believe that Jim took this as a challenge, and he began investigating this aspect of the route's history. During the next few years, he ferreted out a great deal of information that showed that the central route had in fact been used by a significant number of covered wagon emigrants. Before it was over, he had located and obtained copies of twenty-three diaries written by emigrants who had traveled the central trail.

Jim was deciding what to do with these diaries when he started experiencing some serious issues with his eyesight. On the advice of his doctors, he eventually decided that he could not do anything further with the material he had collected. By this time, I had completed my book, *A Route for the Overland Stage: Captain James H. Simpson's 1859 Trail across the Great Basin*, and had some time on my hands. Jim and I had a long discussion, and he handed all his information over to me with the understanding that I would attempt to do something about getting it published.

As I approached this project, I did so with a sense of great responsibility. First, because Jim had already done so much work in locating and obtaining the material, I felt an obligation to do something meaningful with it; and second, I regarded the material as important historical information that has gone largely unnoticed. Many books have been written about emigrants who traveled the Oregon and the California trails, and many have been written about the Overland Stage and the Pony Express. However, to the best of my knowledge, little, if any, information has been published about the emigrants that traveled the Central Overland Trail. This book is a step toward filling that gap.

Acknowledgments

THIS WORK WOULD not have been possible without the contributions of many individuals and historical institutions.

First and foremost, James O. Hall set about to determine whether a significant number of covered-wagon emigrants had traveled the Central Overland Trail, and subsequently located and obtained copies of nineteen out of the twenty-seven documents that appear in this work.

Historian and author Will Bagley encouraged me to continue working with the material that Jim Hall gave me when he learned he was not in a position to do anything further with it.

Historian and archivist Ronald O. Barney provided me with ideas and suggestions on how to go about editing the diaries.

Emigrant trails researcher Roy Tea and the indefatigable researcher of the Pony Express Trail Joe Nardone read the initial draft of this book, made corrections, and suggested ways to improve the editorial comments.

Kathy Franzwa helped me transcribe some of the handwritten material.

The following individuals either provided copies of documents or permission to publish, or both: Diane Cook, who provided a copy of a portion of the diary of Lumin Scott and permission to publish; Dr. Charles G. Hibbard, who provided a copy of a portion of the diary of Charles Scott that he had transcribed from microfilm at the Utah Historical Society; Joyce Holt, who posted the diary of Frederick William Hurst on her website (Joyce Holt's Ancestry Site, http://joyceholt.4t

.com); Paul Pennebaker, who posted the diary of William Gaines Pennebaker on his website http://webpages.charter.net/pepbaker/pennebkr.htm); Sue M. Pennebaker, who gave permission to publish the diary of William Gaines Pennebaker; Loadel Harter Piner, who gave permission to publish the diary of George Harter; Alene M. Thille, who provided a copy of the diary of James Colwell and permission to publish the diaries of Dennis and James Colwell; and George Waltenspiel, who gave permission to publish the diary of Delia Thompson Brown.

The following libraries and historical societies either provided copies or permission to publish, or both: Bancroft Library, which provided copies of the diaries of Lavina Porter, Mary Hall Jatta, and Mary Warner, and permission to publish, and which allowed Jim Hall to transcribe portions of the diary of Albert Jefferson Young; California State Library at Sacramento, which provided copies of the diaries of Mary Karchner, B.P. Lewis, and H.D. Barton, and permission to publish them, and copies of the diaries of George Harter and Lucretia Epperson; Columbia Gorge Genealogical Society provided a copy of the diary of Dennis and James Colwell; Library of Congress, which had posted the diary of Mary Ringo on its website (http://memory.loc.gov); Missouri Historical Society, which provided a copy of the diary of John G. Fackler and permission to publish; Nevada Historical Society, which provided copies of the diaries of Edward James Mathews, Delia Thompson Brown, and Flora Bender; Oregon-California Trails Association and the Merril J. Mates Research Library, which provided a copy of the diary of George Bushnell and permission to publish; State Historical Society of Iowa, which provided a copy of the diary of Wilson Fryberger and permission to publish; University of Kansas; Kenneth Spencer Research Library provided a copy of the diary of Elizabeth Duncan and permission to publish; Washington State Historical Society, which provided a copy of the diary of Phebe Carleton and permission to publish; Western Historical Manuscript Collection—Columbia, University of Missouri provided a copy of the diary of Martha Logan and permission to publish; and Wisconsin Historical Society, which provided a copy of the diary of Charles Tuttle and permission to publish.

If any of the individuals or institutions that have provided me with copies of the diaries or permission to publish them, or both, are missing from this list, that error is mine alone.

Introduction

The wagon road that historians sometimes refer to as the Central Overland Trail passed through Salt Lake City and California via what would become west-central Utah and central Nevada. The earliest documented travel by non-Indians into the corridor that would later become part of the Central Overland Trail took place in 1827, when Jedediah Smith, Robert Evans, and Silas Gobel traveled east from California to the fur trappers' and traders' rendezvous at Bear Lake. Smith and his companions crossed the Sierra Nevada through Ebbetts Pass, then followed a route across modern-day Nevada that approximates U.S. Highway 6. After entering what is now Utah, they turned north, then east, and made their way past the southern shore of the Great Salt Lake.[1]

The next recorded journey through this area was led by Joseph R. Walker, who in 1833 traveled westward with a group of mountain men along the Humboldt River as far as the river's sink, then turned south to cut across the western edge of central Nevada.[2] A small group known as the Bidwell-Bartleson party, generally considered the first overland emigrants to California, traveled a similar route in 1841.[3]

[1]Dale L. Morgan, *Jedediah Smith and the Opening of the West* (Lincoln: University of Nebraska Press, 1953), 210–214; Jedediah Smith, *The Southwest Expedition of Jedediah Smith: His Personal Account of the Journey to California, 1826–1827*, ed. and with an introduction by George R. Brooks (Lincoln: University of Nebraska Press, 1989), 182–194.

[2]Bil Gilbert, *Westering Man, the Life of Joseph Walker* (Norman: University of Oklahoma Press, 1985), 127–133.

[3]Doyce B. Nunis, Jr., *The Bidwell-Bartleson Party: 1841 California Emigrant Adventure* (Santa Cruz: Western Tanager Press, 1991), 70, 88–90.

In 1845, John Charles Frémont and a party of about sixty men were on their way to California with the intention of following the Humboldt River. When they reached Mound Springs, about forty miles west of Wendover, the party split up. Frémont and a group of ten men turned south and crossed the central corridor while traveling through Ruby Valley.[4]

In 1846, Lansford Hastings led the first of several emigrant parties along what would become known as the Hastings Road. This route went west from Salt Lake City, staying north of the central corridor until it reached the southern part of Ruby Valley. While going around the southern end of the Ruby Mountains, the Hastings Road followed an eight-mile section of the route that was later used by the Central Overland Trail. Once past these mountains, the Hastings Road turned north, leaving the central corridor. The Donner-Reed party followed this route a few weeks after Hastings, and a number of travelers used the road during the California gold rush years of 1849 and 1850.[5]

In 1854, Capt. E. G. Beckwith led a small railroad surveying expedition across west-central Utah and into central Nevada, for the most part paralleling a few miles to the north of what would later be the Central Overland Trail. In Ruby Valley, he joined the Hastings Road, then left it after reaching the western base of the Ruby Mountains. From that point, Beckwith veered northwest and left the central corridor.[6] Also in 1854, Colonel Edward Steptoe of the U.S. Army and a force of about three hundred men spent some time in the Salt Lake City area. Knowing that he would soon be marching to California, he hired Oliver B. Huntington to find a route shorter than the Salt Lake Cutoff–Humboldt River route. Huntington took a party of about six men and traveled west, primarily following Beckwith's route to the Humboldt River, then turned southwest to the settlement of Genoa, located at the eastern base of the Sierra Nevada. Steptoe decided not

[4]Ferol Egan, *Frémont, Explorer for a Restless Nation* (Reno: University of Nevada Press, 1985), 302.

[5]Dale L. Morgan, *Overland in 1846: Diaries and Letters of the California-Oregon Trail* (Lincoln: University of Nebraska Press, 1993), 437–439.

[6]James H. Simpson, *Report of Explorations across the Great Basin in 1859* (Reno: University of Nevada Press, 1983), 24.

to use Huntington's route and instead marched his men to California along the Humboldt River route.[7]

During the late 1840s and '50s, Howard Egan, a well-known Mormon frontiersman, made several trips through the central area, including a celebrated ten-day mule ride between Salt Lake City and Sacramento. Although Egan's exact route during this challenging ride remains somewhat uncertain, he probably followed what later became the Central Overland Trail between the Deep Creek Mountains in Utah and the Ruby Mountains in central Nevada. Other than this trip, his travels prior to 1858 took him some distance to the north of the central corridor.[8]

None of these explorations resulted in the establishment of a wagon road that could be used by the army, commercial freighters, or California-bound emigrants. Until 1859, travelers wanting to travel west from Salt Lake City had to choose between two roundabout routes. After the settlement of Salt Lake City in 1847, the most-used route was the Salt Lake Cutoff, which went north to southern Idaho where it joined the California Trail near City of Rocks. The California Trail was also known as the Humboldt route because it followed the Humboldt River across most of what is now the state of Nevada. In 1849, a southern route to California was developed that went south from Salt Lake City and followed the so-called Mormon Corridor down the length of the territory and then joined the Old Spanish Trail near Cedar City. This route terminated at Los Angeles and was primarily used by people traveling late in the season, when the trails crossing the Sierra Nevada were closed because of deep snow. Thus, for roughly a decade, there existed a northern route and a southern route between Salt Lake City and California, both of which were much longer than a central route would have been.

The Origin of the Central Overland Trail

In 1857, President James Buchanan responded to reports of a purported insurrection by sending a military expedition to the Utah territory. In

[7] Simpson, *Report of Explorations*, 24–25.

[8] Howard R. Egan, *Pioneering the West* (Salt Lake City: Skelton Publishing Company, 1917), 193–197.

the summer of 1858, the expedition, under the command of Brig. Gen. Albert Sidney Johnston, reached Salt Lake City. Johnston established his military headquarters at Camp Floyd in Cedar Valley, about forty miles southwest of Salt Lake City. He soon decided that to obtain supplies and possibly reinforcements from California, it would be advantageous to develop a shorter wagon route between Camp Floyd and Sacramento and the San Francisco Bay area. At that time, the only existing wagon route to California went back to Salt Lake City, then north along the Salt Lake Cutoff, then down the Humboldt River, on to the settlement of Genoa at the eastern foot of the Sierra Nevada, and then across the Sierras to Sacramento. According to Johnston's best information, the distance along this route was about 800 miles. On the other hand, he calculated that a route heading west from Camp Floyd to Genoa would be only about 500 miles. He wanted such a route found, and he assigned Capt. James Simpson to do it.[9]

Simpson took his first step in this project in October 1858, when he led a group of thirty-eight men with six army-style freight wagons into Utah's west desert on a reconnaissance mission. It was his and Johnston's understanding that this section would be the most difficult of the proposed route, and they wanted to get a look at it before the main expedition got started. They traveled about eighty miles into the desert when the approaching winter forced them to turn around at Dugway Mountain.[10] Simpson's report to Johnston indicated that he had located a practical route through the first part of the desert. Johnston instructed him to request the War Department's approval for a full-scale exploratory expedition that would go all the way to Genoa.

At about this same time, a businessman by the name of George Chorpenning got into the act. Chorpenning had a contract with the U.S. Post Office to carry the mail between Salt Lake City and Sacramento. Because he had started out using pack mules, his operation was sometimes referred to as the Jackass Mail. Chorpenning had been using the Salt Lake Cutoff–Humboldt River route most of the

[9]Simpson, *Report of Explorations*, 26, 94.

[10]James H. Simpson, *Wagon Road Routes in Utah Territory*, Senate Executive Document No. 40, 35th Congress, 2nd Session (1859).

time, but during winter had been forced to take a more southern route using the Mormon Corridor and the Old Spanish Trail. He too was vitally interested in a central route. As soon as Simpson had returned from his successful reconnaissance trip, General Johnston contacted Chorpenning, suggesting that he take a look at the route that Simpson had located. Chorpenning did so, liked what he saw, and decided to see if this route could be taken further west. Within two months, Chorpenning and his employees had opened a new trail and shifted their operations. The route that Chorpenning discovered continued west from the Dugway Mountains to the southern end of the Ruby Mountains, then turned northwest and struck the Humboldt River at Gravelly Ford. This change resulted in a route that was only about twenty miles shorter, but eliminated the Goose Creek section of the California Trail that had caused Chorpenning a great deal of trouble during the winter months.[11]

In May 1859, Captain Simpson was ready to begin his military expedition. Unlike the reconnaissance of the previous fall, this was to be a major undertaking. Leaving Camp Floyd with sixty-four people and fourteen wagons, he headed west along the route he had followed the previous fall to Dugway Mountain. He began to follow the route the Chorpenning mail company had opened between there and the southern end of the Ruby Mountains, where the Chorpenning route turned northwest. From that point, the Simpson expedition headed southwest across essentially unexplored territory. After crossing the Diamond Mountains, Simpson and his men followed a generally westward route until they struck Carson Lake, where they turned south to the Walker River at present-day Weber Reservoir. The expedition followed the Walker River to its big bend at the north end of Mason Valley, and then left it and turned north until the men struck the Carson River near the future site of Fort Churchill. Turning west once again, they followed the Carson River to Genoa.

This westward journey is generally referred to as Simpson's outbound

---

[11]Simpson, *Wagon Road Routes*, 35; John M. Townley, "Stalking Horse for the Pony Express, the Chorpenning Mail Contracts Between California and Utah, 1851–1860," *Arizona and the West* (1982), 224–246.

route. Except for the westbound trail across the Desatoya Mountains and the diversion along the Walker River, it is the route that developed into the Central Overland Trail. During the expedition's return to Camp Floyd, the soldiers retraced their steps along the outbound trail until they reached the Desatoya Mountains, where they found a better route through this mountain range. This section of their return route was later adopted as a part of the Central Overland Trail. Rejoining their outbound route on the east side of the mountains, they followed it for another seventy miles before leaving it for a route that led well south of the outbound route for the remainder of the journey. This route is referred to as the return route and saw only a small amount of subsequent use. The editor has found only three diaries written by emigrants who used the return route. Charles Tuttle, Lumin Scott, and Edward Mathews came through Camp Floyd within days of Simpson's return, and it appears that Simpson, who was promoting the return route over the outbound route, influenced their choice.

How Many Emigrants?

One of the major objectives of this work is to document the fact that the Central Overland Trail was used by more emigrants than has commonly been realized. As mentioned previously, when the editor first began researching the Simpson expedition, it was his impression that this trail was never used by covered wagon emigrants. Thanks to the diaries that Jim Hall located and a few other documents the editor found, we now know that the central route was used by a significant number of emigrants. Just how many will never be known, but a few of these diaries suggest that the number was substantial.

Delia Brown wrote about seeing other emigrants along the route:

> July 22, 1860 "Here we are at the foot of a mountain in plain sight of the Salt Lake. We only came about five miles yesterday morning and camped here where is a large company. I believe there are 46 wagons here and I don't know how many horses or persons either"
>
> July 26, 1860 "There were 3 or 4 companies camped here last night"

Mary Warner:

JUNE 11, 1864 ". . . when we came to the place where we were to camp. Found four companys allready there."

Lucretia Epperson:

JULY 6, 1864 "Had plenty of company . . . quite a number had camped here upward of one week, in order to let the stock rest."

JULY 18, 1864 There are a great many camped in the valley."

JULY 21, 1864 "Thirty wagons near by, and enough of crying children to disturb a camp meeting."

Flora Bender:

JULY 10, 1863 "A number of trains have come in and all are in good spirits."

JULY 16, 1863 "There are eight trains here, among them the Beloit, also a large freight train from Salt Lake."

Martha Logan:

AUGUST 19, 1864 "Here in a canyon, such a pretty place. The mountains so high—there are a great many campers here."

AUGUST 23, 1864 "Camped in a Canyon where there are a good many others.

AUGUST 24, 1864 "A great many in camp at this place."

Route Variations

At several points along the Central Overland Trail, our diarists had to choose between alternate routes for relatively short distances. The first choice came at the very beginning. Upon leaving Salt Lake City, emigrants who intended to follow the Central Overland Trail could go south and turn west to Camp Floyd, which during the years 1858–61 was the headquarters of the U.S. army in Utah Territory. Or they could head west to the southeast shore of the Great Salt Lake and turn south through the town of Tooele. (See map 2.) The Overland Stage had originally used the Camp Floyd route, but changed its route in 1866 after the army abandoned that camp. These two routes rejoined at Faust Station in Rush Valley. Over the years, nine of the emigrants whose diaries appear in this book took the Camp Floyd route, and fifteen the Tooele route. The first to go through Tooele was Delia Brown in July 1860. After that, only three diarists chose to take the Camp Floyd route. John Fackler took neither, deciding instead to take the Salt Lake Cutoff–Humboldt River route. His diary is included in this collection because he eventually got onto the central route at Austin in central Nevada.

When they reached Skull Valley, the first three of the emigrants whose diaries appear in this collection (Charles Tuttle, Lumin Scott, and Edward Mathews) left Simpson's outbound trail and turned south to get onto his return trail. Although these three diaries are the only accounts of emigrants on this trail that the editor is aware of, they were not the only emigrants to follow that route. Another was Bolivar Roberts, whose letter to the *Deseret News* is included in this collection. Roberts indicated that he had encountered a number of emigrants on Simpson's return trail.

A few miles farther to the west, early travelers encountered another variation in the trail. (See map 3.) Simpson, Chorpenning, and all other travelers until late 1862 followed what became the stage route around the northern end of the Simpson Mountains to Simpson Springs. Among these travelers were Lavina Porter, Frederick Hurst, Delia Brown, Mary Karchner, and Albert Young. In October 1862, soldiers under the command of Colonel Patrick Connor were making their way from California to Salt Lake City. Somehow they knew about the existence of Indian Spring, located in the Simpson Mountains about five miles southeast of Simpson Springs. The soldiers camped there for a few days, and Connor had them construct a new road that went directly east into Skull Valley. This new road bypassed Simpson Springs, making it possible for emigrants to go past Government Spring and then over the mountain to Indian Spring. Among those who followed this new route were diarists B. P. Lewis, Flora Bender, George Harter, Mary Warner, Phebe Carleton, Wilson Fryberger, George Bushnell, Martha Logan, Mary Ringo, H. D. Barton, Dennis and James Colwell, Elizabeth Duncan, and Mary Jatta. After resting their stock at Indian Spring for one or two days, these emigrants rejoined the main route about five miles west of Simpson Springs.

West of Fish Springs at a place called Boyds Station, emigrants faced another choice. (See map 4.) When Chorpenning and Simpson came this way, they continued in a southwest direction, circling around the southern end of the Deep Creek Mountains. One of our diarists, Lavina Porter, came past this spot fairly early in the traveling season in 1859 and followed the Chorpenning-Simpson route to Pleasant Valley. In September 1859, the Chorpenning mail company decided to change its route through this area. Turning northwest from Boyds Station, the new route went through present-day Callao, around the north end of the Deep Creek Mountains, and rejoined the older road near the southern end of the Antelope Mountains in Nevada.

The next decision point was at Antelope Spring at the eastern base of the Antelope Mountains. (See map 4.) From here, the stage road turned south around the southern end of the mountain, then back north until it reached the mouth of Stage Canyon, where it turned west again. Phebe Carleton, Wilson Fryberger, and Martha Logan followed this route. The other choice was to head west from Antelope Spring on a road that went directly into the mountains and followed a series of canyons that took them over the ridge. This route was very steep in some places, but it was about three and a half miles shorter than the stage road, and there was a good spring with plenty of grass near the summit. Eight of our diarists took this route.

Lavina Porter left the Central Overland Trail somewhere west of Diamond Springs and found a way to the Humboldt River.

When the emigrants reached Dry Creek near the center of Nevada, they could choose between the stage route that went south and then circled back to the north past the Cape Horn stage station and then went on to Simpson Park Canyon, or they could take the old Pony Express route that went almost due west past Eagle Butte. (See map 5.) The Eagle Butte route was about seven miles shorter, but much steeper in places. Diarists Dennis and James Colwell, and William Pennebaker took the Cape Horn route. All the others went past Eagle Butte.

From Salt Lake City, John Fackler and the small party he was traveling with followed the Salt Lake Cutoff and the Humboldt River route to the area of Battle Mountain, where they left that trail and followed the Reese River to Austin, where they joined the Central Overland Trail.

Just west of Austin, three of the diarists left the Central Overland Trail. George Harter headed north along the Reese River and eventually got onto the Humboldt River route. George Bushnell and H. D. Barton went south for some distance, and then turned west until they reached the Walker River not far from Walker Lake. Bushnell then turned north and rejoined the Central Overland Trail near Fort Churchill. Barton continued west.

Heading west from Austin, the earliest version of the Central Overland Trail followed Simpson's return route across Smith Creek Valley, up Smith Creek Canyon, and down Edwards Creek Canyon. (See map 6.) In 1862, a new route was opened that went past Mount Airy, across New Pass Summit, and then rejoined the old route just north of Cold Springs. The parties of Martha Logan and William Pennebaker chose this route. Even though the Overland Stage had made this switch and the later route appears to have been much easier, diarists Colwell, Duncan, and Jatta followed the earlier route.

At Sand Springs, the emigrants could chose between three routes. (See map 7.) The first followed the Simpson expedition's outbound trail to the northern shore of Carson Lake. Pvt. Charles Scott, Karchner, Young, Carleton, Epperson, Pennebaker, and Jatta took this route. The second option was to follow the expedition's return route, which crossed Four-Mile Flat, turned north at Rock Springs, then turned west to cross the northern end of the Bunejug ridge. Lumin Scott and Mathews followed this trail. The third possibility was to follow the stage road across Simpson Pass and around the southern side of Carson Lake. Brown, Lewis, Bender, Fackler, and Logan followed this route.

Those who came over Simpson Pass had to make a decision when they reached the Carson Sink stage station. From here, they could head west, following Simpson's return trail through the Dead Camel Mountains, or go north along the western side of Carson Lake and reach the Carson River near Ragtown. Lumin Scott, Brown, Lewis, Carleton, and Logan chose the mountain road. Mathews, Pvt. Charles Scott, Bender, and Fackler went to Ragtown.

Finally, the Central Overland Trail travelers who had made their way past Ragtown would have to choose between following the Carson River to Dayton or crossing the Twenty-Six Mile Desert. (See map 9.) The river route was about four miles longer, but its advantages were a dependable supply of water and grass and the fact that it went past Fort Churchill, where some supplies would be available. Of the ten diarists who went through Ragtown, three followed the river, and seven chose to cross the desert.

Writers' Gender

Our collection of diaries includes nineteen diaries written by male emigrants and nine written by females. The editor's opinion is that the women's diaries are the most interesting. At least three of the female diarists were pregnant during their journey. Lavina Porter and Lucretia Epperson delivered their babies after reaching California. Mary Ringo's child was stillborn when she reached Austin.

Encounters with Indians

There does not seem to be anything unique about the Central Overland Trail emigrant's experiences with American Indians. There is probably not enough information to determine whether their encounters with Indians were better or worse than what emigrants on other wagon routes experienced. However, the experiences of the diarists in this collection are quite interesting.

Pvt. Charles Scott was the only diarist who became involved in any sort of hostile action with the Natives. Out of the twenty-four diaries written by emigrants, six did not mention any encounters with Indians. Of course, this does not mean that they did not see any Indians; it just means that if they did, they did not consider the circumstances significant enough to mention. The eighteen diarists who did write about Indians mentioned fifty-two encounters. Of those incidents, eighteen were described as friendly or beneficial, while twelve were either unpleasant or hostile, including five incidents of horse theft. Twenty-two of the incidents can be considered neutral.

Delia Brown, who made the trip in 1860, just a year after the trail had been opened, wrote the most about Indians, but most of the time she was anticipating troubles that never materialized. It appears that the fear of Indian troubles was a major factor in her party's decision to take the Central Overland Trail. While they were laying over in Salt Lake City, someone convinced them that there was a greater risk of Indian trouble along the Humboldt River route than on the central route. In spite of all her fears, her party had only one dangerous encounter. On July 30, 1860, while they were camped at Indian Spring, a few Indians attempted to run off some horses. When the emigrants gave chase, the Indians took several shots at them, but missed. All but two of the horses were recovered.

In August 1862, when Mary Karchner's party reached Sand Springs, they became so worried about possible Indian troubles that they sent a man back to Middlegate to send a telegram to the army, presumably at Fort Churchill, requesting an escort through the Carson Lake area. As it turned out, no troops ever showed up, and Karchner's party had no problems with Indians.

Mary Warner, who made the trip in 1864, was the only one of our Central Overland Trail diarists to comment on her philosophy of the proper relationship with the Indians: "So far we have treated them well and they have us which I think the true way to get along with them."

Probably the most gruesome incident experienced by any of the diarists occurred on June 24, 1863, when B. P. Lewis was traveling between Government Spring and Indian Spring and passed the bodies of five Indians who had been killed and left where they had fallen several days before by U.S. soldiers. Two weeks later, on July 5, 1863, Flora Bender's party had stopped for noon somewhere near Point Lookout when a soldier showed them what Flora described as "an Indian's scalp what had been taken two weeks before." The soldier then related how he had gotten the scalp. Flora recorded the incident thus: "A number of soldiers were out on a hunting expedition. During the night ten Indians visited their camp. They were soon surrounded by the soldiers and guarded. When day broke, they were all killed but one squaw. They took her prisoner. She was kept a few days and then shot."

Diary Entry Dates

The writers of these diaries used various methods for indicating the dates of their entries. Some dates are very clear and easy to understand, but others are not. Most of the diarists failed to indicate the month, except perhaps on the first day of the month. Many included the day of the week, sometimes failing to include the day of the month. To avoid confusion, the editor has substituted a standard method for the writers' methods. All substituted dates include the month, the day, and the year.

Order, Footnotes, and Brackets

The diaries in this collection appear in chronological order, beginning with Lt. J. L. Kirby Smith's report of his trail improvement detail, which was written in August 1859, and ending with the diary of Mary Jatta, who made the overland journey in 1868. Whenever the earliest of our travelers comes to a point on the trail that requires or deserves some additional description and expansion, this information has been footnoted. When the diaries of subsequent travelers arrive at this same point, the reader will be referred to the first footnote, i.e., "See ch. 10, n1."

The editor of this book worked mostly from typewritten transcriptions of the diaries, but in several cases had copies of the original handwritten pages. In all cases, every attempt was made to copy the material exactly as it appeared. Misspellings and punctuation were left as they were. When necessary, brackets were used to indicate the proper spelling of place names and to insert proper spellings and missing words for clarity. All words within brackets were inserted by the editor. All parentheses and the words and phrases within them were put there by the writer of the diary or, possibly by whoever transcribed the original handwritten document. In cases in which the editor found the handwritten words illegible, ellipses (. . .) have been substituted.

There is something unique to be found in every emigrant diary, but in a general way there seems to be very little difference between the experiences of those who traveled the Central Overland Trail and those who followed any of the other emigrant trails. Aside from the differences of landscape and geography, the day-to-day living conditions were essentially the same.

Surprisingly, only two of the emigrant diaries included any sort of explanation about why they chose to follow the central route rather than the older, more established Humboldt River route. Delia Brown included a short sentence that indicated that her party had been told about Indian troubles on the California Trail. Charles Tuttle stated that he had heard that the central route was shorter by about 250 miles. Although the other emigrants left their reasons unstated, it is probably safe to assume that either the distance factor or the concern about Indians, or a combination of both, played a part in the choice of routes. One thing that we can be certain of is that those who followed the Central Overland Trail were people who were willing to take the road less traveled.

Maps

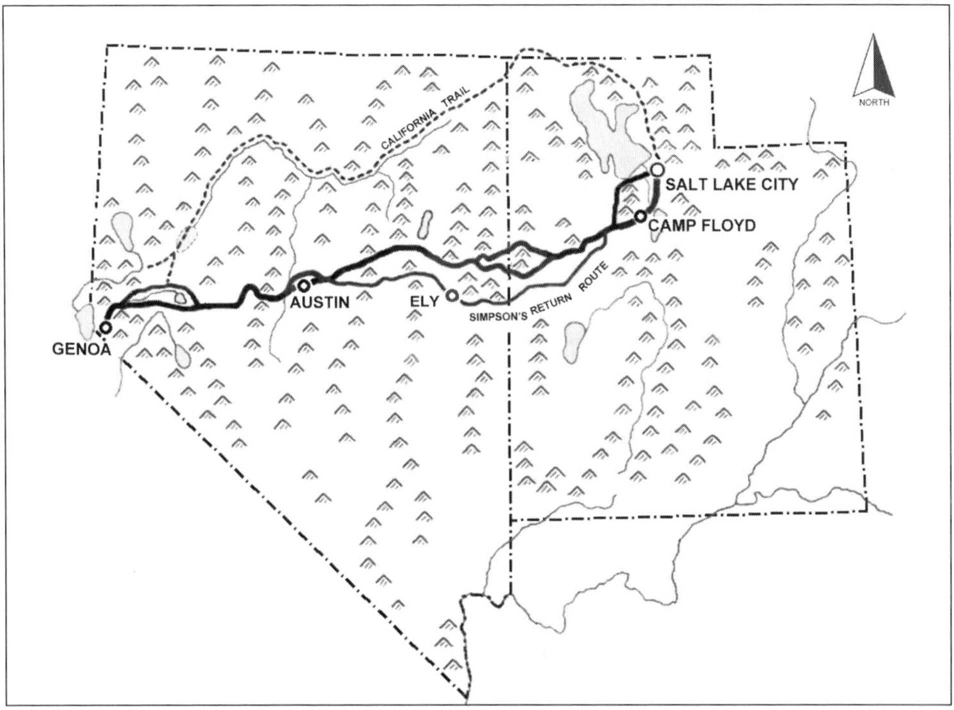

Map 1. The Central Overland Trail in Utah and Nevada

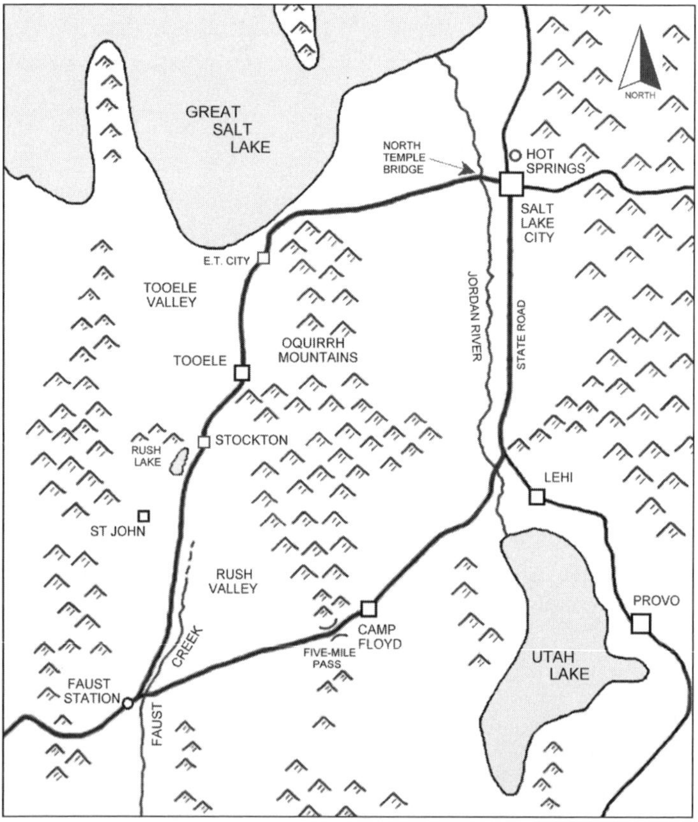

Map 2. Salt Lake City to Faust Station

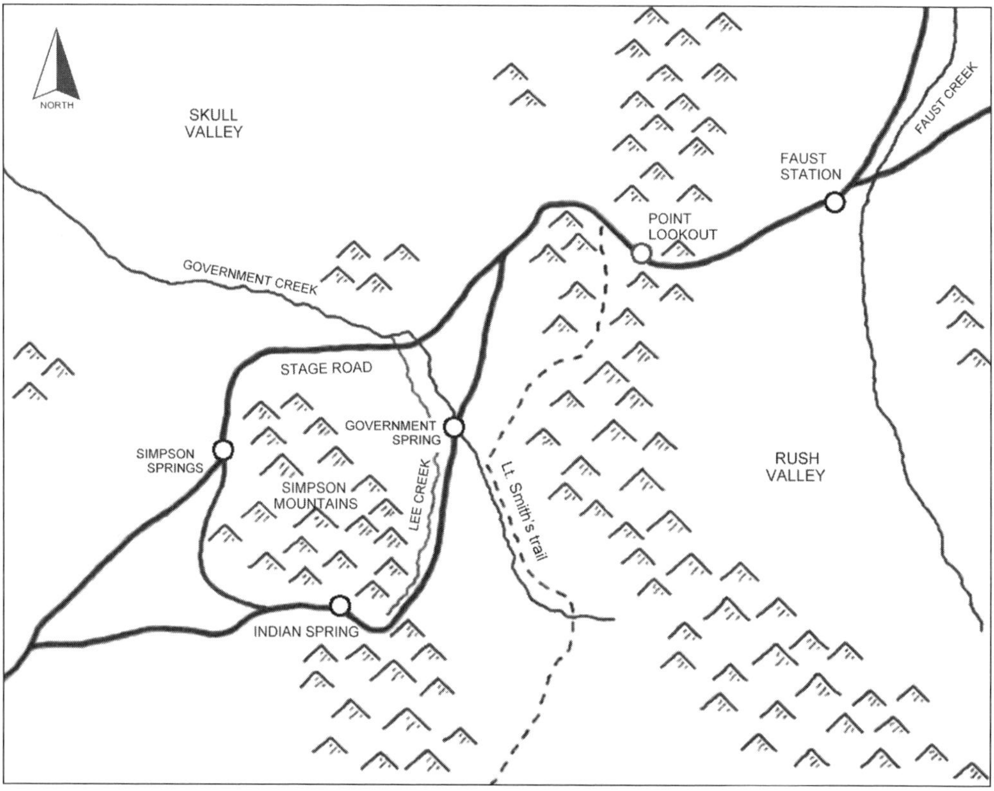

Map 3. Faust Station to Simpson Springs

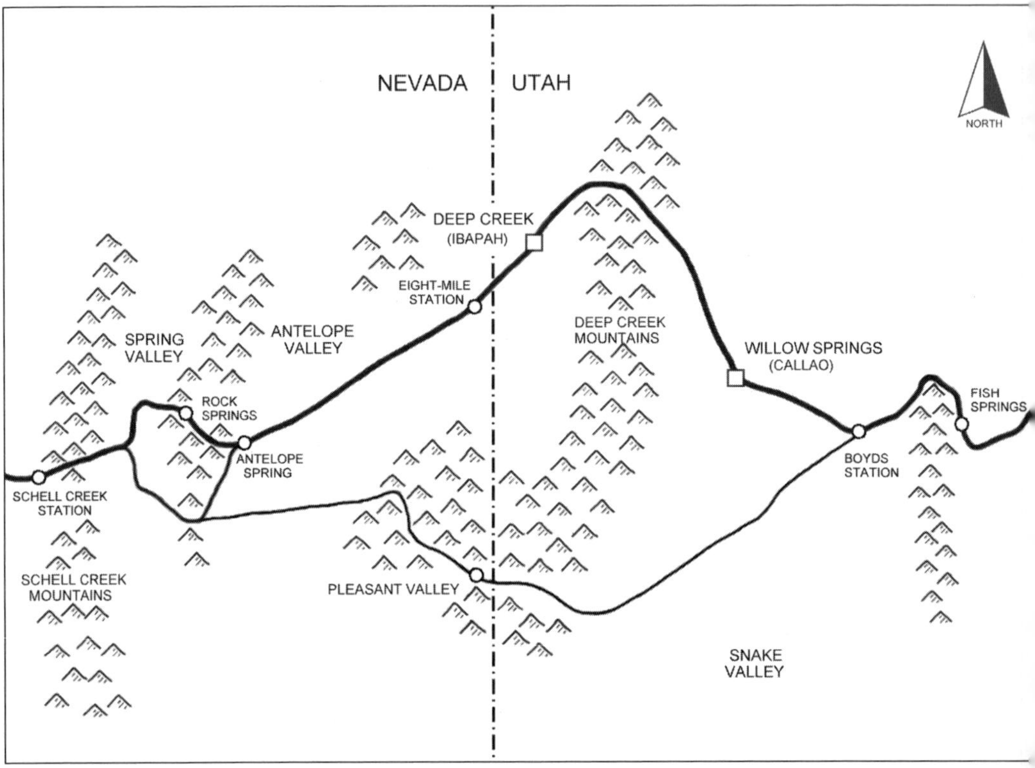

Map 4. Fish Springs to Schellbourne

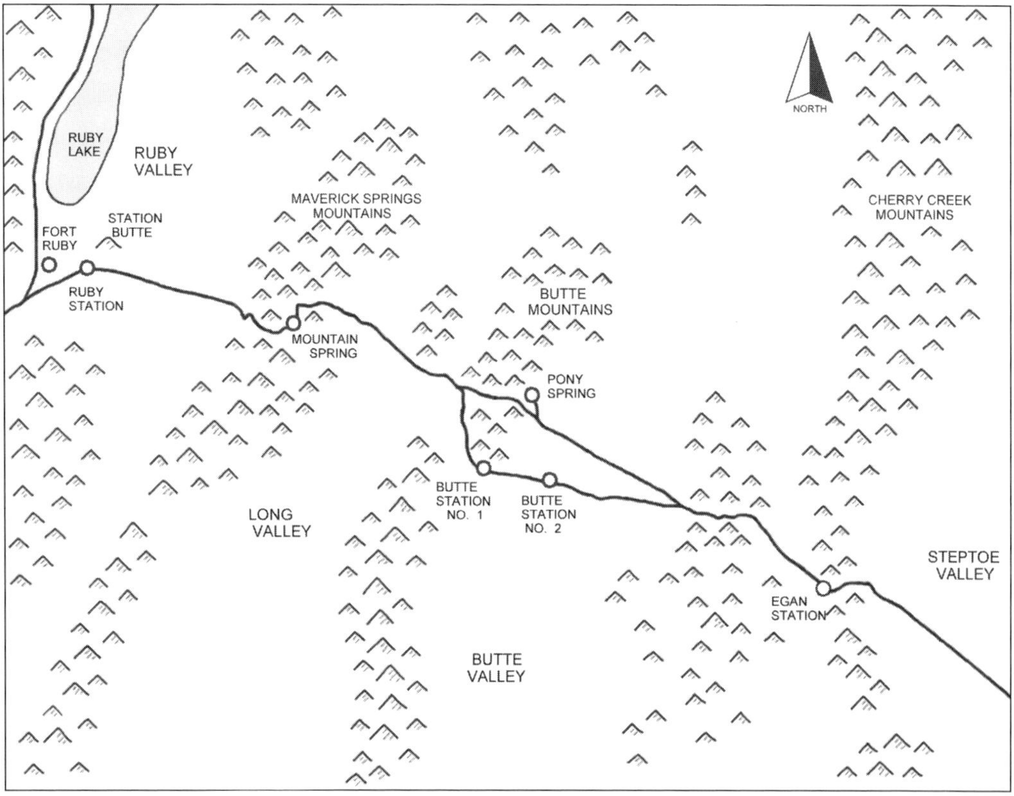

Map 5. Steptoe Valley to Ruby Valley

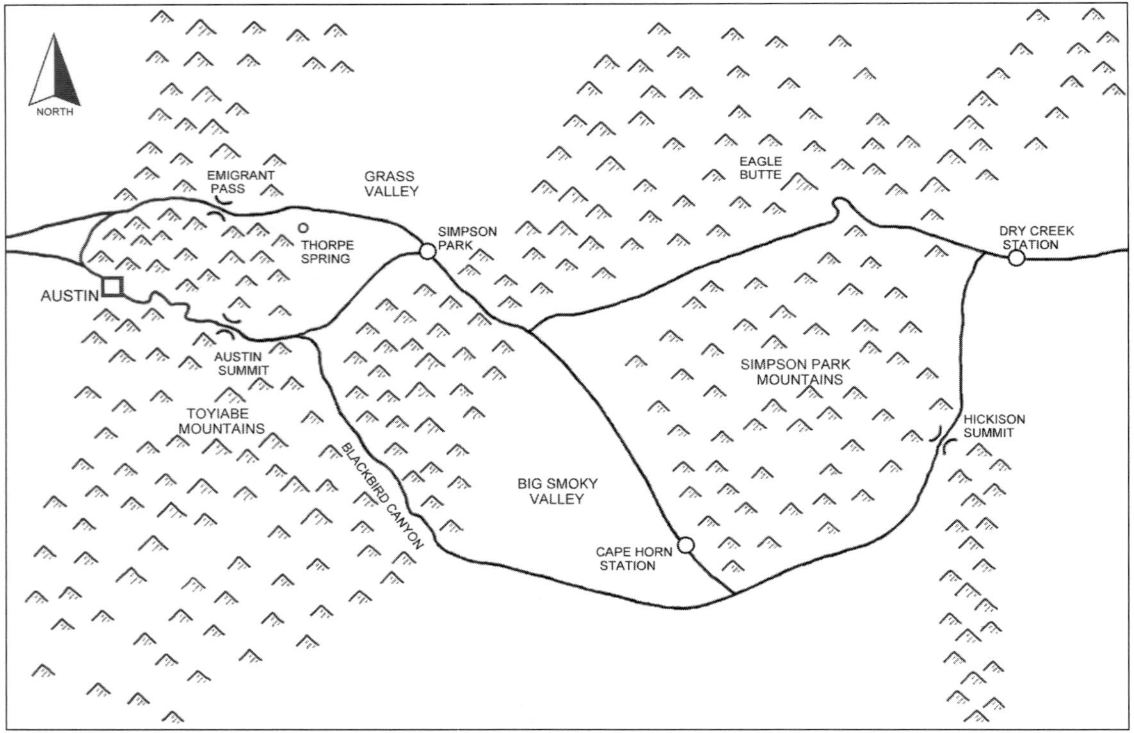

Map 6. Dry Creek to Austin

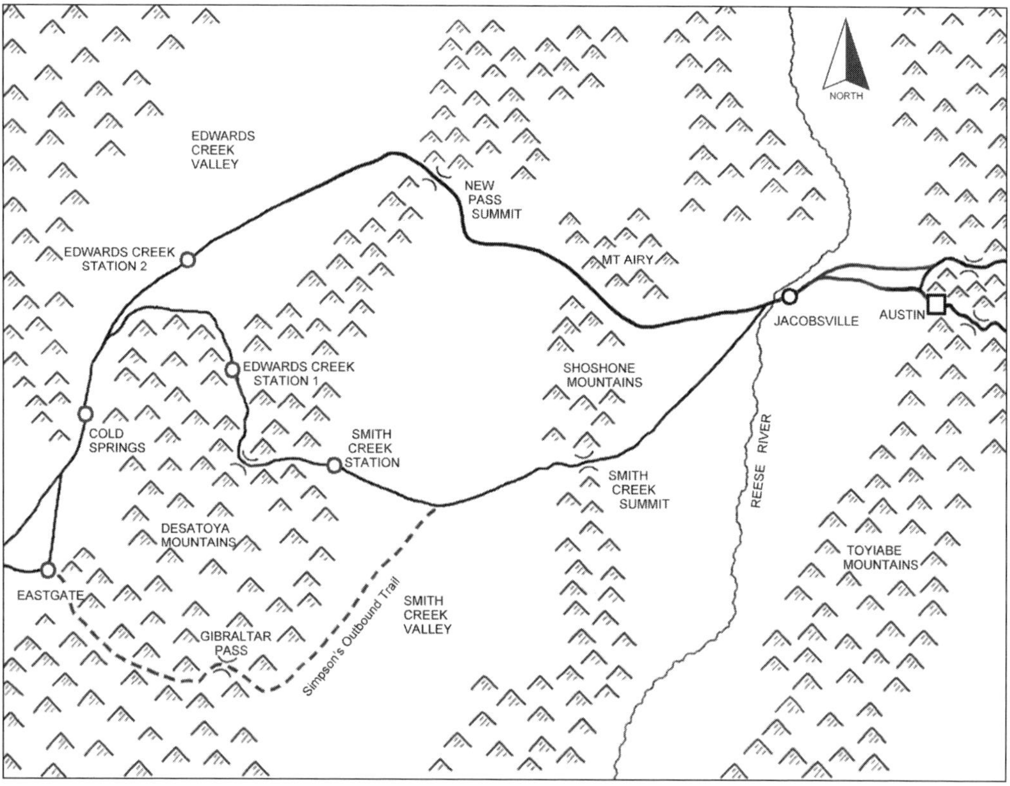

Map 7. Austin to Eastgate

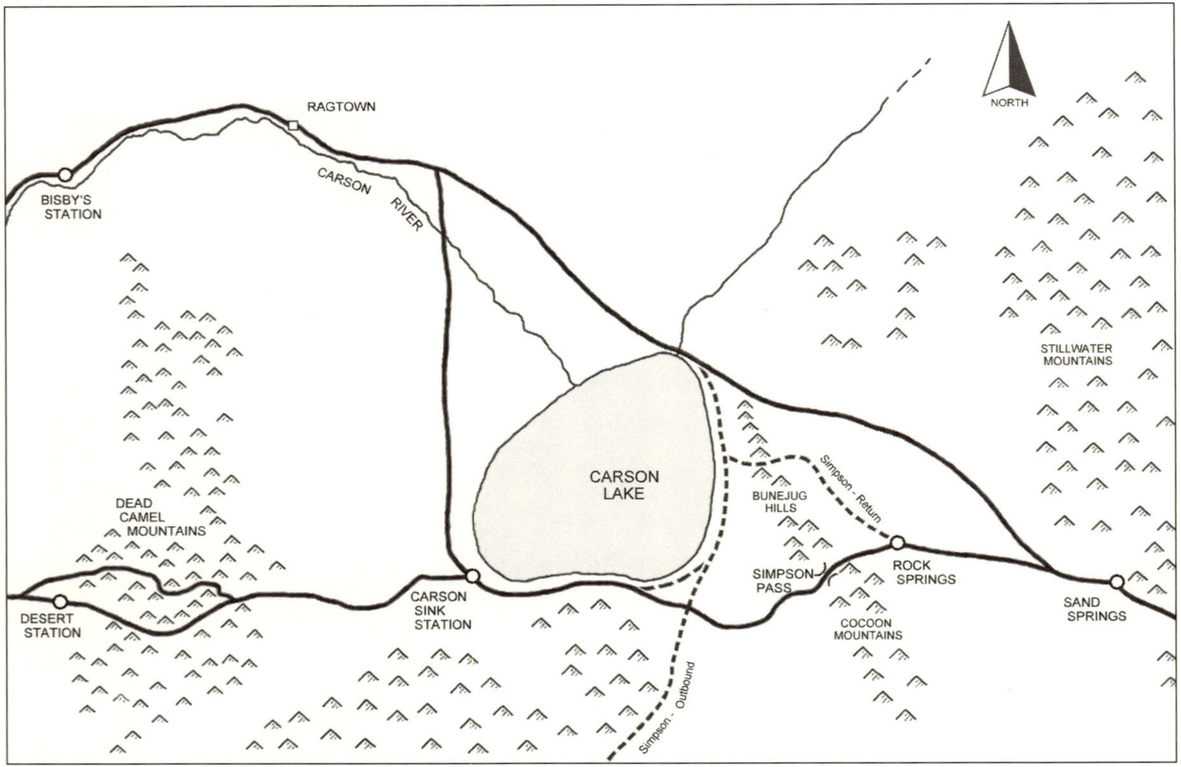

Map 8. Sand Springs to Ragtown

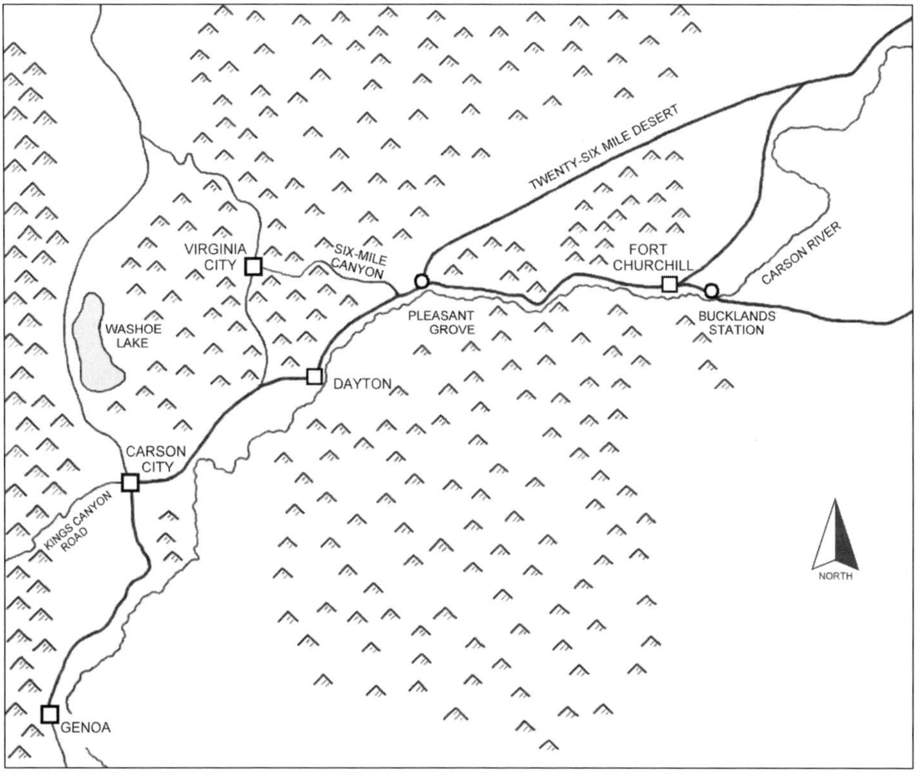

Map 9. Fort Churchill to Genoa

CHAPTER 1

Lt. J. L. Kirby Smith

1859

IMMEDIATELY FOLLOWING the return of Capt. James Simpson's expedition to California, Simpson sent Lt. J. L. Kirby Smith, along with a small work detail, back along the last one hundred miles of the return route with orders to improve several springs and find shortcuts. Simpson and Gen. Albert Sidney Johnston fully anticipated that emigrants would soon be using this new route. Upon completing this assignment, Lieutenant Smith sent a report to Simpson, who was already en route to Fort Leavenworth. Smith's document was included in the report that Simpson later prepared for the United States Congress. Although Smith's report is not an emigrant diary, it is included in this collection because it describes several parties of emigrants who were traveling on the southern variant of the Central Overland Trail.

Smith's report is found in James Hervey Simpson, Report of Explorations across the Great Basin in 1859 *(Reno: University of Nevada Press, 1983), 142–143.*

Captain:

I have the honor to submit the following report of the fulfillment of your instructions to me, dated Camp Floyd, Utah territory, August

5, 1859, a copy of which is herewith inclosed. In obedience to those instructions I left Camp Floyd on the 6th instant, reaching Meadow Creek,[1] in Rush Valley, the same evening. I was provided with four large troughs, destined to collect the water of Marmaduke Spring, and with the tools and material for erecting guideboards to mark the new and direct trail.

On the morning of the 7th I moved west, through Johnston's Pass, to its west foot. Here, as directed by you, I left the beaten road, and turning to the left, moved up a ravine which leads into Johnston's Pass from the south,[2] and furnishes a path thence into the ravine of Brewer's Spring and Creek. The distance by the odometer from the point where I left Johnston's Pass to the point where I struck the ravine of Brewer's Creek is eight miles and four-tenths.[3] The trail over this portion of the route is tolerably direct, but it is somewhat hilly in its southern half, crossing a number of ravines, which presented themselves at right angles and could not be turned without too great a detour.

From the point where I struck the ravine of Brewer's Creek I moved up that ravine to your recent return-trail from California, a distance of three miles.[4] I encamped near here on the 7th; Mr. Reese, the guide, whom I had sent forward in the morning to examine a supposed pass through the Champlin Mountains, returned at night and reported it impracticable for wagons.[5] On the 8th I proceeded by your trail to

[1]Now known as Faust Creek.

[2]At 1.8 miles west from the Lookout Pass summit, an unimproved dirt road leaves the Pony Express road and heads south up a canyon known as Little Valley. This is where Lieutenant Smith left the Simpson expedition's outbound route to get to the expedition's return route. (See map 3.)

[3]What Lieutenant Smith called Brewer's Creek is now known as Government Creek. The place where Smith reached the creek is 5.8 miles south of where the road to Erickson Pass leaves Pony Express Road.

[4]Coming from the south just four days before, Simpson had followed the upper portion of Government Creek to a spring he named Brewer's Spring, and had then turned east (Simpson, *Report of Explorations*, 131). Smith, who was moving south along Government Creek, had reached Brewer's Spring when he indicated that he had come to Simpson's "recent return-trail." The name "Brewer's Spring" is no longer used, but the editor believes he has found its location, 8.1 miles south of where the road to Erickson Pass leaves Pony Express Road.

[5]This pass was almost certainly what is now known as Lee Canyon. Three years later, a detail of soldiers, members of the California Volunteers under the command of Colonel Patrick Connor, built a road through this pass, and emigrants immediately began to use it on their way to Indian Spring, the last watering place before entering the Great Salt Lake Desert (Rogers, *Soldiers of the Overland*, 40).

the point three miles from William's Spring, alluded to in your letter of instructions as camp "No. 32."[6] On the morning of the 9th three mules from one of the teams were found to be missing, and the day was passed in an unsuccessful attempt to find them. Leaving Stephenson, one of the guides, with my mule, to continue the search for the lost animals, I moved on at nightfall for Marmaduke or Big Horn Spring. I followed your trail for about a mile and a half, and then diverged from it to the right. Our road now lay through the range of hills in which Indian Spring[7] is situated, and was necessarily somewhat tortuous, though its general direction was nearly correct. I halted when the moon set (about midnight), and continued the march on the morning of the 10th. We soon emerged from the hills and moved west of south across the valley west of Good Indian Spring, reaching Marmaduke Spring about 3 P.M.[8] We found here, by digging, sufficient water for our immediate wants, but the holes soon ceased to fill up, and the water gave out entirely before night. It seemed evident to me, on examination of the locality, that the supposed spring at this point was nothing more than a reservoir of rain-water, retained in a natural basin of rocks and protected from evaporation by the sand which fills the basin. I found the distance from the camp near William's Spring to this point to be 24.4 miles, verifying nearly your previous estimate.

On the 11th I proceeded to Tyler's Spring[9] by the most direct route possible, finding a good pass through the mountain west of Big Horn Spring. I improved Tyler's Spring by digging several new reservoirs there, and on the 12th commenced my return. I adopted a pass through the mountain west of Big Horn Spring, a little north of the pass I used going out, and preferable to it in some respects.

Being forced to abandon Big Horn Spring as a camping or watering place, it seemed necessary to make the Good Indian Spring a point of

[6]The location of Williams Spring is uncertain, but the camp was on the north bank of Death Canyon Wash, about two and a half miles from the mouth of Death Canyon, which is on the southwest slope of the Simpson Mountains.

[7]Smith is referring to the spring that Simpson named Simpson's Good Indian Spring, which later became known as Keg Spring. Smith traveled through the northern foothills of Keg Mountain, but did not go to Keg Spring at this time.

[8]The exact location of Marmaduke Spring, also known as Big Horn Spring, is uncertain, but is somewhere in the northern end of the Drum Mountains.

[9]Now known as Mud Spring

the route, and decided to carry the troughs thither. I sent Mr. Reese forward, accordingly, to ascertain the best route to Indian Spring. He found a very direct eligible route thither, and we reached that point on the morning of the 13th instant. The distance from Tyler's Spring to Good Indian Spring, by the trail I followed, is 35 miles. I remained at the latter spring during the 13th and 14th, placing the troughs and perfecting their arrangement as far as possible. On the night of the 14th Stephenson arrived with the lost mules.

I left Good Indian Spring on the 15th, following your trail to within two and a half miles of Camp 32, near William's Spring. Here I diverged to the right, striking your trail again about two miles this side of the camp near William's Spring, cutting off between one and two miles of the distance from Indian Spring to Prince's Creek, and to Camp Floyd, which post I reached on the 17th instant. Wherever the trail I adopted intersected or diverged from any other wagon-trail, the route to Carson's Valley was indicated by a guide-board, and if the other fork was a trail which I had abandoned, it was ditched across and further obstructed by sage or cedar brush.

A party of emigrants, with six wagons, overtook me going out, near William's Spring, and followed my outward trail to Tyler's Spring.[10] Returning I met upon the proper trail five other parties, having in all, I should think, about thirty wagons,[11] and one herd of cattle numbering a thousand head. I gave them all such information as they required about the route ahead of them, and have no doubt they followed the trail I recommended to Tyler's Spring, making that the most marked and best beaten road.

In compliance with your instructions I have added to your itinerary of the route from Genoa to Tyler's Spring my notes of the route from that point to Camp Floyd.

I am, sir, very respectfully, your obedient servant,

J. L. Kirby Smith,
Second Lieutenant Topographical Engineers

[10]This would have been the party that included Charles Tuttle and Lumin Scott, whose diaries are included in this collection.

[11]One of these parties may have included Edward Mathews, whose diary is included in this collection.

CHAPTER 2

Charles M. Tuttle

1859

Charles Tuttle left his home in Union, Wisconsin, on April 26, 1859, traveling with three companions. After crossing the central plains, they arrived at Salt Lake City on July 29. Tuttle's diary entry for that day describes how they left the previous night's campsite in the Mountain Dell area, climbed over Little Mountain, and traveled down Emigration Canyon to enter the city.

The available portion of Charles Tuttle's diary was published in the Wisconsin Magazine of History *in two installments in 1931. The second installment ends abruptly when Tuttle was less than halfway across Nevada. Whether or not the last third of his diary was ever published is unknown to the editor.*

Permission to use the Tuttle diary in this work was granted by the Wisconsin Historical Society.

July 29, 1859 We commenced the ascent of the mountain early this morning we found it steeper of ascent than the one of the previous day but the road was not so rough we made the ascent and decended to the valley on the other side and encamped for noon in sight of

Great Salt Lake City we drove through the city this afternoon and camped for night within half a mile of the city The city is regularly laid out in squares with water running around each square and shade trees set out around most of them the buildings are mostly small though they look clean and neat Brigham Young's residence is quite a nice building there is a large Eagle carved out over the gateway leading to it and a large Lion over the portico of the front door he has several other buildings though none of the others are quite so nice The Temple Block has a very nice wall around it. it is about 250 yards square and about 10 or 12 feet high it is made out of stone and brick and then cemented over with cement

JULY 30, 1859 We left our encampment about noon and came a distance of about 4 miles and encamped we remained here all day there is good grass upon the mountains about 2 miles from our encampment there is hot springs about half a mile from our camp they are Sulphur Springs.[1]

JULY 31, 1859 There was a fine shower of rain last night accompanied by thunder and lightening the weather is vary warm this morning. We remained at our encampment all day to day.

AUGUST 1, 1859 We remained to day at our camp all day the weather is pleasant

AUGUST 2, 1859 Moved back into the city and traded off our cattle for mules, and encamped in the city to night

AUGUST 3, 1859 Still at our camp where we have remained all day

AUGUST 4, 1859 Remained at our encampment all day to day

AUGUST 5, 1859 To day we started on our way again. we are going the new mail route as they say it is 250 miles nearer[2] About 6 miles from the city we crossed Big Cottonwood Creek a stream about 80 feet wide and 2 feet deep[3] it has a mill on it where we bought some

---

[1]The location of these springs is uncertain, but it does not appear that they were the ones that later became known as Beck's Hot Springs.

[2]Tuttle refers to the Central Overland Trail as the "new mail route" because the Chorpenning mail company had quit using the upper Humboldt River route and began using the Central Overland Trail during the previous December (Townley, *Stalking Horse*, 244–245) (see map 2).

[3]Big Cottonwood Creek crosses present-day State Street, which was the old wagon road, just about six miles from where the center of Salt Lake City would have been in 1859.

feed for our mules leaving here we came on about 17 miles farther and encamped for the night on the bank of the River Jordan[4] It has been very windy to day. The dust has blown so that it was almost impossible to travel.

August 6, 1859 We were off in good season this morning. we crossed the river Jordan[5] about 6 miles from our encampment we got to Camp Belazes[6] about 4 oclock this afternoon, and came on from here about 5 miles farther and encamped for the night[7] the distance traveled today is about 25 miles. Camp Belazes is where the United States Troops are stationed that came out to Salt Lake There is about 4,000 soldiers here at present There had a party just arrived from California.[8] They came a new route which they say is about 250 miles nearer than the old mail route There was a company of 14 wagons (commanded by Capt Simpson) which had just arrived being the only ones that had come this route. Capt Simpson very kindly offered to let us have an Indian guide to lead us to the right road we gratefully accepted his offer and accordingly he sent one along[9]

---

[4]Tuttle's distance was a little off because seventeen miles would have put him in the Jordan Narrows or on the ridge of the Point of the Mountain, neither of which would have been a good place to camp. More than likely, the camp was a short distance to the north of the narrows.

[5]Most of the traffic heading for Camp Floyd crossed the Jordan River about a mile and a half south of the Jordan Narrows. The Thanksgiving Point Golf Course now occupies the east bank of the river at this location. When Tuttle made his crossing, it was probably only a ford. However, Mary Karchner, whose diary appears in this collection, mentioned that in 1862 she made the crossing on a ferry. See ch. 10, n3.

[6]When Brig. Gen. Albert Sidney Johnston arrived in Utah in June 1858 to put down the so-called Mormon Rebellion, he took his force of about 2,500 men to Cedar Valley, about forty miles southwest of Salt Lake City, and established an army post that was named after the Secretary of War, John B. Floyd (Moorman and Sessions, *Camp Floyd and the Mormons*, 45–58). It was from here that Capt. James Simpson began his 1859 expedition that established the route of the Central Overland Trail. The camp flourished for just over four years and was then abandoned when the Civil War began in the east. Following the camp's closure, most, but not all, of our emigrant diarists bypassed Camp Floyd by traveling west from Salt Lake City and taking the Tooele Valley and Rush Valley route to Faust Station. Camp Floyd had a number of nicknames, but Tuttle's diary is the only place the editor has seen the name "Camp Belazes."

[7]This camp would have been somewhere in the Five Mile Pass area.

[8]Tuttle is referring to the Simpson expedition.

[9]On this same date, Capt. James Simpson wrote, "A party of California emigrants, with seven wagons, take, also, my return-route. I have furnished them with an itinerary" (Simpson, *Report of Explorations*, 133). This tells us that Tuttle's party may have been the first to use the trail made by the Simpson expedition during its return trip.

August 7, 1859 We were early on the road this morning we came a distance of about 14 miles and encamped on a small stream called Medow Creek for noon Leaving this place we came on about 11 miles and encamped for night. the road so far has been on the mail road[10]

August 8, 1859 We came to day about a mile from our camp when we came to the track which the guide came to show us here he left us and went back and we proceeded on our way. this new track which we are following is only the faint track made by two waggons. we are only going to follow this track for a day or two when it will strike a more beaten way where there has been fourteen wagons along[11] we encamped for noon on a small stream where was a large herd of cattle kept they are principally cattle which have been brought through by government trains and Freight Trains[12] leaving this place we came on and encamped near a good spring the distance traveled today is about 18 miles[13] the road has been very rough, but we have plenty of grass and water for our mules.

August 9, 1859 We came today about 15 miles and encamped with the government Wagons which made the track which we have been following. there is neither water nor grass here but we have to go up into the mountains about 2 miles for both.[14] the two government wagons start on tonight and two of our company are to accompany them abut 30 miles to help fix some troughs into a spring where we could not otherwise obtain enough for our stock The two wagons started about dark and I accompanied them we traveled until about 3 oclock in the morning and then waited for day. When day light

[10]The stream that was known as Meadow Creek in 1859 later became Faust Creek.

[11]The Indian guide accompanied Tuttle's party to the western base of Lookout Pass, where he pointed out the tracks that had been made by Lieutenant Smith's two wagons the day before. They followed these tracks up a shallow canyon now known as Little Valley. They had been told that this trail would lead them to the trail that had been made by the fourteen wagons of the Simpson expedition (see map 3).

[12]Lieutenant Smith called this stream "Brewer's Creek," but it later became known as Government Creek. There was, and still is, a spring in the channel of Government Creek that Simpson named after Assistant Surgeon Charles Brewer, who in 1859 was stationed at Camp Floyd (Simpson, *Report of Explorations*, 131).

[13]Tuttle was at Black Spring, a mile and a half south of Erickson Pass, but the distance traveled would have been closer to sixteen miles.

[14]Tuttle's party had caught up with the military detail commanded by Lieutenant Smith.

came we started on and reached Big Horne Springs about 2 oclock in the afternoon.[15] here we found but little water and could obtain that only by digging. the road traveled last night and today has been very rough and barren of every green thing except Sage Brush which grows in abundance

AUGUST 10, 1859 The road traveled to day by our teams is the same as the one just described they reached Big Horne Spring about 5 oclock this afternoon tired and thirsty not having had any water since morning only what they brought along. we remained up all night to obtain water for our stock all the water we could get we obtained by digging about 9 feet deep and then dipping the water out as fast as it ran in, (which was very slow

AUGUST 11, 1859 We started early this morning on our way. the next point where we can obtain water is Tyler springs[16] a distance of about 20 miles The two government wagons started about an hour before we did bound for the same place we arrived at Tyler Springs about 7 oclock P.M. here we found plenty of wood, Water & grass.

AUGUST 12, 1859 We remained at the Tyler Springs all day to day. The Government Wagons started back to day

AUGUST 13, 1859 We started to day again on our way we came to day about 15 miles and encamped at Chapin Springs Creek & Canyon.[17] here we found good grass and water. the roads have been as good as we could expect considering it was a new one.

---

[15] This entry gives us no useful information about the route they traveled or the location of Big Horn Spring (also called "Marmaduke Spring"), but Lieutenant Smith's report indicates that it was 24.4 miles from the previous camp, and Tuttle's entry for the next day said that it was about twenty miles to Tyler's Spring. After plotting the likely trails between these places, the editor has concluded that Marmaduke Spring was in a shallow canyon on the northeastern slope of the Drum Mountains.

[16] The Simpson expedition had camped at this spring just two weeks before, and Simpson named it after Lt. Charles H. Tyler of the Second Dragoons (Simpson, *Report of Explorations*, 126). It is now known as Mud Spring and is on the northeastern slope of Swasey Mountain, in the House Range.

[17] Leaving Mud Spring, Tuttle's party dropped into Whirlwind Valley, circled around the eastern and southern base of Swasey Mountain, climbed back into the House Range, and camped at what Simpson called Chapin Spring after Lt. Gurden Chapin of the Seventh Infantry (Simpson, *Report of Explorations*, 125). Chapin Spring does not appear on modern maps, and the water that was its source has been piped. The road going through this area is shaped like an upside down U, with the spring at the upper end.

August 14, 1859 We traveled on to day. we came about 15 miles to Rush Pond[18] where we encamped for noon there is not much grass here but there is plenty of water. We staid here two hours and then proceeded on our way. We came from here 20½ miles to Plympton Springs where we encamped for the night[19] We have had splendid roads to day the most of the way has been across a desert We arrived here about 1 oclock at night.

August 15, 1859 We started on our way about noon to day and came about 10 miles and encamped on Crosman Creek for the night[20] the road to day has been level but rather sandy

August 16, 1859 We came to day a distance of 22 miles and encamped near Tamley's Springs and Canyan.[21] we crossed Dry branch[22] about 9 miles from our camp this morning and about 5 miles from Dry branch we came to Ungohah or Red springs[23] about 7 miles from red springs we came to the summit of Jashoat Mountain[24] and 2 miles from here we came to camp

August 17, 1859 We came today about 23 miles and encamped in about a mile of the summit of Ungo-we-ah or Pine Range[25] about 8 miles from our camp of last evening we came to a very fine spring in

[18]"Rush Pond" was Simpson's name for present-day South Tule Spring, which is located near the center of Tule Valley (Simpson, *Report of Explorations*, 124).

[19]Simpson named a group of springs on the east side of Snake Valley "Plympton's Springs," after Lt. Peter W. L. Plympton of the Seventh Infantry (Simpson, *Report of Explorations*, 122). The main springs in this group are now known as Knoll Spring and North Knoll Spring. The distance from South Tule Spring to North Knoll Spring, where Tuttle probably camped, is 20.3 miles.

[20]Simpson named the stream and the valley after Deputy Quartermaster-General George H. Crosman, who was then stationed at Camp Floyd (Simpson, *Report of Explorations*, 121). The stream is now called Baker Creek. The campsite was about a mile and a quarter northwest of the small community of Eskdale.

[21]Simpson called them "Turnley's Springs" after Cap. P. T. Turnley, the assistant quartermaster at Camp Floyd, and they have retained that name (Simpson, *Report of Explorations*, 120).

[22]Silver Creek. Simpson described this streambed as a dry branch.

[23]Present-day Strawberry Ranch, which is located just north of U.S. 50 and 6, about ten miles west of the Utah-Nevada state line.

[24]The summit was present-day Sacramento Pass. "Jashoat" would have been Tuttle's spelling of "Go-shoot," which was Simpson's name for the Snake Mountains.

[25]Simpson's names for the Schell Creek Mountains. Although conclusive evidence is lacking, the editor believes that this camp was at an unnamed spring located 1.7 miles north of Cooper Meadows, which are at the head of Cooper Canyon.

Hutchins Valley[26] the road to day has been very good considering the newness of it [27]

AUGUST 18, 1859 We came to day a distance of 14 miles and encamped on Stephens Creek we crossed this creek several times the forenoon and also camped on it at noon[28] the road to day has been very mountainous though it is what you might call passable

AUGUST 19, 1859 We came to day about 19 miles and encamped in Spring Canyan We crossed Murry's Creek about 3 miles from our encampment of last night[29] we also passed the Gate of Hercules[30] there is five springs in the compass of one half mile in Spring Canyan where we are camped[31] the road to day has been vary good

AUGUST 20, 1859 We came to day about 12 miles and encamped near Hunt's Spring[32]

AUGUST 21, 1859 We started about 12 oclock last night on our way as we have a desert of 35 miles to cross to day we came about 18

---

[26]The spring that Tuttle mentioned as being in Hutchins Valley was present-day Layton Spring. The origin of the name "Hutchins" is unknown. Simpson called this area "Antelope Valley," thinking it was an extension of the Antelope Valley that the expedition had crossed some forty miles to the north during the outbound part of his expedition. The area soon became known as Spring Valley.

[27]As far as Tuttle knew, the section of the road that his party was traveling had been made by the Simpson expedition only a month before. He was not aware that it had been made a year previously by a group of Mormons scouting for a place where the residents of Salt Lake City could move to if they were forced to flee from the federal army that was then on its way to Utah. In May 1858, a group of twenty-eight men under the leadership of Orson B. Adams broke a trail over Sacramento Pass and then over the Schell Creek Mountains by way of Cooper and Steptoe Canyons. When Simpson came this way in 1859, he used this trail and remarked on how good the road was (Stott, *Search For Sanctuary*, 131–132; Simpson, *Report of Explorations*, 118).

[28]The stream is now Steptoe Creek, but Simpson had named it "Stevenson Creek" after Capt. Carter L. Stevenson of the Fifth Infantry (Simpson, *Report of Explorations*, 118). The campsite was about three miles south of Ely.

[29]The crossing of Murry Creek took place near what is now the sixth hole of the White Pine County Golf Course. Simpson named this stream after Lt. Alexander Murry, who commanded the expedition's military personnel (Simpson, *Report of Explorations*, 117).

[30]Tuttle's "Gate of Hercules" is about six miles north of Ely. It is a gap in a low ridge through which a small stream flows. Simpson's name for it was The Gates of Hercules; it is now known as Hercules Gap (Simpson, *Report of Explorations*, 117).

[31]Tuttle's Spring Canyon was the upper part of present-day Smith Valley, north of Ely.

[32]In the southeast corner of Butte Valley, the Simpson expedition had entered a canyon through which flowed a stream that Simpson named after Garland Hurt, the agent at that time for the Ute Indians (Simpson, *Report of Explorations*, 117). Tuttle's "Hunt's Spring" is apparently a misspelling of "Hurt." The camp was near the mouth of what is now Combs Canyon.

miles when we stoped for our breakfast we came the other 17 miles by 3 oclock P.M. when we camped on Niell's Creek[33] the road has been good except where the sage brush bothered and the last 10 miles which were sandy[34]

---

[33]This stream is located on the eastern slope of the southern part of the Diamond Mountains. Simpson named it "Neill's Creek," after Capt. Thomas H. Neill of the Fifth Infantry (Simpson, *Report of Explorations*, 114). The stream is now known as Pinto Creek.

[34]At this point, the available portion of Charles Tuttle's diary comes to an abrupt stop. The reason for this is unknown, but it is difficult to believe that he simply quit writing. The more likely explanation is that the remaining portion of the diary has been lost.

CHAPTER 3

Lumin A. Scott

1859

DURING THE SUMMER OF 1859, Lumin Scott traveled westward to California. His diary is one of only three known to the editor that were written by emigrants who followed the Simpson expedition's return trail. We take up Scott's diary on July 29, the day he arrived at Salt Lake City. Although they do not mention each other, Scott was a member of the same party as Charles Tuttle, whose diary also appears in this book.

A transcribed copy of the Scott diary and permission to publish it was obtained from Cappy Cook, a direct descendent of Lumin Scott.

JULY 29, 1859 En rout to California from Salt Lake July 29th passed through Salt Lake City and went out about two miles and camp grass is very poor clost to the city went to a circus in the evening.

JULY 30, 1859 Went on a mile or two and laid over went to the warm spring, wrote letters and climbed mts.

JULY 31, 1859 Write another letter and went up to the hot springs.[1]

[1]These springs were visited by six of the emigrants whose diaries appear in this collection. (For a detailed history of the springs as a recreational attraction, see "Warm Springs and the First Bath House in Salt Lake City," *Utah Historical Quarterly* 76(3): 212.) (See map 2.)

This spring is situated about four miles from the city and is hot enough to scald a man's hand in a few seconds.

August 1, 1859 Went to the city and loafed all day and got a slight squint of Brigham in his office. We hear of cattle, mules, and horses being stolen every night, men shot, etc.

August 2, 1859 Watched the cattle up on the mountain until they were sold. The most of the train went on and the rest went to the city to stay a day or two.

August 3, 1859 We took our wagon to the city and are going to get mules.

August 4, 1859 Bought our mules and rigged up for a fresh start. We have made up our minds to go the new route south of the lake and by Camp Floyd. The last night in the city.

August 5, 1859 Hitched up our four mule team and drove on up on to mains st. and stopped to get a few necessaries and then left for Camp Floyd. There is four mule teams and one two mule team in our company now and Mr. Monday is still our captain. As for the roads, they are very good except the dust which the wind raises in such quantities that we cannot see anything that we pass scarcely. The country is wholly unproductive without irrigation. Camped on Jordan River about twenty miles from the city.[2] No wood but plenty of grass.

August 6, 1859 Took an early start in the morning and rolled along four or five miles and crossed Jourdan[3] and passed Utah Lake on the west. Here the road turns to the right and leaves the Great Salt Lake Valley and passes over an elevation of land into Cedar Valley. There is no road or water from here to Camp Floyd, a distance of sixteen miles.[4] Camp Floyd about four o'clock.[5] This is an ill looking place but there appears to be considerable business going on. It is garrisoned with about twenty-five hundred soldiers. We left the camp and went about eight miles and camped without water—good grass and sage.[6]

---

[2]This would have put Scott on the east bank of the Jordan River, in the area of present-day Draper.

[3]See ch. 2, n5.

[4]Scott was referring to the place near Utah Lake where he turned west. His comment about there being no road is curious because the road to Camp Floyd had been used by numerous freight wagons for over a year.

[5]See ch. 2, n6.

[6]This would have put Scott and his party about three miles west of Five Mile Pass. (See map 2.)

August 7, 1859 Took an early start for Rush Valley a distance of sixteen miles where we camped for dinner with plenty of water and grass but no wood or sage brush.[7] Camped in a little canyon—good spring, wood, and water.[8]

August 8, 1859 Here we take to the left on a new road that has just been serviced. We are the first emigrants that ever traveled it.[9] Roads very rough on account of not being travelled. Passed several groves of mountain cedars. By going this new road we shun all of the deserts and alkali ground of the Humboldt River. The greatest distance we have to go without water being thirty two miles. Camped at Marmaduke or Big Horn Springs.[10] Plenty of good wood, water, and grass.

August 9, 1859 Road very rough and stoney in the morning. Strike on to a small desert about ten miles across. Camp about midway and took our mules up into the mountains and staid all night.[11] Good grass but no wood. We can here see mountains in every direction and the whole country is just good for nothing from Fort Laramie to here and how much further I don't know!

August 10, 1859 Rolled on over and through sand, sagebrush, and stones twenty five miles to water and but very little of it. When we got to it there was not enough to water half our mules. But we gave what we could get to them and tied them to the wagon and gave them a little ground feed and let them stand all night without grass.[12]

---

[7]This dinner stop was on Faust Creek. (See map 3.)

[8]This camp was at Point Lookout, about three-quarters of a mile west of Lookout Pass. Simpson had discovered this pass, which lies between the Onaqui and Sheeprock Mountains, during his 1858 reconnaissance; he named it "Gen. Johnston's Pass" in honor of the commander of Camp Floyd (Simpson, *Wagon Road Routes in Utah Territory*, 34–35). The 1859 Simpson expedition camped here for one night because of the level area and a small spring (Simpson, *Report of Explorations*, 46). For reasons unknown to the editor, this area soon became known as Point Lookout.

[9]Although Scott called it a road, it was actually just a track that had been made the previous day by Lt. J. L. Kirby Smith and a work detail consisting of a few men and two wagons. (See map 3.)

[10]Scott is confused about the name of the spring. They still had a long way to go before reaching Marmaduke Spring. This camp may have been at Black Spring, which is a mile and a half south of Erickson Pass.

[11]The small desert was the area immediately south of the Simpson Mountains, with the camp being about three miles southwest from the mouth of Death Canyon. When Scott took the mules into the mountains, he probably went into Death Canyon, which is on the southwest slope of the Simpson Mountains.

[12]Scott was now at Marmaduke Spring, sometimes called "Horn," "Big Horn," or "Horne Spring." This was the spring that Lieutenant Smith had been sent back to improve. See more about this in Lieutenant Smith's report. See ch. 1, n8.

August 11, 1859 Got up before daylight and took the stock around a point of the mountain to a small patch of grass about two miles off. After letting them eat about an hour we took them back to the wagons and harnessed them up and started for Tylors Springs which are about twenty one miles distant, and twelve of it across a desert. Five of us took two canteens of water and started off ahead of the teams to go through to the springs, supposing it would be enough to last us there but when we got to the desert our water was all gone and we were very dry and the wagons five miles back. What to do—we did not know, but after a brief consultation we concluded that we mite as well go on as to wate for the teams. So we set out again for the springs and when we were about two thirds of the way acrost one of the men gave out and we had to go on and leave him by the side of the road. And after going two or three miles farther two more failed so fast that they could not keep up—and myself and another man went on to the spring where we arrived just as near dead as any two men could be and walk. After we had been there about ½ hour the two men came up nearer gone than we were. I then took a canteen of water and went back and met the fellow we had left by the side of the road coming along very slow. He drank the water and we came back to the springs where the teams all arrived in good time but not without suffering some for want of water. Here we found plenty of wood, water, and grass and concluded to lay over a day.[13]

August 12, 1859 Set our wagon tire and fixed other necessaries. There were some Indians camped here and they had killed three mountain sheep and were drying the meat.

August 13, 1859 Went on fifteen miles and camped at a good spring where there is good wood and grass.[14]

August 14, 1859 Traveled up a mountain over very rough roads. Then down a steep crooked canyon[15] for four or five miles out on to a desert covered with a saltish substance. About midway of this desert is a

[13]They had crossed Whirlwind Valley and were at present-day Mud Spring. This spring is fairly high in the foothills, on the northeast slope of Swasey Mountain, which is near the center of the House Range.

[14]Simpson named this spring "Chapin Spring." See ch. 2, n27.

[15]Dome Canyon, sometimes called "Death Canyon."

rush pond[16] where there is water for stock but not for any other use. We staid here until about 5 o'clock and then started for Plymptons Springs[17] a distance of twenty one miles where we arrived about one o'clock in the morning. Good roads, plenty of water and grass, but no wood.

AUGUST 15, 1859 Let our mules rest until noon then hitched up and drove ten miles to Crosman's Creek.[18] Good water and grass but nothing but willows for fuel.

AUGUST 16, 1859 Crossed the valley and struck into a wide canyon and went up five or six miles and stopped for dinner on a small creek coming from Red Springs.[19] After going five or six miles further we passed the summit of the mountain and came into the head of a small canyon and went down it about two miles and camped.[20] Plenty of water and grass and sage for fuel.

AUGUST 17, 1859 Went down the canyon into Antelope Valley[21] then down it to a spring[22] and then cross over into another small crooked canyon[23] and eat our dinner. Then up the canyon over rocks and goulies and through places where the rocks came nearly together at the bottom making it almost impassable to a small spring[24] Good wood, water, and grass.

AUGUST 18, 1859 Passed on up the mountain and over the summit down into a canyon that is more steeper and more crooked than the one we came up. After going down a mile or two we came to a small rivelette which we have to cross several times. And once in crossing Mr. Monday broke his wagon tongue which detained us a short time.

---

[16]The "rush pond" was present-day South Tule Spring. This spring was also mentioned by Simpson, Bolivar Roberts, Charles Tuttle, and Edward Mathews, none of whom complained about the quality of the water.

[17]See ch. 2, n19.

[18]See ch. 2, n20.

[19]This stream is now known as Weaver Creek. Red Springs is located on the property of the Strawberry Ranch, near U.S. 50 and 6, about ten miles west of the Utah-Nevada border.

[20]The summit was Sacramento Pass. The camp was at Turnley Springs.

[21]Scott called it Antelope Valley because that was Simpson's name for it. See ch. 2, n26. It soon became known as Spring Valley.

[22]Although Simpson camped at this spring overnight, he did not name it. It is now known as Layton Spring.

[23]Cooper Canyon, on the eastern slope of the Schell Creek Mountains.

[24]See ch. 2, n25.

But again all was ready and the train moved on down the mountain. Some of the time we were in the mud and water and then out up on the rocks. This place is called Stephins Crik and Canyon.[25] Here our train split and one wagon and two others went on ahead and camped on Murry's Creek[26] while the other wagons camped at a spring about three miles back. Good water and a little grass but no wood.

August 19, 1859 Passed along over a good road into what is call Five Springs Canyon[27] and eat our dinner.

August 20, 1859 Then passing over the mountains and camped at Heart's Spring.[28] This is the last watering place before crossing the thirty two mile desert. Here we laid in some water and cut some grass for our mules and about 5 o'clock in the afternoon we set out. It being rather dark in the forepart of the night we were compeled to go ahead of the teams in order to keep the road which was very blind in some places. About one o'clock we stopped and fed our mules and let them rest an hour or two and then started on and about seven o'clock in the morning we arrived at the spot where the guide stated we could get water by digging two or three feet. But it was so dry there was no water and consequently we had to drive on eight miles farther to a creek where we laid over for the remainder of the day, it being Sunday the 21st.[29]

August 22, 1859 Rolled out at an early hour and went up the creek to its source in a small canyon which leads up a mountain that is

---

[25]Simpson named this stream "Stevenson's Creek." Later, it became Steptoe Creek.

[26]They were probably camped at the same place where the Simpson expedition had camped exactly one month earlier (Simpson, *Report of Explorations*, 118). This site is in the northern part of the city of Ely, and is now occupied by the White Pine County Golf Course.

[27]They were in upper Smith Valley, near Archie Spring. The editor has found no other use of the name "Five Springs Canyon."

[28]Simpson named the stream "Hurt's Creek," but did not mention a spring in this area. See ch. 2, n32.

[29]Simpson had named the creek on which they were camped Neill's Creek. Tuttle, who was still traveling with Scott, referred to it as "Niell Creek." Today it is known as Pinto Creek. The area where they attempted to find water by digging can be identified by measuring back from the Pinto Creek campsite. The guide that Scott mentioned was a written itinerary his party had obtained from Simpson when they passed through Camp Floyd. There is no mention of the presence of water in this area in Simpson's report or in his published itineraries, which means the guide they had was different from the versions that can be found today.

rather hard to climb passing over the mountain we came into a very rough canyon that leads out on to desert.[30] Passing over this we came into a small valley covered with grass, the only one we have passed through since leaving Salt Lake. Camped at Lee Springs[31]—good grass and sage.

August 23, 1859 Travile along over a levil but rather sandy road to Twin Springs[32] dinner. Very little grass but no wood. Our guide book stated that there was water ten miles from Twin Springs but it being very dry there was no water to be found. Then consiquently we had to move on and it being dark we missed the next spring, it being off from the road a waise which left us in a rather bad position for the night.[33] But there was no other way for us only keep moving until we did find water and feed for the mules so we kept on untill about twelve o'clock at night when some of the mules became so weak and tired that we could hardly get them along and coming to the summit of a small mountain we unharnessed and hitched the animals up to sage brush and let them stand untill morning.[34]

August 24, 1859 Left our mountain camp at daylight and traveled about ten miles acrost a desert to a small creek and canyon where we lay up the remainder of the day[35] and was visited by about thirty natives who behaved themselves very sivil and wanted to swap antelope hides and other notions for old clothes. Water and grass in abundance.

August 25, 1959 Went on up the canyon which is very wide and

---

[30] They traveled upstream along Pinto Creek until they passed Pinto Spring, and then continued across the ridge of the Diamond Mountains. From there, they dropped down Simpson Creek canyon into the southern end of Diamond Valley.

[31] Lee's Springs are just off U.S. Highway 50, about twelve miles west of Eureka, but they are no longer known by this name. Simpson named them after William Lee, one of the civilian members of his expedition (Simpson, *Report of Explorations*, 112).

[32] Twin Springs is located just north of U.S. 50 and twenty-six miles west of Eureka.

[33] The guide was probably referring to the small stream that flows through present-day Willow Creek Ranch, and the spring they missed in the dark would have been Jackrabbit Spring, which is another mile and a quarter to the west and about a half mile to the south.

[34] It would appear that this stop was at the summit of the Toquima Mountains, about three miles south of where U.S. 50 crosses Hickison Summit. About fifty-five years later, travelers on the Lincoln Highway called this ridge "Ford's Defeat."

[35] This camp was in the mouth of Simpson Park Canyon. The stream that flows through this canyon is one of a number of Willow Creeks in Nevada.

not very steep with now and then a small level valley covered with the very best of grass.[36] On going over the summit[37] the descent was more abrupt down into the valley where after traveling five or six miles we came to the Reasses [Reese] River[38] which is a very handsome little brook with plenty of speckled trout in it. Good grass but no wood.

AUGUST 26, 1859 Laid over and done our laundry and caught a mess of trout for supper. The largest weighing nearly three pounds.

AUGUST 27, 1859 Took an early start and after traveling all day without water we came to Smith's Creek where we found plenty of water and a little grass and sage. Roads very hard the most of the way and over a small range of mountain and also a small desert.[39]

AUGUST 28, 1859 Rolled on up the creek and canyon which is very crooked and steep in places and stopped for dinner in a most beautiful meadow of wilde clover and along one side was some wilde cherry bushes loaded with the very best of cherries. Passing over the summit we came into another canyon and after going down a mile or two came to Edwards Creek and followed it down several miles and camped where there is plenty of wood, water, and grass.[40]

---

[36]This is a good description of Simpson Park. (See map 6.)

[37]Emigrant Pass.

[38]During its outbound trip, the Simpson expedition crossed Emigrant Pass, then traveled straight across the valley and forded the Reese River at a point about three and a half miles downstream from the U.S. Highway 50 bridge. On the return trip, they crossed the river about a quarter of a mile upstream from the bridge. Sometime during the next few months, a bridge was built between Simpson's fords, and a mail station was established on the west bank. The old bridge is gone, but the stone abutments are still visible. All of the diarists who traveled this part of the Central Overland Trail had to cross the Reese River, but none provide details as to exactly where they did so. We can only assume that most of them used the bridge. Exceptions were George Bushnell, who crossed it a few miles to the south, and George Harter, who was somewhere between Austin and Battle Mountain when he crossed this river. (See map 7.)

[39]The "small range of mountains" was the Shoshone Mountains, which Scott's party crossed by way of Smith Creek Summit, about a mile and a half north of Railroad Pass, which is on State Route 722. The "small desert" was the northern section of a very large playa. They would have reached Smith Creek about halfway across the valley, at the point where Simpson's return route rejoined his outbound route.

[40]The Simpson expedition's outbound route crossed Smith Creek Valley and came to the eastern base of the Desatoya Mountains near the mouth of Campbell Creek Canyon. From there, they found a route that crossed the ridge through what Simpson called Gibraltar Pass, which is 1.2 miles south of Carroll Summit on State Route 722 (Simpson, *Report of Explorations*, 81). (See map 7.) This proved to be a very difficult route for wagons, and during the expedition's return

August 29, 1859 Passing out of the canyon we went up a valley between two ranges of mountains twelve miles to Cold Springs[41] where we laid over and prepared for crossing the sixty mile desert by cutting grass and filling our kegs with water this being the last place where we can get good water for within that distance.

August, 30, 1859 Hitched up as soon as we could see and rolled on for the next place where the guide (book) said perhaps we could get water by digging a few feet. On arriving there we did get a little water but of a very poor quality. There being plenty of good grass here we stopped a few hours for our mules to eat.[42] About five o'clock in the afternoon we set out for a Sulfher Spring thirty miles distant. After traviling untill about eleven o'clock we stopped and feed the mules and let them rest an hour or two and then went on to the spring[43] where we arrived about nine o'clock next morning. Very hard roads.

---

trip, Simpson looked for a better one. Circling around the northern end of the mountain, he found a route through Edwards Creek and Smith Creek Canyons, which brought him back to his outbound trail at the point where it had crossed Smith Creek. This section of the return trail was adopted by the Overland Stage and the Pony Express and used until 1862, when the Mount Airy–New Pass route came into use. Scott traveled Simpson's return trail through Smith Creek Canyon to Basque Summit, and then dropped down Edwards Creek Canyon into Edwards Creek Valley. The camp was probably somewhere just above the mouth of the canyon.

[41]In the Cold Springs area, Scott's party probably camped at or near the site that was later occupied by the Cold Springs telegraph station. This same site had been used by the Simpson expedition during the night of June 30, 1859 (Simpson, *Report of Explorations*, 106).

[42]Middlegate got its name from a naturally occurring gap in a low ridge that extends to the south from the Clan Alpine Mountains. During the outbound journey, the Simpson expedition reached this spot after passing through Eastgate. Four weeks later, they returned to Middlegate and then turned northeast toward Cold Springs. In his report, Simpson stated, "It should be remarked that there is not the slightest doubt that water in abundance could be got at this point (Middle Gate) by sinking suitable wells. Indeed it exists now in springs in an arroyo near, and we got it in another easily accessible place by digging not more than two feet deep" (Simpson, *Report of Explorations*, 106). Although he does not identify it by name, Scott was the first of our diarists to reach this spot, and it was here that he and his party spent some time digging for water.

[43]They were now at Sand Springs on the eastern side of Four Mile Flat, and at the base of Sand Mountain. (See map 8.) The Simpson expedition arrived here on June 4, 1859. Simpson described it thus: ". . . we come to our camp-ground, where the guide party, which is in advance of us, has dug a number of small wells. The water is found in an efflorescent sand-flat, and lies 3 feet below the surface. In some of the holes it is strongly alkaline; in others just tolerable. The addition of vinegar improves it very much. . . . altogether this is a miserable camping-place, the worst we have had" (Simpson, *Report of Explorations*, 84).

August 31, 1859 Very poor water being that it is so strong of Sulpher that it is not fit for use. After letting the mules rest a few hours we went on to Carson Lake and camped.[44] This lake is very shallow and is surrounded by a belt of bulrushes through which the ground is very soft and mirey—making it very difficult to get to the water and it is hardly fit for use after so much trouble to get it. It being brackish and warm. No wood and but little grass.

September 1, 1859 Traviled around the south side of the lake for twelve miles and coming to where there was good grass we laid over untill morning.[45]

September 2, 1859 Hitched up at fore o'clock and set out for Carson River twenty five mils distant where we arrived at dark after traviling through sixteen miles of deep sand.[46] A man belonging to

[44]The Simpson expedition made two trails between Sand Springs and Carson Lake. The outbound trail traveled along the eastern edge of Fallon Sink and reached Carson Lake at its northeastern shore. The return trail left the eastern shore of the lake, climbed over a low place in the Bunejug hills, passed Rock Springs, and rejoined the outbound trail just south of Sand Springs. A third route was established about a year later, when a stage road was opened going west from Rock Springs across the Cocoon Mountains by way of Simpson Pass. (See map 8.) Of the twenty diarists who traveled through this part of the country, seven followed Simpson's outbound trail, two took Simpson's return trail, and six went over Simpson Pass. The routes taken by the remaining five cannot be determined. Lumin Scott's entry for the following day makes it clear that his party followed Simpson's return trail over the Bunejug ridge. After reaching the lake, they turned south and then west, following the southern shore of the lake.

[45]The camp was probably at the spot where the Simpson expedition camped for the night of June 27 during their return trip. This was also where the Pony Express established its Carson Sink station. During this period, the body of water now named Carson Lake was known by two different names, so it can get a little confusing. In June 1859, Simpson called it "Carson Lake" and mentioned that its outlet flowed northward into "the sink of Carson" (Simpson, *Report of Explorations*, 85). However, within a short time, travelers had begun to refer to the lake as the sink. The stage and Pony Express station located near the southwest shore of the lake was officially named the Carson Sink Station. Today, what is left of the lake is called Carson Lake, and Carson Sink is about 30 miles to the north, not far from the Humboldt Sink.

[46]From Carson Lake, two routes would take the emigrants and the stagecoaches west. One followed Simpson's return trail through the Dead Camel Mountains. The other headed north along the western shore of the lake and then turned west and passed by the small settlement of Ragtown, where it joined the Carson route section of the California Trail. (See map 8.) This second route eventually came to a split, with the northern route going through the present-day town of Stagecoach and the southern going past Fort Churchill. Of our diarists who wrote about this section of their route, five crossed the Dead Camel Mountains and nine went through Ragtown. Lumin Scott's party followed Simpson's return trail across the Dead Camel Mountains and came to the Carson River somewhere near the point where it is crossed by U.S. Highway 95A.

another wagon took an Indian trail leading off to the right into the mountains and this evening at nine o'clock had not been heard of.

SEPTEMBER 3, 1859 The lost man returned. Traviled along up Carson River three or four miles and then crossed over to the other road[47] which we found much (better) than traviling over sage brush as we have been fore the last five hundred miles. Carson River is a handsome mountain stream running into Carson lake. The valley presents a very handsome appearance the river running acrost from one mountain to the other and is skirted along with gigantic cottonwood trees that afford splendid shade for camping. Plenty of good grass.[48]

SEPTEMBER 4, 1859 Passing along up the valley over very good roads we came to a little place called Chine Town at the mouth of Gold Canyon where they are doing considerable mining though there are but two or three companys that are making it pay very well. Flower is selling at from ten to fifteen cents per pound and potatoes at from six to ten and all other things in proportion. Camped out of town about two or three miles at a handsome spring.[49] Plenty of wood and grass.

SEPTEMBER 5, 1859 Took an early start for Genoa and traveled along passing several nice farms and ranches which they are called here with nice buildings which looked quite natural. Passing to the right (north) of Carson City in Eagle Valley about four miles and camped on the Carson River two or three miles below Genoa.[50] Good wood, water, and grass.

SEPTEMBER 6, 1859 Went on up to the city (Genoa) which is situated just at the foot of the Sierra Nevada Mountains. And after staying there an hour or two rolled on up the valley seven or eight miles and camped.[51]

---

[47]When the Simpson expedition reached the Carson River near this spot during the previous June, the river was running so high that they could not ford it, and they were forced to build a raft to ferry the wagons across (Simpson, *Report of Explorations*, 89).

[48]Scott does not tell us where they made camp for the night, but we can surmise that it was on the north bank of the Carson River, somewhere between Bucklands Station and Dayton. (See map 9.)

[49]This campsite could have been in Spring Valley, about two miles almost due west of Dayton.

[50]This would have put Scott and his party near the southern end of Jacks Valley.

[51]At Genoa, Scott came to the western end of the Central Overland Trail. He was one of only five of our diarists to travel the entire trail from Salt Lake City to Genoa. His diary continued until September 10, 1859 when he reached Placerville, where he ended it with the statement, "Considering myself fairly into California I shall not trouble my mind to keep a diary any longer."

CHAPTER 4

Edward James Mathews

1859

The diary of Edward James Mathews may be the most entertaining of the diaries in this collection. It is also one of the three known diaries written by persons who followed the Simpson expedition's return route through western Utah and eastern Nevada. In April 1859, Mathews left Iowa City, Iowa, and headed west. When he began the trip, his intended destination was the Pikes Peak gold fields of Colorado. Along the way, he changed his mind and decided to go to California. At the beginning of his journey, he was with a group of single men, sharing ownership of some livestock and a wagon. After reaching Salt Lake City, he got out of this arrangement and began paying another wagon owner for his passage. Mathews arrived in Salt Lake City on July 28. This put him in the city one day before Charles Tuttle and Lumin Scott arrived, but he did not leave the city until four days following their departure.

The Mathews diary was transcribed and privately published by unidentified descendents under the title Crossing the Plains. *A copy of the diary was obtained from the Nevada Historical Society.*

JULY 27, 1859 Started up the little mountain roads, better through canyons and gorges. Got within sight of the Great City. Sat for a long time looking. It is worth all the trip to get such beautiful views. The grandest in the world. Cannot express myself, so fine is the scenery.

JULY 28, 1859 Fine day. Camped near the city. Went to the auctioneer about selling our cattle as we decided to set out and hire our passage to California. Got sick of being with Durand. Auctioneer charged five per cent for selling. Sold four yoke of them, left old Brindy and the cow to be sold some other day. A great many Mormons trying to sell us mules. The rest of the company went on.

JULY 29, 1859 Fine day. Had our tents pitched in the street. Selling goods fast, beat all. All of our company split up. Sy Paterson, Simon Shoup, Burr, and Slocum the only ones of the company who went on with the cattle. Was on a little bust at night. Saw some gambling. Williams was showing us around. Found him a Mason, also Hutchison. Brother Brigham, a Mason also. Town very pretty, laid out in ten acre square lots, shade-trees all around, fine flowers and vegetables. A fine stream of water runs in every street, all the gardens irrigated from it. Charley and I went out to herd cattle, found one gone.

JULY 30, 1859 Fine morning. Nearly sold out. Went after the ox, had a big hunt for him. Finally found him in the pound, and had to pay $3.50 to get him out. Beloit boys sold their cattle. We sold balance of ours at five o'clock, cow $27.00, and ox $20.50, "very cheap." Slept in the tent for the last time, was glad of it. Took some beer with Beloit boys, good time. Got a horse from Mr. Shell, who was Stage Agent for California Stage Co., fine fellow, a Pennsylvanian.

JULY 31, 1859 Took a bath and dressed myself as well as I could for I had sold most of my clothes. Went to church, heard Brigham preach, or lecture, to his people. Fine looking man, light complexion, about my height. After church I took dinner with Mr. Hutchison, and had a very pleasant time. They tried to make a Mormon of me, but had little effect. Think them very nice people. Got back to supper. Retired at half past ten o'clock. Slept on the floor of the first class hotel kept by Mr. Hawkins, a jolly Englishman. Liked him and his wife very well.

AUGUST 1, 1859 Fine morning. Went and settled with Williams, and found that the ox was not sold. Somewhat surprised, but he finally settled all right. Finally sold the ox for $21.50. Settled up and felt free once more. Sold my rifle to Mr. Hutchison for $8. Left some money with him to send papers home. Went and called on Bishop Hunter of Delaware County. Had a long talk with him, he treated me very kindly. Took some Valley Tan.[1] Got to the hotel late, had a talk and a great time with the girl at the hotel, raised the whole house.

AUGUST 2, 1859 Fine morning, but very hot. Joe and I paid our fare, $50. each for California. I did not like the style of going. Some fellow told me of the big chances to make money at Camp Floyd, so I got my fare back and concluded to go in that style.[2]

AUGUST 3, 1859 Fine morning. Joe and I getting ready to get off. Got off about four o'clock. Bade them all good-bye. Parker got his money back and got tight as a brick. We did not decide how to go, but were glad we had not gone with the others as it was rough.

AUGUST 4, 1859 Fine morning. Felt rather badly, kind of diarrhea. Dieted, felt better. Things around town looked very dull. Felt as though we ought to have gone yesterday. Offered $100. for a pony. Did not get him. Concluded finally not to buy animals.

AUGUST 5, 1859 Fine day. Took a ride to Warm Springs after dinner.[3] Splendid place to bathe. Felt much better. Got home, took tea, read the papers, played some euchre. Retired outside, as it was so warm in the house.

AUGUST 6, 1859 Fine day. Stayed in the house all day. Some trouble in town. Williams trying to shoot a Mormon for meddling with his business. All blew over. Played euchre with Parker for beer, got beaten.

AUGUST 7, 1859 Went to church. Heard a good sermon by Mr. Gibson in the morning. Went in the afternoon, heard Heber Kimball and Orson Pratt. Did not like Kimball, very heavy on U.S. Government. Saw Brigham's family, some 28 or 30 children. Looked very nice. Got home, retired early on a soft board in the kitchen.

---

[1] "Valley Tan" was a locally produced whiskey that had a reputation for being cheap and strong. It was also the name of a Salt Lake City newspaper.

[2] It appears that Mathews had paid someone for transportation to California and then changed his mind, deciding instead to go to Camp Floyd to see what sort of arrangement he could make there.

[3] See ch. 3, n1.

August 8, 1859 Fine day. Went to see Read about taking us to Sacramento. Had ten fine horses. Agreed to take us for $75., to start on Tuesday morning. A good wagon, in stage style. Paid him $50. each. Had a princely dinner and a fine time. At night had music and singing. Played whist with the same lady. Retired at twelve o'clock.

August 9, 1859 Fine day. Ran around town. Loaned Read $70. at two per cent a month. Got started at three o'clock. Read met a woman on the road with a little boy. She had run away from her husband. Did not like Salt Lake or the Mormons. Camped fifteen miles from town.[4] Woman kept in the wagon, afraid of being seen.

August 10, 1859 Very warm day. Traveled thirty miles to Camp Floyd.[5] Got in about six o'clock Frogtown on the opposite side, and it is properly named.[6] Awfully dirty place. People living in houses under ground. Saw the soldiers on parade. Looked well. A great deal of gambling going on, hard place.

August 11, 1859 Fine day. Stayed at Camp Floyd. Sent a paper home. Every house a gambling house. Parker bet some, said he won, but I think he lost. Had fresh meat for dinner. Retired at ten o'clock, all prepared to start in the morning.[7]

August 12, 1859 Fine day. Started out at six o'clock. Got on the wrong road, soldiers turned us back. Got the mule to work. Gray horse sick, gave him a shower bath. Stopped at Jackson for dinner. No water for 24 miles. Got to camp at eight o'clock. Made 32 miles. Cow doctor by name of Clark in Company. Awfully glad to get to camp.[8]

---

[4]Mathews and his companions headed south from Salt Lake City, following what became known for a time as the state road. The camp was not far from the Jordan River, somewhere within the present limits of Draper. (See map 2.)

[5]See ch. 2, n6.

[6]"Frogtown" was a nickname for Fairfield, which was on the north side of the small creek that flowed eastward from Big Spring. The military post was on the south side of this stream. The name of the town had nothing to do with small green amphibians. During this period of time, "Frog" was a common euphemism for prostitute, and Frogtown had more than its fair share of brothels (Moorman and Sessions, *Camp Floyd*, 67).

[7]Mathews does not say anything about it, but at Camp Floyd, his party obtained information about the Simpson expedition's return route. They also obtained a written copy of an itinerary of the route that Simpson had compiled (Simpson, *Report of Explorations*, 133).

[8]During this day and the following two days, Mathews's mileage figures are unreliable, and the route his party followed is uncertain. When they first started out from Camp Floyd, they got

August 13, 1859 Fine day. Lay over. Howell after horses. Lew and Parker hunting, got two rabbits. I on watch, beautiful night, moonlight. Woke Read at half past twelve, horses all right.

August 14, 1859 Fine day. Started at eight o'clock. Got on the new road, had a rough time of it. Started for Johnson's Pass, stopped at Creek in Porter's Valley. Several springs. Took dinner sixteen and three-fourths miles from Camp Floyd.[9] Camped on Prince's Creek[10] in canyon three and one-half miles. Hen and I slept together.

August 15, 1859 Fine day. Started out at seven o'clock. Passed Williams Springs and creek, a fine stream of water.[11] Roads rough. Met Len Smith and guide.[12] Mr. Read took a cut off to Indian Springs,[13] twelve miles from Williams Springs. Had to walk a great deal. Got to camp at four o'clock, awfully tired.

August 16, 1859 Fine day. Got up late, felt tired. Lots of Indians, one lame, one named Jack—a smart fellow. Taught him how to count.

---

onto the wrong road. Where they went, and where they were turned back by the soldiers, cannot be determined with any degree of confidence. However, if we ignore his mileage figures, it would seem that the most logical place for this night's camp would have been at the mouth of Little Valley, at the western base of Lookout Pass. (See map 3.) This conclusion is supported by Mathews's entry for the fourteenth, when he said that they "got on the new road." This new road was almost certainly the route first traveled by Lt. J. L. Kirby Smith, who had gone through Little Valley on August 7, just a week earlier (Simpson, *Report of Explorations*, 142).

[9]The sixteen and three-fourths figure is clearly a misstatement by either Mathews or his transcriber. He was about forty-six miles from Camp Floyd at this time.

[10]The Simpson expedition had camped here eleven days before the Mathews party arrived. Simpson had named the stream after Maj. Henry Prince. It is now known as Judd Creek. The spot where the Simpson expedition camped on Judd Creek is exactly 3.5 miles from the point where the trail crossed Porter's Creek (Simpson, *Report of Explorations*, 131).

[11]Williams Creek is now known as Death Canyon Wash. The location of Williams Spring is uncertain, but was probably a short distance from the mouth of Death Canyon, which is on the southwest slope of the Simpson Mountains. Simpson had named the spring after Assistant Surgeon Thomas H. Williams (Simpson, *Report of Explorations*, 130).

[12]It seems likely that the transcriber changed "Lt. Smith" to "Len Smith." According to his official report, Lt. J. L. Kirby Smith was traveling back to Camp Floyd along this same section of the trail on this same day. Accompanying him was John Reese, the chief guide for the Simpson expedition (Simpson, *Report of Explorations*, 143).

[13]When the Simpson expedition was camped at present-day Keg Spring on July 31, he named it "Good Indian Spring" in honor of the Indian who led the expedition's guide to it (Simpson, *Report of Explorations*, 129). Mathews and others soon shortened this name to "Indian Spring." It is important not to confuse this spring with the Indian Spring in the interior of the Simpson Mountains, where almost all Central Overland Trail emigrants camped after 1862.

He called Brigham Young a Son of a B.[14] Holladay's cattle came up, water scarce. Started at five o'clock to cross desert 35 miles. 45 miles to Tyler's Springs or Creek and Canyon. I rode horse Jack all the way. Three ponies belonging to some Packers gave out. We met Frenchman again.[15]

August 17, 1859 Fine morning. After getting up took breakfast with the Packers. Took blankets and slept until three o'clock. Took a good wash, also a smoke after supper and went to Holladay's camp. Had some good singing by a fellow named Charley. Sang a great many songs. Packers bought three ponies, one for $2., one for $8.50, and one for $10., saddles and bridles included. Water plenty and very good. Retired at ten o'clock. Hen on watch, thought he heard Indians and woke up the camp. Robinson and lady camped with us, fine people.

August 18, 1859 Fine day. Roads awfully rough. Started out at seven o'clock, got to Chapin's Springs at three o'clock—distance sixteen miles.[16] Just got through supper when Al ran to camp and said Indian had stolen a horse. Saw him riding off. Everybody excited. Read got the mule Jaco and started after the Indian, others on foot. Tracked the horse some four miles, gaining on him all the time, over a very rough mountain trail. Got to the top of the mountain, found the horse but no Indian. Horse just able to walk a hundred feet or so when he fell dead. The Indian had stabbed him to the heart. The boys piled a lot of brush and dry wood over and under the horse to burn him up, so that the Indians should not eat him. All felt badly to think that an Indian should get the advantage of us.

August 19, 1859 Cloudy day. Started out at eight o'clock. Good road. Got to Rush Pond[17] at one o'clock. Just a watering place, no wood

---

[14] There can be little doubt that the lame Indian was Quah-not, the cripple who led Simpson's guide to Keg Spring. Perhaps Jack, the "smart fellow," was Quah-not's son, whose real name was Ah-pon (Simpson, *Report of Explorations*, 130).

[15] The Simpson expedition had camped at Tyler's Spring, now known as Mud Spring, on the night of July 27 (Simpson, *Report of Explorations*, 126). See ch. 2, n16. The actual distance along the trail between Keg Spring and Mud Spring is very close to thirty-five miles. Mathews's mention of the "Packers" indicates that in addition to his party, there were other travelers using Simpson's return route.

[16] See ch. 2, n17.

[17] See ch. 2, n18.

or grass. Started at four o'clock, got to Plympton's Springs,[18] twenty miles, at eleven o'clock. Water strong with sulphur. Good roads but feed very scarce.

August 20, 1859 Fine day. Started out without dinner. Did not like it much. Got to Crosman's Creek at six o'clock.[19] Feed good. Small stream. Distance about eleven miles. Heard awful yells, coyotes and Indians howling, could not sleep.

August 21, 1859 Fine day. Started at eight o'clock Roads good. Rush Springs in Crosman's Valley, four mile crossing of dry creek. Water about 5 1/2 miles away at forks of roads. 23 1/2 miles to Red Springs.[20] Several in vicinity. Camped at noon, roads very heavy. Started at four o'clock. Seven and a half miles to summit of High Springs.[21] Got there at eight o'clock, very dark. Read was mad. Water good. Got supper. Some Indians showed themselves. Snake tribe, good Indians. Read and I on watch first. I had a hard time to keep stock together. Found them all right in the morning, though hard work.

August 22, 1859 Fine day. Started out at half past seven o'clock, got to spring in Antelope Valley at half past ten o'clock. Passed good feed but little at the Spring. Took dinner. Roads heavy. Lots of Indians around, called themselves Snakes. Got within four miles of high mountain range, Read discovered good spring. Traveled ten miles from Antelope Springs, saw lots of antelope. Roads heavy. Lew rode horseback all afternoon. Felt unwell and could not walk.[22]

August 23, 1859 Fine day. Started out at seven o'clock. Rough roads, fine stream of water running alongside named Stevenson's Creek.[23] Gathered lots of choke berries, very good, ate plenty of them. Camped

[18]See ch. 2, n19.

[19]See ch. 2, n20.

[20]Mathews overestimated the distance. It is only 14.5 miles from the campsite on Baker Creek to Red Springs.

[21]From Red Springs to Turnley Springs, which is probably what Mathews called "High Springs," it is nine miles rather than the 7.5 given by Mathews.

[22]They were now in present-day Spring Valley. The spring they came to at 10:30 is now known as Layton Spring. The overnight camp was probably at a small spring 1.7 miles above Cooper Meadows. See ch. 2, n25.

[23]After leaving camp, Mathews's party climbed over the ridge of the Schell Creek Mountains, dropped into Cave Lake Canyon, and then into present-day Steptoe Canyon, through which flows the stream that Simpson had named "Stevenson's Creek."

for dinner at ford of Steven's Creek, ten miles from last camp. Started at one o'clock, feed good all the way, roads rough. Clark's cart, or tender, upset. Clark very mad. Had a good laugh, lots of fun. Traveled to Murray's, four miles.[24] Beautiful springs, good feed, caught the other train.

AUGUST 24, 1859 Weather cloudy. Started at seven o'clock. Roads middling good. Got to Hercules Gate,[25] water scarce eight miles from camp, rather curiosity. Camped at dinner. Rained hard in the afternoon. Camp Springs and Canyon eight and one fourth miles. Five Springs in vicinity.[26] Rained while getting supper.

AUGUST 25, 1859 Fine day. Started at seven o'clock. Passed summit of mountain range three miles. Harts Springs and Canyon three and a half miles.[27] Took dinner. No water nor feed. Camped among the Ute tribe in canyon at four o'clock. Twelve miles. All camped together, company killed beef. All felt good. Water and feed fine.[28]

AUGUST 26, 1859 Fine day. Started for the desert at six o'clock. Crossed Summit of Blackhead Mountains, one mile. Thirty-two miles to Bluff Creek. Camped for dinner halfway. No feed. Rode the black colt for the first time. All thought he would throw me, but no go, though he tried hard. Got to Bluff Creek at seven o'clock.[29] Team did not get in until ten. Clark got in at half past eleven. Very hard road for eight miles, sage and sand. All glad to camp. Felt tired. Water good. Feed scarce. Did not watch, all so tired.

AUGUST 27, 1859 Fine morning. Did not get up until nine o'clock. Got breakfast. Howell very sick, put him in the wagons when we started. O'Neal's Creek in Canyon four miles.[30] Found good feed and water. Lay over, took a good wash and change. Retired at eight

---

[24] After leaving the canyon, they turned north and came to Murry Creek, near Ely, Nevada.

[25] Mathews's "Hercules Gate" is about six miles north of Ely. It is a gap in a low ridge through which a small stream flows. See ch. 2, n30.

[26] This camp was in the upper end of Smith Valley where there is a cluster of springs, of which the most prominent and easiest to reach is Archie Spring.

[27] Mathews has changed the name from "Hurt's Creek" to "Hart's Creek." See ch. 2, n32.

[28] Simpson had named the springs where they camped with the Indians "Pete's Springs," after one of the expedition's guides, an Indian who went by the name of Ute Pete (Simpson, *Report of Explorations*, 116). This area is now known as Thirty-Mile.

[29] This camp was at the eastern base of the Diamond Mountains, near present-day Water Canyon.

[30] The Simpson expedition followed a stream that he named "Neill's Creek" down the eastern slope of the Diamond Mountains. Mathews changed this to O'Neal's Creek. It is now known as Pinto Creek.

o'clock. At ten o'clock other teams came in. Had an awful time, woke us all up. Horses running all about. I saw the fine looking girl who was married in Salt Lake.

AUGUST 28, 1859 Fine day. Had a very sick horse. Could not leave it. I bet he would die in ten minutes from the time I saw him. I lost. He died about three o'clock. Thought he was poisoned with wild carrot or hemlock. Gave him a good deal of medicine, no use. As soon as he died, Indians went to skinning him. Lots of them about. Some Shawnees, fine looking fellows, very clean. The Company traded some with them. Got some beef from Brown. Clark and Brown ran a foot-race for $1.00. Clark got beaten.

AUGUST 29, 1859 Somewhat cloudy. Had quite a shower at noon. Passed summit of Macoby's Range of Mountains one mile and Macoby's Creek 1 3/4 miles.[31] Stopped for dinner at Lee's Springs, 6 1/2 miles. Roads good, camped, lots of Indians around. I slept in Robinson's tent.

AUGUST 30, 1859 Cloudy morning. Passed Clay Creek.[32] Water in holes, did not look good, 5 1/4 miles, Junction Springs, twenty acres of grass. Marsh 6 1/2 miles. Camped for dinner. Alkali crossing, outward route one mile. Valley Tan Springs, good water, grass scarce, 2 miles. Struck outward route, 5 miles.[33] Antelope Creek, 1 1/2 miles, rough road. Had a great time blowing abut the road. Read talked hard about Howell. Does not think him sick. Antelope Creek almost dry. Boys a good distance ahead with the horses. Indian told us there was plenty of water up the creek Found it. Water rather scarce[34] I slept with Ned. Very warm. Retired at nine o'clock. Blew up and hailed some.

AUGUST 31, 1859 Fine day. Started out at seven o'clock. Took the outer road and got stuck. Did not get water for 19 miles on right road, 35 miles on wrong road. Very foolish. Did not get to camp until eleven

---

[31]Simpson had named the stream "McCarthy's Creek" after Charles S. McCarthy, a civilian taxidermist who was traveling with the expedition. It is now known as Simpson Creek. The mountains are the Diamond Mountains (Simpson, *Report of Explorations*, 113).

[32]Clay Creek was Simpson's name for what is now known as Slough Creek.

[33]Mathews is talking about crossing Simpson's outbound trail. Since leaving Camp Floyd, his party had been following the trail that Simpson had made during his return trip. About twenty-two miles west of Eureka, the two trails crossed at a point where the outbound trail was heading south and the return trail was heading east.

[34]Simpson named this stream "Antelope Creek." It is now known as Willow Creek. It flows northward out of the Monitor Mountains into the southern part of Kobeh Valley (Simpson, *Report of Explorations*, 75, 111).

o'clock. Met some new packers, told us there was water 5 miles ahead at junction of outward route.[35] Horses very tired, feed not good, water plenty.

SEPTEMBER 1, 1859 Fine day. Got a late start. Intended to stop as soon as good grass was found. Went on to Rus [Reese] River.[36] Road leaves 2 1/2 miles on outward road. Take left hand. Monoponope Springs 3 miles. Numerous parks and lakes, water 5 miles. Feed fine. Stopped for dinner summit of high mountain range 5 miles above outward road. Take left hand 4 1/2 miles. Rus River crossing. Follow 1/2 mile. Camped 5 miles. Late. Good water. Feed scarce.[37]

SEPTEMBER 2, 1859 Fine day. Camped all day at Rus River. Caught some fine trout. Clark, self and Robinson out hunting. Had a good time. George and High camped with us for the last time, good fellows. Read on watch. Shot at a coyote. Made an awful fuss about others shooting while on watch.

SEPTEMBER3, 1859 Looked like rain. Started quarter to seven. Roads good. Junction of outward 1 ½ miles. Forks of road take right hand 17 miles to mouth of canyon or Smith's Creek, 3 ½ miles. Fine stream of good water, feed and wood plenty. Rained and snowed some.[38]

SEPTEMBER 4, 1859 Fine day. Started at seven. Woodruff Valley 3 1/2 miles, 1 3/4 summit to Lookout Mountain, 3 1/2 miles Edwards Creek.[39] Follow Creek for seven miles. Camped three o'clock. Piutes plenty around. Gave us lots of pine nuts. I ran one a race and beat him. Traded for furs. Good deal of fun.

SEPTEMBER 5, 1859 Fine day. Started at seven o'clock. Camped

---

[35]The words "outer road" probably referred to Simpson's westbound trail. The "junction of outward route" may have been in Big Smoky Valley where Simpson's return trail left his outbound trail about a mile north of Cape Horn. (See map 6.) Mathews's camp for the night was probably in Simpson Park.

[36]See ch. 3, n38.

[37]Mathews is going back to events that occurred earlier in the day. Simpson's name for the Simpson Park area was "Won-a-ho-nupe," so that seems to indicate where they were when they started. They probably had their dinner at the summit of Emigrant Pass, and then descended into the Reese River Valley.

[38]This somewhat confusing entry makes sense if it is interpreted to mean that after going 1.5 miles, they came to where Simpson's return trail left his outbound trail to cross the Reese River. After traveling another 17 miles, they came to another fork in Simpson's trails, where they took the right hand route, went 3.5 miles, and came to the mouth of Smith Creek Canyon. (See map 7.)

[39]The camp was near the point where Edwards Creek comes out of the canyon. See ch. 3, n40.

at Cold Springs.[40] Saw some Indians who talked good English. One's name was Buffalo Jim. Piute Spring good way from the road. Robinson hit Wilobie in the eye. Quite a gale. Retired at eight o'clock.

SEPTEMBER, 6 1859 Fine day. Started at eleven o'clock for Middle Gate. Passed Small Branch gate nine miles, 1 3/4 miles to water. Got by gate,[41] saw lots of Indians, squaws and papooses. Treated us very well. Awfully dirty tribe. Could not trade with them, know too much for us

SEPTEMBER 7, 1859 Fine day but rather cool. Started across the desert. Had grain along with us for animals. Stopped for dinner, fed stock. Started out, found some bunch grass, let the stock feed. Forks of outward road took left hand, 23 1/2 miles to Sulphur Springs.[42] No grass. Clark and Robinson stayed back. Got to springs at ten o'clock. Roads heavy, water strong with sulphur. Next place to H--ll. Could not drink water. Wall and Evans teams caught up with us. Slept awfully cold. As Ned was not with us, had to sleep alone.

SEPTEMBER 8, 1859 Fine day. Started out at eight o'clock. Felt very tired. Got to Carson Lake at eleven o'clock. Rested. No feed. Carson Lake and junction of outward road.[43] Warm Springs. Camped on east shore of Carson Lake.

---

[40]In the Cold Springs area, there are three sets of ruins: a Pony Express station, a stage station, and a telegraph station. Mathews and his party could have camped near any of these, or anywhere else in the area.

[41]Mathews had his gates mixed up. The "small Branch gate" that he came to first was Middlegate. From there, he went on to Westgate, where he camped. See ch. 3, n42.

[42]These springs are now known as Rock Springs. Mathews bypassed Sand Springs by taking Simpson's return trail and camped at Rock Springs, which is on the west side of Four Mile Flat. See ch. 3, n44.

[43]Mathews's statement about coming to the junction of Simpson's outward road needs some explanation. The Simpson expedition had been traveling in a northwestern direction when it reached the northeastern corner of Carson Lake. (See map 8.) They camped for a night on the eastern bank of the stream that left the lake and flowed north. Upon leaving this camp, the expedition headed south, following the eastern shore of the lake. After passing the lake, they continued in a southerly direction until they came to the Walker River, where they turned northwest to follow the river for some distance. During their return journey, the expedition crossed the Dead Camel Mountains and then traveled along the southern shore of the lake. When they reached the southeast corner of the lake, they turned north, rejoining their outbound trail for a few miles. About halfway along the eastern shore, they made an abrupt turn to the east, leaving the outbound trail and crossing the low ridge of the Bunejug hills. Mathews was traveling west on Simpson's eastbound trail when he crossed this ridge and came to the spot where Simpson's return trail left his outbound trail. This intersection of Simpson's outbound trail and his return trail is the "junction" that Mathews referred to. The location of Warm Springs is unknown, but the Mathews camp was somewhere near the junction.

SEPTEMBER 9, 1859 Fine day. Started at eight o'clock for south shore of lake. Arrived at two o'clock.[44] Found other company there.[45] Provisions all out and ours most gone. Clark and Read started out on mules for something to eat. Had supper and dinner together. Tried to fish and shoot something, but no go. Retired at eight o'clock, hungry. Touched my weak point.

SEPTEMBER 10, 1859 Got up late. Fine day. Took breakfast at ten, ate the last flour. Clark gave us some meal, made out a breakfast. Tom and I went out in the lake with the cart to sit on and fish. Did not get a bite. I fell in about five feet deep. Discovered the bottom was covered with mussels. Got a lot and had them cooked for supper. Tasted very good as we were all hungry. Read and Clark got back with the provisions, brought some fresh beef. Ate a big supper. Some Indians camped close by. Two squaws took supper with us, took a walk. Retired at ten o'clock feeling fine.

SEPTEMBER 11, 1859 Fine day. Started out without breakfast for Carson River. Did not get to river until ten o'clock. Roads very sandy. Very fine stream. Took a bath. Felt badly. Took dinner. We crossed the river, and got to Ragtown at three o'clock.[46] Took supper at station, had buttermilk and sugar, very good meal.

SEPTEMBER, 12, 1859 Cloudy day. Started out at eight o'clock. Six horses gone, traveled ten miles and waited for them to come up. Got to camp at three o'clock.[47] Clark and Robinson back. Parker and I fished some. Washed our clothes. Rained a little. Retired early.

---

[44]Since they had traveled for six hours, they could have gotten as far as the southwest corner of the lake, where they would have been near the Carson Sink Pony Express and stage station. See ch. 3, n45.

[45]Who could this "other company" have been? Was it part of the same loosely joined group that left Camp Floyd at the same time as Mathews, or was it a different group entirely? We know of the party that diarists Tuttle and Scott were traveling with, but Scott indicates that this party had passed this area on September 1. This entry may indicate that at least one other group of emigrants that has yet to be identified was traveling this route at this early date.

[46]This entry makes it clear that Mathews and his party took the Ragtown route. Although he does not specifically say so, it might be safe to assume that they camped somewhere near Ragtown. See ch. 3, n46.

[47]Early travelers could follow two different trails between Ragtown and Dayton. They could stay with the Carson River or take a shortcut across what became known as the Twenty-Six Mile Desert (Mattes, *Overland Journal* 10(4): 31). The latter route left the river near the present-day

SEPTEMBER 13, 1859 Fine day. Started at seven o'clock. Roads very sandy on the Old Imigrant Road. Camped on the river for dinner. Traveled about nine miles. Old horse gave out, fed him some flour. Started for station, seven miles. Got to camp at dark.[48] Ate some melons. Getting into civilization.

SEPTEMBER 14, 1859 Fine day. Started at one o'clock. Roads very good. Camped on river for dinner. Traveled six miles, hailed hard in afternoon. Camped on river. Feed scarce. Clark and Robinson ahead.

SEPTEMBER 15, 1859 Started early, got to Chinatown,[49] bought some things. Caught up to Clark at Dutch Necks at noon. Lew and I walked over to Carson City, got there ahead of the teams. Met a man by the name of Curry, wanted me to go to work for $75. per month, found teams. Camped in town.

SEPTEMBER 16, 1859 Dressed up a little. Talked a good deal to Curry. Advised me not to go over to California as there were good mines in Opher, some sixteen miles east by north. Finally made up my mind to stay.[50]

---

small community of Silver Springs and remained quite close to the route of U.S. Highway 50 until it rejoined the river route near Pleasant Grove, about seven miles northeast of Dayton. Simpson was referring to this section of road when he said that just after leaving Pleasant Grove, the expedition "for the first time, got into the old Humboldt River and Carson Valley emigrant-road." He further described the road as being "as well beaten as any in the states" (Simpson, *Report of Explorations*, 89). Mathews's comment about doing some fishing after going into camp indicates that he had taken the river route, rather than the shorter, waterless route across the Twenty-Six Mile Desert. (See map 9.) Based on the next entry, the camp was about two miles east of where U.S. Highway 95A crosses the river, not far from where Samuel Buckland built a bridge the following winter (Townley, *Pony Express Guidebook*, 240).

[48]This was one of the early Chorpenning mail stations, established when he was still using the Humboldt River route to carry the mail between Salt Lake City and Sacramento. It was on the north bank of the Carson River, just before the river entered the canyon that leads to Fort Churchill. Simpson called this area "Pleasant Grove," and it was at various times called "Miller's Station," "Reed's Station," and "Clugagis Station."

[49]Dayton.

[50]This was the end of Mathews's travel on the Central Overland Trail.

CHAPTER 5

Bolivar Roberts

1859

In August of 1859, Bolivar Roberts, an employee of George Chorpenning's Salt Lake and California Mail Company, learned about the route that the Simpson expedition had used during its recent return from Genoa. Roberts learned that Simpson and Gen. Albert Sidney Johnston were saying that this southern route would be a better wagon road than the expedition's outbound route that the mail company was using. Roberts decided to take a look at the section of this return route that traversed the desert of western Utah. After traveling this section of Simpson's return trail, he wrote a letter to the Deseret News, *a Salt Lake City newspaper. Even though Roberts's letter is not a diary, it is being included in this collection because he mentions encountering emigrants on the trail.*

The Deseret News, September 14, 1859, 4.

NEW CALIFORNIA ROUTE

By request we insert the following letter from Mr. Roberts, an agent or sub-agent of the Salt Lake and California Mail line, in relation to the eastern portion of Captain Simpson's new route to Carson Valley. It will be seen by comparing Mr. Roberts' description of the road with Captain Simpson's itinerary, that the distances very nearly correspond, but there is not as much water as might be supposed at [Good] Indian Spring, in the absence of a definite statement as to the amount in Capt. Simpson's report. Mr. Roberts says that the road in some places is not good and that grass is not so very plenty. Of these the captain says nothing on that portion of the route referred to by Roberts and, of course, emigrants should understand that neither are to be found there, and make calculations accordingly before entering upon those desert places that are thus made to appear:

Pleasant Valley, C. and S. L. M. Route Aug 26, 1859

Ed. News—Dear Sir:

Much has been said lately about the new route which Capt. Simpson has recently explored from your city to Carson Valley. As I have just returned from a trip over a portion of that road, perhaps a brief description of it, so far as I went, may prove beneficial to a portion of the late emigration. And permit me to say that in penning these lines, I am not actuated by any selfish or jealous motive, but simply desire to benefit the traveling public.

Capt. Simpson's road leaves the mail route thirty miles west of Camp Floyd, bearing southwest.[1] It is uneven and very rocky for about twenty miles. At this point there is a small mountain stream, called Prince's creek, which affords plenty of water, there is bunch grass north in the kanyon.[2] From there it is nineteen miles to [Good] Indian spring over very heavy road, rock and sand all the way.[3] I found a few emigrants

[1]At almost exactly thirty miles from Camp Floyd, the Little Valley Road leaves the main road and heads south. (See map 3.) This is the route that Lt. Kirby Smith followed on August 6, 1859, when he took a work detail back along the last 100 miles of the return route. It was Smith's trail that Roberts referred to as "Capt. Simpson's road."

[2]Judd Creek is twenty miles from where Smith's new trail left the Simpson expedition's outbound route. Simpson named this stream Prince's Creek after Maj. Henry Prince, the army paymaster at Camp Floyd (Simpson, *Report of Explorations*, 131).

[3]Depending on the route taken through the Death Canyon Wash area, it is seventeen to nineteen miles from Judd Creek to Keg Spring, which Simpson named "Good Indian Spring" and Roberts called "Indian Spring."

camped here, who informed me they had been there thirty six hours trying to water twenty head of animals.[4] The spring affords barely sufficient water for camp use. Thence to Tyler's springs it is thirty five miles.[5] Neither grass nor water on the way. At this place, also, there were emigrants camped.[6] Their stock was very much jaded, as they had driven fifty four miles without water. There is plenty of water for camp use here; the animals have to be driven one mile and a half up the kanyon to water; bunch grass on side of the mountains.

About ten miles from these springs, and near the same distance west of Sevier lake is the junction with the old road leading to the White Mountains. I was told that Captain Simpson's route follows this road about one hundred miles. Five and a half miles north west of the junction is the Chapin springs. There is but little feed here. Thence, forty miles to Plympton [Knoll] spring; water once on the way, but no grass.

On arriving at this point, I became satisfied that it was unfit for an emigrant road, much less a mail route, therefore I took across the country to Pleasant Valley, which is about twenty five miles north west. All travelers going to California by said route, should start with their animals well shod, and a good supply of water casks.

B. Roberts

---

[4]The identity of these emigrants is unknown. We do know of two emigrant parties that passed through Camp Floyd on August 6 and 7 because they were mentioned in Simpson's report. The first group included Charles Tuttle and Lumin Scott, whose diaries appear in this book. This party did not go to Keg Spring. We also have information relating to a third emigrant party that passed through Camp Floyd on August 11 and spent the night of August 15 at Keg Spring (Simpson, *Report of Explorations*, 133). Another of our diarists, Edward Mathews, was with this group, but they would have been gone from Keg Spring before Roberts arrived.

[5]See ch. 2, n16. The distance between Keg Spring and Mud Spring, which was then known as Tyler's Spring, is very close to thirty-five miles.

[6]The identity of these emigrants is also unknown. This is important because that it shows that Simpson's return trail was used by more emigrants than has been previously realized.

CHAPTER 6

Lavina Porter

1859

Lavina Honeyman Porter and her family made the westward journey in 1859. She undoubtedly kept some sort of diary or journal and some years later referred to it when she wrote an account of the trip. Porter's account is long on descriptions of daily activities and the sights along the trail, but very short on the details that would tell us where she was and when she was there. Due to the length of her account and the lack of pertinent detail, the editor has included only those brief excerpts that provide some information about the party's locations as they traveled westward along the Central Overland Trail. The route followed by Porter's party was unusual in that soon after crossing the Diamond Mountains, they left the Central Overland Trail and traveled northward to the Humboldt River.

Porter's account was published under the title Westward Journeys: Memoirs of Jesse A. Applegate and Lavina Honeyman Porter Who Traveled the Overland Trail *(Chicago: Lakeside Classics, 1989). The title of Porter's section of this book is "By Ox-Team to California." The Bancroft Library provided a copy of a portion of the Porter account and granted permission to publish it (banc mss c–d, By ox-team to California, Lavina Honeyman Porter).*

Emerging from the hills we came out on the broad plateau that overlooked the valley of the Great Salt Lake. The city was still several miles from us, and although we had two or three hours of daylight before us, we had to curb our desire to enjoy the comforts and luxuries that we had hoped to find within its boundaries. It was not until almost noon of the following day that we descended—weary, dusty, and browned with over a thousand miles of jolting, fording, and camping—into the veritable city that so long had seemed a myth. To us poor emigrants it bore a most delightful aspect. It was regularly and handsomely laid out on a level plain. Little irrigating canals flowed on either side of the streets, whose clear, cold waters were led into the orchards and gardens surrounding every home. The houses of that time were generally small, one story buildings of adobe, and every householder had an acre of ground to cultivate around his home. . . .

We camped for several days in the outskirts of the city, and enjoyed to our heart's content the luscious fruit and fresh vegetables that we were able to buy or trade from the Mormon women. These women thronged into our camp with everything in the way of produce, which they were glad to exchange for any articles the emigrants desired to part with. . . .

We lingered for several days in Salt Lake City and cleaned house so to speak. That is we unloaded and rearranged our stores, repacked our depleted boxes, aired and cleaned our bedding, which was impossible when we traveled each day, brushed out the accumulated sand and alkali dust, repaired the wagon which the constant wear over the bad roads made necessary, and had our faithful, old horse newly shod. We were very soon to find that we had overstocked ourselves with fresh fruit and vegetables. We hoped that they might last us a month, but had not counted on the hot sun across the Utah desert, which so wilted and shriveled them that they were no longer appetizing and we threw them away. The tub of fresh butter, which looked so hard and firm when stowed away in our wagon, was soon turned by the hot sun of the desert into liquid oil by day, though it hardened a little at night. For a while we used it even in its liquid state, but eventually it became so rancid that it, too, was left by the wayside. . . .

Leaving Salt Lake City, our road crossed the River Jordan.[1] We did not get a view of the Great Salt Lake as it lay some twenty miles and a good day's travel beyond our direct route.[2] We left the green and fertile land around the near neighborhood of the city and again came on a desert as barren as the great Sahara. Here we encountered sixty miles of almost pure sand. Seas of water would not have produced verdure on its barren soil. The scanty vegetation was the everlasting sagebrush and greasewood which I am tired of mentioning. The mountains and plains seemed to divide the ground equally. The valleys were from ten to fifteen miles across, though in the clear air of Utah they seemed only half that distance. But the arid land produced little food for our stock. Here and there grew the bunch grass on which depended the life and sustenance of our cattle. Only at rare intervals would we reach a stream whose banks afforded forage for our stock, and rest and refreshment for weary and thirsty travelers. Springs were most infrequent and often we had to dig a considerable depth in the shallow, dry bed of the streams for water, finding barely enough to partially slack the thirst of our cattle. And, oh the suffering from the scorching, burning alkali dust. It filled the air, penetrated through everything, covered our bodies, found its dusty way into our food boxes, bedding and clothing. . . . It was over six hundred miles from Salt Lake to the base of the Sierras, but the roundabout way that sometimes we had to travel in order to find food and water for our stock made the distance much longer. . . .

Time hung heavily on our hands as we plodded along over the barren stretches of Utah. We became almost lifeless as the country over which we were traveling. Even by day there was an all-pervading silence. No chirp of bird, no hum of insect. Far ahead of us a white line marked our road. It seemed to ever beckon us on over more arid stretches of desert sand and sagebrush. This part of our journey was one perpetual search for water, and when we were fortunate enough to find it, we did nothing but condemn and criticize it all night, grumbling at its quality and lack of quantity. Yet we left it in the morning with fear

[1]The crossing took place near present-day Thanksgiving Point. See ch. 2, n5.

[2]From Salt Lake City, the Porters traveled south on the old state road to the Jordan River crossing, then southwest to Camp Floyd. (See map 2.)

that we might not again find any so good. . . . Just before reaching Fish Springs, we passed one of the salt wells that were common to this part of the country.[3] Its depth was unknown, but the water contained therein was so strongly impregnated with salt that it was like a strong brine. This well was six or eight feet in diameter, and all around it the vegetation was covered with a white incrustation. The suction of this strange well was so intense that it would draw in anything used in attempting to explore its depths. A rude fence had been thrown around it to guard the unwary traveler.

Fish Springs[4] was a large pool of water lying at the base of a low mountain. For three or four miles it sent out a large and copious stream, but the thirsty sands soon absorbed it. The water, while brackish, was said to abound in fish. We threw in our line and tried to coax a bite from the finny denizens, but the only bite we got was from the swarming mosquitoes, immense in size and venomous as starved creatures. They stung our cattle to the verge of madness, and at early dawn we were glad to get beyond their onslaughts. A rude stage station was established at Fish Springs, and the lonesome keeper greeted us warmly. The sight of travelers to pass the night brought some variety into his isolated life, which had no companionship save the horses and his dogs and cats. We filled his heart with gratitude by leaving with him some of our tattered and torn literature. From the keeper

[3]On their way from Dugway Mountain to Fish Springs on May 6, 1859, the Simpson expedition took a roundabout route, following the Chorpenning trace, which circled to the south of the Black Rock Hills to avoid the marshy area to the east and south of the springs. After crossing the southern part of Fish Springs Flat, the expedition moved north along the eastern base of the Fish Springs Mountains, passing a deep and brackish pool that Simpson called "Devil's Hole" (Simpson, *Report of Explorations*, 50; Greeley, *An Overland Journey*, 203). Porter described this pool as a "salt well," indicating that her party was following the Chorpenning-Simpson trail to Fish Springs. They may have been among the last to use the route past Devil's Hole because within a few months, a passable road was established across the swampy area.

[4]When the Simpson expedition reached Fish Springs, they probably camped at the first large pool they came to, which now is known as South Spring. The next day, they passed by a Chorpenning mail station near Middle Spring (Simpson, *Report of Explorations*, 51). All but six of our diarists stopped at Fish Springs. It is interesting to note that among those who described the water, their opinions varied considerably. Some thought it was fine, while others said it was undrinkable. This might have had something to do with from which of the several pools they tried to drink. The degree of mineralization varies between the different pools, and perhaps the emigrants who did not like the taste of the water should have tried other pools before moving on.

we learned that the nearest water was over thirty miles away, and he urged us, if possible, to make the drive in one day.

The next morning, long before the sun was up, we were traveling through a dusty, sandy pass. The sky was overcast with heavy leaden clouds and the dry heart was intense. Peal after peal of thunder shook the air, but only a slight shower overtook us. However, we hailed it with delight for while there was more thunder than shower, we were gratified for any moisture. This unusual rain served to cool the air, and we hurried along with renewed zeal, hoping to reach by nightfall the point already described to us as Pleasant Valley. Darkness overtook us long before we reached its precious locality. We knew, however, that it could not be far off by the way our thirsty cattle snuffed the air, and by their increased gait, which required no urging. A little later we drove into the valley, where the pure and sparkling water of Willow Springs greeted us with its refreshing coolness.[5] How we reveled in its pure, sweet depths. Our thirsty cattle drank again and again, stopped to graze awhile, then returned to dip their brown muzzles into its leaping waters. The vegetation around Willow Springs was the most luxurious we had seen since we left Salt Lake, and as we had overdriven our stock, we stayed there for two or three days.

We were told by the keeper of this station that we were now across the Utah Desert, that is the northeast corner of it, though it extended some two or three hundred miles south of us. For a time after departing Pleasant Valley, our road lay over the mountains of Utah, which brought us some relief from the everlasting sagebrush and sand of the desert. . . .

Our route through these Utah mountains[6] led us over innumerable ranges. We seldom lacked for water there, but the way was devious and

---

[5]The Porters were now in Pleasant Valley, which is just west of the Utah-Nevada border. (See map 4.) In this valley, there is a large spring now known as Cane Spring. This may have been what Porter called "Willow Springs." Probably because of her use of this name, the editor of the Lakeside Classics mistakenly thought the Porters followed the route that went past the Willow Springs that are within the town of Callao. A few months later, Chorpenning's company dropped the Pleasant Valley route and started going through Callao. The editor is not aware of any other emigrant party that used the Pleasant Valley route.

[6]Although they had crossed into what is now the state of Nevada, at that time the Territory of Utah still occupied the eastern third of present-day Nevada.

wild. One afternoon, leaving the higher ranges behind us, we struck a level plain, and saw ahead of us a drive of five or six hundred cattle which their drivers were urging along a low, marshy piece of ground over which had been built a rough pole bridge.[7] Such a large number crossing at one time had torn the frail structure to pieces. As the ground was too miry and uncertain for us to attempt the crossing, we were compelled to hold up for a day until James with the help of the herdsman repaired the bridge over which our timid oxen reluctantly trod. Our horse for a time utterly refused to trust his precious bones on the uncertain structure.

When we arrived at Ruby Valley,[8] we were told that we were in Nevada Territory. I looked in vain for the precious stones that I supposed had given name to the little station. On Reaching Diamond Springs, I found them also lacking in the sparkling gems whose name they bore.

Finally, we arrived at the banks of the Humboldt River.[9]

---

[7]The existence of a bridge on the Central Overland Trail in 1859 would have been highly unusual, but there is a record of one being constructed in Steptoe Valley. On May 1, 1859, using poles cut by employees of the Chorpenning mail company, the soldiers of the Simpson expedition built a bridge across what is now known as Duck Creek (Simpson, *Report of Explorations*, 58).

[8]Ruby Valley was one of the most important places on the Central Overland Trail. There was plenty of water and grass, and some other provisions soon became available for purchase or trade. All of our diarists who followed Simpson's outbound route indicated that they at least passed through here, and most of them stayed for two or three days. The Chorpenning mail company had a station near Station Spring, as did the later Overland Stage and the Pony Express. Col. Patrick Connor with about 600 soldiers of the California Volunteers arrived in Ruby Valley on September 1, 1862, and established Fort Ruby about two miles west of the station (Varley, *Brigham and the Brigadier*, 47). Connor left Ruby Valley on October 2, leaving 160 men behind as a garrison force. Four of our diarists mentioned that they saw some of these soldiers. When westbound travelers left Ruby Valley, they got onto the old Hastings Road, which had been traveled by the Donner-Reed party during the summer of 1846. These later emigrants stayed on the Hastings Road for about eight miles until it turned north to follow the western base of the Ruby Mountains and the South Fork of the Humboldt River. From the point where the Hastings Road turned north, the Central Overland Trail turned southwest.

[9]This statement makes it clear that the Porter's party left the Central Overland Trail and traveled north to intersect the Humboldt River at some point, but the route they used is unknown. Two routes that connected the Central Overland Trail and the Humboldt River route were the Hastings Road and Chorpenning's route to Gravelly Ford, but we can be quite certain that the Porters did not use either of these because Lavina tells us that they continued west on the central trail as far as Diamond Springs before turning north.

CHAPTER 7

Frederick William Hurst

1860

Frederick Hurst was a twenty-seven-year-old resident of Salt Lake City when he obtained employment with George Chorpenning's Salt Lake and California Mail Company. During late 1859 and early 1860, Chorpenning was in the process of changing his route to the Central Overland Trail and was setting up stations along the new route. Hurst's job required him to travel to Ruby Valley, where he was to help manage the station; his primary responsibility would be to plant and care for a vegetable garden. Although Hurst was not an emigrant, his diary is included in this collection because it contains important descriptions of the early use of the Central Overland Trail.

The original copy of the Hurst diary is in the archives of the Church of Jesus Christ of Latter-day Saints Church History Library. The editor was given access to a microfilmed copy and also obtained a transcript made by Samuel and Ida Hurst in 1961 and later digitized by Joyce Holt and posted on her website.

April 8, 1860 On 8th of April I received a letter from Brother Shearman stating that he had got me a situation out at Ruby Valley, Western

Route to California. I saw Mr. Egan.[1] He told me he wanted me to start with the first team which would start on the 13th of April, on Friday. He also said he would give me 35 dollars per month to start on, etc. I am going out for the express purpose of making a garden. I made arrangements for my wife to stay with her mother while I am away. Not having time I left everything for Creighton to move. I rented the house to Mr Hooper for 3 dollars per month. I also wrote out a list of debts due me the amount of 31 dollars and left it with my brother Clement to collect.

April 13, 1860 I started April 13th with Constantine, a Frenchman, he was teamster. Drove one of these large freight wagons with six mules, . . . also a young man, Joseph Wintle. I understood Mr. Egan that I was to ride out to Ruby, but after we started we were given to understand that the wagon was too heavily loaded, consequently we had to walk. Although I was so sick and weak it seemed that I would give out. By the time I had traveled five miles, Constantine very kindly let me ride. Accordingly drove down the state road.[2] We reached Majors at the Warm Spring[3] about four o'clock just in time to see the Bar Keeper and his boss have a quarrel and fight. Pistols were drawn but it ended without shooting. Having no orders, we had quite a fuss to get supper. We were all in a starving condition having had nothing to eat since early morning.

April 14, 1860 Next morning we started at three o'clock and arrived at Camp Floyd[4] at 12. Breakfasted at one thirty at Thomas Drun's Saloon. The place appeared to me to be worse than a Saloon. How men that call themselves Mormons can live in such a place is a mystery to me. It was a perfect hell to me. Talk of cursing, and swearing, I have never seen it beat, not even in the Gold Mines.

April 15, 1860 Next morning, Sunday, April 15th. We drove over to Gilbert and Gerrish's store and took in a quantity of bacon, some sugar, lumber for well curbs, and in fact we filled the wagon to the

[1]Howard Egan, the manager of the eastern half of the Chorpenning mail company's route.

[2]The state road was what later became known as State Street through the length of the Salt Lake Valley. (See map 2.)

[3]This stage station was sometimes known as Hot Springs and sometimes Rockwell's because it was owned and operated by Orrin Porter Rockwell. It was located just to the south of the present-day state prison.

[4]See ch. 2, n6.

top of the box. Mr. Egan also hired ten or a dozen of the worst black guards and black legs, loafers that could be scared up around Camp Floyd. I guess I just have to say too much. Suffice it to say I kept myself to myself as much as possible. We reached Jackson's station in Brush Hollow[5] before sundown, after a weary walk over a perfect sandy rocky desert without water. Distance, 25 miles, 75 miles from the City.

APRIL 16, 1860 Next day traveled about ten miles and then broke down. Constantine left Joe Wintle and I to mind the goods, etc., while he went back to Camp Floyd for another wagon. The balance of the crowd went on to Simpson Springs.

APRIL 17, 1860 Next day 900 head of cattle passed us, also three rough looking fellows, stating they had been hired by Mr. Egan, which statement afterward proved false.

APRIL 19, 1860 On Thursday, April 19th, Constantine arrived with the running gears of a wagon. We put the bed of the other wagon, had them loaded up, and although it was three o'clock we started for Simpson Springs,[6] where we arrived at 11. I was in hell all night for the men carried on shamefully and kept me awake most all night.

APRIL 20, 1860 On the 20th we started at four in the evening to cross what they call the 40 mile desert. We reached the Dugway Station[7] after midnight. We had no shelter and it kept storming. Nothing but a very little sagebrush to burn. The wagon did not arrive until about three in the morning. I thought I would perish with the cold. I never shivered more before in my life.

---

[5]Brush Hollow may have been an early name for what later became known as Point Lookout. See ch. 3, n8.

[6]Others may have known about Simpson Springs before Capt. James Simpson made his short reconnaissance in October 1858, but his is the first known record of their existence (Simpson, *Wagon Road Routes*, 30) He named this place "Pleasant Spring," but it soon became known as Simpson Springs. The Chorpenning mail company established a station here in late 1858, and it was later used by the Overland Stage and the Pony Express. Horace Greeley, who spent the night of July 21, 1859 at this location, expressed his concern that "the hot suns of August will dry up this spring" (Greeley, *An Overland Journey*, 262). Sir Richard Burton referred to these springs when he wrote, "[we] reached the station which Mormons call Egan's Springs, anti-Mormons Simpson's Springs, and Gentiles Lost Springs" (Burton, *City of the Saints*, 333). The water supply was always meager and there was never much grass in this area. As soon as a better source of water was found a few miles away at Indian Spring, most emigrants began going there to recruit their animals in preparation for crossing the Great Salt Lake Desert.

[7]This "station" consisted of nothing but a small tent at this time.

April 21, 1860 After a scant breakfast we traveled two miles, then had the pleasure of packing a sack of potatoes each up the Dugway, about a quarter of a mile. Then walked 25 miles farther to Fish Springs.[8] We ate up everything on the station before the wagon arrived which was about 11. I and Brother Crossbey took our blankets and went out to the haystack where I really did enjoy a good night's rest. Many of the party complained of sore feet. Saturday evening, after traveling in the rain most of the day we arrived at Willow Springs.[9] No shelter again. Just like the Dugway station, nothing but a small tent. However we had plenty of wood. They had nothing but a little flour. I made some kind of cake till the wagon arrived at 11. I then cooked supper for all hands, the rest being too tired.

April 22, 1860 Sunday. we traveled 18 miles. Camped in the mountains.[10]

April 23, 1860 Next day early, arrived at Deep Creek Station.[11] While resting I wrote letter No. 1 to my wife, Aurelia. Same evening rolled out again and traveled 9 miles. Camped at the Springs with neither wood nor food. The consequence was the mules strayed off while we were eating supper. Hunted till near midnight in the rain. At last we laid down. I had just got fairly to sleep when I was aroused by the cry of "Fire," and sure enough we were all in flames. Some of the bedding was burned considerably. I had lent my quilt to a Brother who had no bedding and it was entirely spoiled.[12]

---

[8]See ch. 6, n4.

[9]After circling the northern tip of the Fish Springs Mountains, the original Chorpenning-Simpson route went southwest to the southern end of the Deep Creek Mountains. (See map 4.) However, in September 1859, the mail route was changed. From Boyd's Station, the mail route then turned northwest to go to Willow Springs and the settlement of Deep Creek (*Deseret News Weekly*, September 28, 1859). A stage and Pony Express station was established at Willow Springs, which later became known as Callao. What is supposed to be the original structure still exists at Willow Springs Ranch, near the center of Callao.

[10]Traveling eighteen miles from Willow Springs would have taken Hurst through Overland Canyon and put him just west of the Deep Creek summit.

[11]When the Chorpenning mail company dropped the section of the trail that went to Pleasant Valley in September 1859, the new route went through Overland Canyon, over the summit at the north end of the Deep Creek Mountains, and then to the small settlement of Deep Creek, where a mail station was established. The station was about two miles north of present-day Ibapah. For nearly eight miles, the banks of the stream were lined with lush growths of grass, making it an ideal area for emigrants to recruit their livestock.

[12]The camp was near the site of Eight-Mile stage station, which may not have been operating when Hurst traveled this route.

April 24, 1860 At early dawn next morning, Constantine and I tracked the mules for about seven miles. We had a great deal of trouble to catch them. Got back to the wagons about nine. I rode a good part of the way for I really was too tired to walk. When we got within 7 miles of Antelope Springs we met Brother W. H. Shearman. We had a short chat together. I gave him the letter I wrote to Aurelia at Deep Creek Station. I did not catch the wagon till we got to Antelope Springs.[13]

April 25, 1860 Next day we laid by and I wrote to Clement

April 26, 1860 Next day when we got to Pete Neil's I left it to him to put in the mail. We laid out one to Brother Shearman from his wife. We narrowly escaped a fuss with the Indians through that hot-headed fellow, Constantine. They were begging as usual and wanted to trade. Constantine only answered them with curses. At last one of them said he was like a wolf running away. It was downhill at the time and the mules were on the lope. With that, Constantine stopped the team, jumped down, seized his revolver and ran to the hind end of wagon as the Indians (there were two of them) started to run. We drove on, we got about 100 yards and one of them stopped and drew a bead on us but didn't fire. We reached Shell Creek about three.

April 27, 1860 Next day drove on to Egan's Station,[14]

April 28, 1860 Saturday to Butte,[15] and on

April 29, 1860 Sunday, April 29th, 1860 we arrived at Ruby Valley Station,[16] etc., etc., etc. There are six rooms and a Blacksmith Shop at this Station. During Brother Shearman's absence Mr. E. N. Dillion had charge and Brother George Aly, assistant. Also one express rider, Brother William Fisher or James Carlow. After noting my new

---

[13]Antelope Spring is near the western edge of Antelope Valley and the eastern base of the Antelope Mountains. Along the current maintained road, it is 28.8 miles from Ibapah and 3.8 miles southwest of the old Tippett Ranch. These springs were the site of an Overland Stage and a Pony Express station. Lucretia Epperson, one of our diarists who camped here in 1864, mentioned the existence of a military fort. See ch. 17, n14.

[14]Egan's Station was just west of the west end of Egan Canyon, which is at the southern end of the Cherry Creek Mountains. (See map 5.)

[15]Hurst may have been at the old Chorpenning mail station that was at the south end of the Butte Mountains and was on the original Chorpenning-Simpson trail, or he could have been at Pony Springs, which was discovered some time after Simpson had passed this way on May 16, 1859. See ch. 8, n12; and map 5.

[16]This station was near Station Spring. See ch. 6, n8. His arrival at Ruby Valley marked the end of Hurst's travel on the Central Overland Trail.

home it put me in mind of a prison, built wholly of logs and the never failing dirt roof. Next day, Brother George and I fixed up what few tools there were around and the balance of the day we spent gardening. Last week we expected a fuss with the Indians for we heard they were going to drive off our stock. We watched all night but they did not come, however, we have kept our watch ever since. Last Saturday received a letter from Aurelia and was truly glad to hear from home. Both her and the little child are well. I also received a nice letter from Howard Egan telling me to take charge of the station and all of the mail properly belonging to the same, and give Mr. Dillon a receipt, and proceed with all the necessary improvements as fast as possible. Yesterday morning Brother James Carlow arrived from Diamond Springs and stated that the Indians had killed Raphael Lazier at Dry Creek, John Applegate and James Aulcoutt at Simpson Fork, and set fire to the Station. That Lafayetter Ball and Silas McCandless had run on foot all the way from Dry Creek to Roberts Creek. That they also left that station at 12 last night and came over to Diamond, 25 miles from here. He also stated that all the stations from Diamond to Carson were deserted, also that 60 men had been killed by the Indians near Carson. I sat down and wrote to H. Egan explaining the particulars and sent it off by express.

CHAPTER 8

Pvt. Charles A. Scott

1860

In 1860, Charles Scott was an enlisted soldier stationed at Camp Floyd. In late May, he was assigned to a detachment commanded by Lt. Stephen H. Weed that had the duty of patrolling the Central Overland Trail to protect emigrants from marauding Indians. Scott's diary takes us all the way from Camp Floyd to Carson City and back again. Although Scott was not an emigrant himself, his diary is included in this collection because of his frequent references to emigrants he encountered traveling the Central Overland Trail.

Scott's entire handwritten diary for the time he spent in Utah Territory is on microfilm at the Utah Historical Society. Dr. Charles Hibbard has transcribed the portion that was written during Scott's travels on the Central Overland Trail, and he graciously provided the editor a copy of his transcription.

May 26, 1860 1st Lieut. Weed with 22 men of the Company left Camp to day mounted as Rifleman to look after the Indians on the California Mail Route[1] who have been committing depredations.

---

[1]Scott is referring to the Central Overland Trail. Because Simpson's new (*continued, next page*)

May 27, 1860 The balance of the Company equipped as Mounted Riflemen left Camp Floyd this morning enroute for Ruby Valley, where I believe it is the intent [to] locate, establish a Post, send out scouting parties in search of Indians, keep the mail route open, and protect emigrants and mail stations. Some delay on the road on account of a wagon breaking down. Got to Rush valley Mail station[2] at sun down and camped it commenced pouring down rain after dark. Distance 23 miles.

May 28, 1860 It rained nearly all night so that bedding and everything else was pretty well soaked when we got up this morning. Started at 7 oclock, more delay by the same wagon breaking down, crossed Skull valley[3] and camped at the foot of Johnston Pass, water scarce, plenty of wood & grass. Distance 10 miles.

May 29, 1860 On guard during the night, the horses got very uneasy about one oclock, heard a horse winnow and our horses pricked up their ears and answered, presently, I thought I heard the sound of voices, and challenged three times. Then waited for the object to show itself before I fired but as I heard the sound of horses feet retreating I called for the Sergt. Of the Guard. A patrol was sent out, without finding anything. During the morning a white man and an Indian passed us in a different direction from the road. Started at six, very bad road for five miles. Considerable delay with the same old wagon. Camped at Simpsons Springs[4] at 3 oclock, water scarce, no wood or grass. Distance 18 miles.

---

route had been adopted by George Chorpenning's California Mail Company, it was referred to as the California Mail Route for some time, even though the mail contract had been given to the firm of Russell, Majors, and Waddell a few months before Scott wrote this.

[2]This was Faust station. (See map 3.) On his way back from his short reconnaissance trip in late 1858, Capt. James Simpson camped for a night on Faust Creek in western Rush Valley (Simpson, *Wagon Road Routes*, 35). When he returned to the same spot in May 1859, he found that Chorpenning's company had established a mail station on the west bank of the stream (Simpson, *Report of Explorations*, 46). A little over a year later, when Chorpenning was forced out of business, the station was taken over by the firm of Majors, Russell, and Waddell, and it became a stop for the Overland Stage and the Pony Express. Nothing remains of the station, but the site is marked by a stainless-steel post at the corner of a large equipment shed. The location is 4.5 miles north of the town of Vernon and a half-mile west of State Route 36. All of our diarists but John Fackler traveled past this station.

[3]Scott was confused about the name of the valley—he was actually still in Rush Valley. Skull Valley is west of what was then known as General Johnston's Pass, now Lookout Pass.

[4]See ch. 7, n6.

MAY 30, 1860 Started at Midnight, level road for 20 miles. Took 4 1/2 hours to get over the Dugaway hill. 20 miles further brought us to the Slough where two wagons stuck. Got a set of ox-teams to haul them out Camped at a pond at ten P.M.[5] Guard mounted at eleven, went on the first relief, fuel scarce, some grass, plenty of bad water. Distance 42 miles.

MAY 31, 1860 Got to bed at ½ past two this morning and had to get up at four. All hands busy during the forenoon, washing the mud from everything. Started at four P.M. Camped 1 1/2 miles beyond the Fish Spring Mail Station plenty of grass plenty of bad water and some wood Distance 5 miles.

JUNE 1, 1860 Started at seven. Passed some poisoned springs easily known by the bones of animals scattered around them. Road level at 12 miles. Came to forks of the road.[6] Took left hand one that leads into Pleasant Valley, owing to false information given to Lieut Perkins by a man at the last station, went four miles on it before we found out that we had been deceived, retraced our steps and resumed our journey. Camped at Willow Springs Mail station[7] at 1/4 past five, a fine bottom about a mile wide with plenty of grass and water, no fuel except willows. Distance 23 miles, considerable alarm at this station, about the Indians; a Boy while herding cattle yesterday, was shot in the arm by Indians concealed among the rocks. A few days ago, an Express Rider was shot through the hand and his mule killed from under him.

JUNE 2, 1860 About 4 oclock this morning an Express came in with the news that Antelope Mail Station was taken by the Indians at 12 oclock last night. Started at six. The road up hill for the first five miles, then through Willow Spring Canon for 15 miles, threw out flankers on each side of the road to guard against an ambush, saw the Express mule that was killed. The Indians had cut off his ears as a trophy of their victory, the road very good all the way to Deep Creek Station[8] where we camped at 2 oclock. Distance 30 miles, plenty of grass & water, wood two miles off. An excellent valley for agricultural

---

[5]This camp was at Fish Springs. See ch. 6, n4.

[6]There was nothing at these forks at this time. Later, it was the site of Boyd's Station. (See map 4.)

[7]See ch. 7, n9.

[8]See ch. 7, n11.

purposes. A large train of Mormon Emigrants in waiting for our protection. Total distance 151 miles.

JUNE 3, 1860 Laid over.

JUNE 4, 1860 Started at six a level road all the way antelope Spring Mail Station[9] where we camped at 2 oclock. Distance 30 miles plenty of wood and water, grass scarce. At the time this station was taken, two friendly Indians left in charge told the hostile ones that the soldiers were coming and that if they disturbed anything they would be hunted through the mountains so they left without troubling anything. They are said to be in Eagan Canon about 150 in number. The Indians in this vicinity are called Go-sha-utes.

JUNE 5, 1860 Started at six. The road led up the Canon for five miles which took us 5 ½ hours to get to the summit which is certainly the hardest and longest pull from here to Leavenworth the balance of the road was down hill.[10] Camped in Spring Valley at 2 1/2 oclock. Distance 12 miles. Plenty of grass and water, wood 1/2 mile off.

JUNE 6, 1860 Started at six. The road up a ravine.[11] Good camping places all along. Camped on the down hill slope; a mile from the Shell Creek Mail Station. Distance 7 miles plenty of wood, water and grass. We have had more or less rain every day since we started.

JUNE 7, 1860 Started at six. Very good road to Eagan Canon. The scenery in the Canon is grand, solemn, and impressive. The rocks on either side piled one on the other in picturesque confusion to a height of two thousand feet. A party passing through the Canon would be completely at the mercy of a concealed foe, who could pick them off at

---

[9]See ch. 7, n13.

[10]When westbound travelers left Antelope Spring, they had a choice of two roads. (See map 4.) The road heading south followed the eastern base of the Antelope Mountains until it came to Tippett Pass, where it turned northwest until it reached Spring Valley at what is now known as Stonehouse. An Overland Stage and Pony Express station was established at this point. The southern route was used by the stage all year round and by the mail riders during the winter. The other road left Antelope Spring heading westward, then climbed over Rock Springs Pass, and dropped into Spring Valley. This route required a lot of hard climbing, but was three and a half miles shorter and had good grass and water, which the Tippett Pass route lacked. Of the twenty-one diarists who traveled between Antelope Spring and Spring Valley, twelve indicated which route they traveled. Three took the stage route, and nine went over the mountain. This entry clearly indicates that the soldiers took the trail over Rock Springs Pass.

[11]Stage Canyon.

leisure. Camped at the Mail Station. Plenty of wood and water. Grass scarce. Distance 18 miles. A lot of half naked and starved Indians hung around the Camp all the evening eating the bacon slush that was thrown away and beggin for more. Rained all the evening and part of the night.

JUNE 8, 1860 Started at eight. Road heavy and up hill for the first five miles then downhill and level then up hill to the Butte Mail Station[12] where we camped at two oclock. Plenty of wood and grass on the hills. A sufficiency of water. Distance 18 miles. Rained most of the day and part of the night.

JUNE 9, 1860 Started at seven. The road up hill and sideling at the start. One of the horse wagons turned over twice, without doing any injury. Got to the top, descended a steep hill and ascended another where we had to double team. Descended across Huntingdon Valley, ascended and crossed. Camped in Long Valley. Plenty of grass and wood. Water not so plenty for large parties. Distance 13 miles.

JUNE 10, 1860 The mail came along last night with the intelligence that three Indians had been killed at Shell Creek, the Station burned, but that all the Stock had been safely driven to Deep Creek. Started at eight. Road down hill. Camped at Ruby Valley Mail Station[13] at 11 oclock. Distance 9 miles. Plenty of water and grass. Wood two miles off. Lieut Weed's party joined us here. An Indian called Leatherhead, whom they took prisoner at Deep Creek, attempted to make his escape two nights ago by throwing ashes in the eyes of the sentinel, but did

---

[12]This station was high up on the southern slope of the Butte Mountains, near Pony Spring. During the years that the Central Overland Trail was in use, two other sites in this area were called Butte, but they were not near any springs. One of the three sites was listed in the records of the Pony Express as "Bates Station." The first of our diarists to use the "Pony Spring" name was Phebe Carleton in July 1864. When the Simpson expedition traveled through this part of the country on May 15, 1859, they skirted the southern tip of the Butte Mountains and made camp near a Chorpenning mail station, missing Pony Spring entirely. Simpson commented in his report that since the water supply at the station was inadequate and undependable, a new source would have to be found, and the route changed (Simpson, *Report of Explorations*, 61). Sometime between then and August 1860, Pony Spring had been discovered in a canyon about three and a half miles northeast of the Simpson campsite, and the route had been changed. Although the new route went through the mountains and was more difficult to travel, the presence of water and grass at Pony Spring made it worth the effort. (See map 5.)

[13]See ch. 6, n8.

not get more than 30 yards before Henry the sentinel fired and shot him through the thigh and then went up to him and put his pistol to the Indian's head and fired three shots, all of which made furrows in the skull but without entering it. He then beat him over the head with his rifle until he was interfered with, as they all thought him dead. Judge the surprise of all, when next morning they found the Indian was still alive. He was taken care of and is living yet.

JUNE 11, 1860 Laying by. Last night, Conly who was sentinel over the wounded Indians says that during the night, the Indians tried to use a hatchet which he had concealed under the head of his bed so he shot him through the body and killed him.

JUNE 12, 1860 Laying by.

JUNE 13, 1860 Laying by.

JUNE 14, 1860 Left Ruby Valley at eight. Road up hill and then down. Crossed a valley. Water at 15 miles. Then up the steepest hill we have met with.[14] Then down is Diamond Spring Mail Station. Camped at five. Distance 25 miles. Plenty of grass and water. Wood two miles off.

JUNE 15, 1860 Started at six. Road level but some parts sandy. Water at 7 miles. Forks of the road at 14 miles, the balance of the road over a rolling country to Roberts Creek where we camped at half past one. Plenty of water, grass and fuel. In coming in sight of Roberts Creek we saw a party of men which we concluded were Indians. Charge was the command, and away we went at a gallop. On near approach we found them to be white men, with the mail from California. They were pretty well frightened, having been under the same impression that we were. Distance 30 miles.

---

[14]This hill is known as Overland Pass. There are two places on the Central Overland Trail that have this name, and they are separated by only fourteen miles. One is at the southern tip of the Ruby Mountains, and very little climbing is needed to reach it. This one is on the ridgeline of the Diamond Mountains, and the road to it is the steepest section of the entire trail. On the eastern approach to this pass, the first three miles were not so bad, rising only 970 feet from the valley floor, making it a six percent grade. But the last half mile to the summit is much steeper—the vertical rise is 480 feet, an 18 percent grade. The road over this summit is passable today, but only by four-wheel drive vehicles in their lowest gear. Simpson's expedition crossed it on May 19, 1859, and he named it Cho-Kup's Pass after a Shoshone chief (Simpson, *Report of Explorations*, 67). Twenty of the diarists in this collection climbed over this pass, and fourteen of them commented on how difficult it was.

JUNE 16, 1860 Laying by. The Emigrants were coming in at all hours of the night, all pretty well worn out, and it is on their account that we are laying by. The Mail Station at this place was burnt by Indians about three weeks ago.

JUNE 17, 1860 Started at 5 ½. Road level but sandy. At 14 miles a little water in holes. Camped on Dry Creek at 1/2 past four. Plenty of grass and water. Sage for fuel. Distance 35 miles. The Mail Station here was burnt and two men killed.

JUNE 18, 1860 The Emigrants were coming in at all hours of the night, so they are not able to start this morning. At twelve oclock, we target practice on horse back with pistols. The shooting was very good. Some of the emigrants reported Indians up the Canon. Accordingly, Lieut Weed took a party and started off on the gallop. Lieut Perkins took 17 of us up the Canon as far as we could go on horseback, dismounted and proceeded on foot. Took us about an hour and a half to climb a bluff. Found plenty of snow on the summit. Distance 16 miles. Descended to some cottonwoods, but no sign of Indians. Got back to Camp at sun down.

JUNE 19, 1860 Started at half past five. Good road to mouth of Simpson's Canon.[15] 4 miles through to Simpson's Park. The Canon is the wildest looking place I ever saw. Camped at Sage Springs 2 1/2 miles west of the Park.[16] Plenty of grass, water scarce, sage for fuel. Distance 26 miles. Lackfey caught and devoured a live snake.

JUNE 20, 1860 Started at 1/2 past six. Road up hill at the start, then down. Camped on Reese's River[17] at 11 oclock. Grass and fuel scarce. Distance 12 miles.

JUNE 21, 1860 Started at five. Road level at first then up hill and

---

[15]When the Simpson expedition left the Dry Creek area, they turned south, crossed Hickison Summit, circled around Cape Horn, then turned back north and entered Simpson Park Canyon (Simpson, *Report of Explorations*, 75–76). (See map 6.) Beginning in July 1861, the Overland Stage used this section of Simpson's route. The riders of the Pony Express took a much steeper route that headed west through the Simpson Park Mountains, passing the base of Eagle Butte. Emigrants used both routes. The stage route was easier, but seven miles longer. Of our diarists who indicated which route they followed, two followed the stage road and eleven took the more difficult Eagle Butte route.

[16]Possibly present-day Thorpe Spring near Emigrant Pass, north of Austin. (See map 6.)

[17]They probably camped somewhere near what would later become the settlement of Jacobsville. (See map 7.) See ch. 3, n38.

then down to Alkilie Flat, which is almost as smooth and level as a billiard table. Camped on Smith's Creek near the point of Lookout [Desatoya] Mountain at two oclock. Distance 30 miles. Plenty of wood, water & grass.

JUNE 22, 1860 Laid over to allow the Emigrants a rest.

JUNE 23, 1860 Started at five. Road up hill to the summit of Lookout Mountain. Then down hill along Edwards Creek[18] for 10 miles. Balance of road good to Cold Springs where we camped at two oclock. Distance 25 miles, plenty of water, sage for fuel, grass scarce. It was at this place that a Mr. Lewis lost 250 head of cattle by the Indians. There is a first rate wagon & camping in the middle of the road, with lots of broken dishes, camp kettles are lying scattered around as though the owners were suddenly called away, without having time to make any preparations for receiving their guests.[19]

JUNE 24, 1860 Laid over.

JUNE 25, 1860 Left Camp at seven. Road down hill, Camped at the Middle Gate at eleven.[20] Distance 10 miles, little water. Fuel & Grass very scarce. Started again at 6 1/2 P.M. Road good during the 1st part of the march.

JUNE 26, 1860 Latter part of the road sandy in places. Stopped at Sand Springs[21] at 2 A.M. fed & watered animals. Animals drank very little on account of so much Sulphur and started again at four. Road very sandy & stony. Mules pretty well fagged out. Camped on the Slough near Carson Lake[22] at 9 1/2 oclock. Distance from Cold Springs 54 miles, plenty of water and grass, no fuel except a little Cattle dung. Total Distance 461 miles.

JUNE 27, 1860 Laying by. Lieut Weed and fifteen men started for Carson City on detached service.

---

[18]See ch. 3, n40.

[19]In reading this description of the litter and abandoned articles beside the trail, one should keep in mind that the Central Overland Trail had been in use for only the last part of the 1859 emigrating season and the early part of the 1860 season. This seems to reinforce the concept that the central route was being used by a significant number of emigrants.

[20]See ch. 3, n42.

[21]See ch. 3, n43.

[22]This slough was probably what Simpson had called the outlet of Carson Lake (Simpson, *Report of Explorations*, 85). If so, it means that Scott's group followed Simpson's outbound trail to the northern shore of the lake. (See map 8.) See ch. 3, n44.

JUNE 28, 1860 Laying by.

JUNE 29, 1860 Lieut Weed's party got back without accomplishing their journey on account of a big mud hole.

JUNE 30, 1860 Mustered at seven oclock and crossed the Slough immediately thereafter on a raft that we had constructed which carried over the wagons and traps. The horses had to swim across. Started on our journey towards Carson City. Road level but sandy. Camped on Carson River about noon. Distance 8 miles. Plenty of wood. Grass scarce.

JULY 1, 1860 Left Camp No. 23 at 6 1/2 oclock. Road very sandy. At 12 miles came to Ragtown and the junction of the Humbolt Road.[23] Ragtown at the present is without an inhabitant. It consists of two houses, one of which I suppose is where the citizens reside and the other for a Store, Blacksmith, Barber, and Carpenter shops, Barn and for all other purposes so necessary to be carried on in a large town. We passed another house. I have not learned yet if it is a Town or only a village. Camped on the River at 11 1/2 oclock. Distance 18 miles. Plenty of wood and grass. Carson River is quite a large stream and I should think navigable for light draft Steamer for about fifty miles. It empties into the Lake of the same name, which has no outlet.[24] A Thunder storm came up about four oclock and drenched all hands. It continued pouring down rain until dark. So we have the very pleasant prospect of sleeping wet blankets.

JULY 2, 1860 Got up this morning thoughily exhausted and still as a poker our Thomsonian mode of treatment, but a little exercise and some hot coffee restored us. Laid up during the heat of the day to dry up. Started at five P.M. Road level but stony. Crossed the Little Desert at a brisk trot and arrived at Slabtown at midnight.

JULY 3, 1860 Camped on the River at one oclock in the morning. Distance 35 miles, plenty of wood and some grass.

JULY 4, 1860 Started at half past five, at nine miles passed through Pintown or China Town at which place the road leaves the River and

---

[23]This entry makes it clear that Charles Scott traveled through Ragtown rather than following the Simpson Road across the Dead Camel Mountains. See ch. 3, n46.

[24]Scott was wrong about Carson Lake having no outlet. The slough his detachment had rafted the wagons across the day before was actually a stream that flowed about fifteen miles to the northeast into the Carson Sink.

we had a good view of the diggings in the direction of Virginia City. There is every indication of a rich mining region, and plenty of claims being taken up to judge from the number of Shanties that dot the hill sides, but I doubt if the miners are making anything as I could see no signs of water. On approaching Carson City we were met by a number of Gentlemen in red and blue scarfs who invited us to join in the celebration, but as we were not in trim, Lieut. Perkins gave our excuses, as we entered the town a large crowd were firing a salute from two old anvils. The Carson Rangers (Mounted), the Carson City Guards, the Masons and Odd Fellows were all turned out. Camped a short distance above the town in an enclosure. . . .

JULY 5, 1860 Laying by. Met Commodire Corlely late of Nicarauan Navy. Had a cruise together over the town the navigation of which fatigued me that I was scarcely able to reach Camp.

JULY 6, 1860 Laying.

JULY 7, 1860 Left Carson City at nine, Camped on the Carson at half past three.[25] Distance 22 miles, plenty of wood grass and Mosquitos.

JULY 8, 1860 Left Camp at half past six, crossed the Little Desert and Camped at Williams Station at half past twelve. Distance 26 miles. No rest from the mosquitos.

JULY 9, 1860 Left Camp at seven Camped at Ragtown at half past twelve. Distance 20 miles nearly tormented to death by Mosquitos.

JULY 10, 1860 Left Camp at 6 3/4 oclock, got to the Slough at 11 1/2 oclock. All got safely across at three and joined the detached party under Workman.

JULY 11, 1860 Left Camp on the Slough 5 1/2 oclock. Met two or three horse droves bound in. Sand Springs at seven oclock. Distance thirteen miles. The Mail Company have built a corral and are rebuilding the Station. They have also sunk a deep well so that there is tolerable good water here now.

JULY 12, 1860 Left Camp at a Quarter past four oclock halted two hours on the Desert where some pepper grass grew. Camped at Middle Gate at half past two oclock. Three mule teams came near

[25]Scott neglected to mention that his detachment was now returning to the east.

giving out. It was more than an hour behind the Rest in getting into Camp. About two more days will dry up, What little water there is now. Distance today Twenty eight miles. We found a young Steer here. And had a lot of fresh beef

JULY 13, 1860 Left Camp at a Quarter past five. Camped at Cold Springs at 9 1/2 oclock. Distance Ten miles. Mule teams traveled very slow. We found a calf here.

JULY 14, 1860 Left Camp at a Quarter to Seven Oclock. On Edward's Creek, met Billy Fairchields with the Pony Express and afterwards the Eastern Mail party. Camped on Smith's Creek at 7 1/2 oclock. Distance Twenty Three miles.

JULY 15, 1860 Out on a Scouting Expedition today. . . . We Started this morning at Six oclock and got back to Camp at Four Oclock. Having traveled Steadily the whole time. All hands pretty well worn out. Distance 30 miles. Shortly after getting back to Camp there was a cry that Millar was drowned and sure enough when we went down two or three men were rolling poor Miller on the bank of the Creek, but life was already extinct. . . . This morning he started with us and seemed in better spirits than usual. He climbed two or three of the highest Mountains and was finally detached to find a Trail up a Ravine. That was the last we saw him alive. He got back to Camp about a quarter of an hour before us and being much heated from the extraordinary exertions he had made. He very imprudently went into the Creek to cool himself and while there must have had a stroke or Appoplexy which caused his death. His untimely death is deeply deplored by his comrades as he has left a vacancy in their ranks which will not be filled by a better man. This is my Thirtieth Berth day.

JULY 16, 1860 We buried Poor Millar at Nine Oclock this morning. The grave was dug five feet deep and then walled up with Stones. The bottom was covered with willow bushes. The Body was lowered in and covered over with boards. The Funeral service was impressively read by Lieutenant Perkins And the usual three rounds of Blank Cartridges were fired over his grave. A board was placed at the head with the following inscription on it. Sacred to the Memory of Joseph Millar of Light Co. "B" 4th Arty. Died July 15th 1860. Age 27 years.

The Location of the grave is a little above where the Road turns off to Edwards Creek, and is on the bank of Smith's Creek. One mile and a quarter distant from the Summit of Lookout Mountain. We left Camp at half past ten oclock and met a . . . train on the Alkali Bottom Camped on Reeses River. At a quarter to six Oclock. Distance Twenty seven miles.

JULY 17, 1860 Left Camp at half past Seven Oclock. Met the Pony Express on the river. They report a large party of Gosh Utes on the Park or near Simpson's park. They have secretly come from the Humbolt. Camped at Sage Springs[26] at half past Eleven oclock. Distance Twelve miles.

JULY 18, 1860 Laid over.

JULY 19, 1860 Went on another Scout in the Ravines and Mountains near Simpsons Canon. Found no signs. Came back to Camp after traveling about fifteen miles.

JULY 20, 1860 Left Camp at half past Six oclock. Got through Simpson's Canon all right. At the mouth of it saw a smoke on top of a hill to the left. The Company was divided. One half going with the wagons. The rest of us went in the direction of the smoke. On gaining the top of the Mountain, it was evident that Indians never camped there as there was no sign of water. Continued our scout through the Mountains without discovering any sign of Indians. Came out on the Road with in a few miles of Dry Creek, where we camped at half past two oclock. Distance from Sage Springs Thirty miles.

JULY 21, 1860 Left Camp at Twenty Minutes to five. At the grass Spot[27] something was observed in the Sage brush. Stewart and West were sent to see what it was. It was soon evident that there was something there, so a lot went to see what it was and brought in three Indians prisoners. The poor devils were very much frightened. A party charged round to see if there was any more, but finding none we resumed our journey when within five miles of the Station a lot more Indians were seen. A couple came up themselves. The rest attempted to run but were soon overtaken and brought back. So that we had

[26]Possibly Thorpe Spring.

[27]Possibly Grubb's Wells.

about a dozen Bucks and one squaw when we got to the Station. They were all let go as the Station Keeper said they were friendly Indians. Camped a mile & a half above the station on Roberts Creek. Distance thirty six and a half miles.

JULY 22, 1860 Laid by.

JULY 23, 1860 Left Camp at Seven oclock. Camped at Diamond Springs at half past Three Oclock. Distance Thirty miles.

JULY 24, 1860 Left Camp at a quarter past Six oclock. Met an Emigrant Train on the big hill.[28] Camped in Ruby valley. . . .

AUGUST 11, 1860 Quite an eventful day—The Company numbering 26 men left Ruby this morning at six, at the Butte Station we met Lieut. Goode with a supply train, & receiving some mail matter from it, we continued our journey and arrived at Egan Canon about five P.M. Distance 42 miles. When we were five miles from the Station, the Pony Express passed us and within three of the Station we met him again. He informed us that the Station was surrounded by two hundred Indians and they had the Keepers of it prisoners; as soon as Lieut. Weed came up we went at full speed, on coming in sight some few of the Indians that were unarmed took to the hills, the rest resolutely stood their ground. The Chief advanced to shake hands, but the Lieutenant insisted that he should lay down his rifle and it said to have been his intention to disarm the whole of them, but at this moment Corpl. Mitchell either without orders or from a misunderstanding of them, charged into the Indians followed by two or three, leaving the rest of us quite unprepared, as we were waiting for the Lieutenant's orders. After the charge; the action became general and quite lively firing kept up for about an hour. The Indians retreating to the hills & rocks where four or five of them were killed at long distance. It was useless to follow them as they could fire on us with impunity without any risk themselves. One Indian was killed at the Station and about five on the Rocks. Two or three more must have been wounded as we saw them carrying off several bodies. . . . All hands kept watch during the night, but nothing occurred to disturb us.

---

[28]The Overland Pass in the Diamond Mountains. See ch. 8, n14.

August 12, 1860 Nine men went back with the wounded. Five men went as an escort to the Pony Express as far as Shell Creek, leaving ten of us to keep the Station. . . . All hands took turn at watching.

August 13, 1860 The Pony express came in last night. Ten oclock. Our boys not come back from Shell Creek yet and we begin to feel quite uneasy about them Beecher was left back. His horse was shot in the back. Wound not dangerous. . . . Lieutenant Good's party have just arrived on their return to Camp Floyd.

August 14, 1860 On Scout this morning. . . . Left Eagan Cannon at Sundown leaving six of our men behind to guard the Station got to Shell Creek Station at Eleven Oclock. . . . Found the party here very much alarmed. All their stock has been driven off. They were very glad to see us

August 15, 1860 Poney [Express] Came in from the west this morning. Twelve of our men started ahead to escort it as far as Spring Valley. We left Shell Creek at eleven o'clock leaving behind Seven of Lieutenant Good's party to protect the Station. Camped in Spring Valley. Distance Eight Miles. No signs of Indians during the night.

August 16, 1860 Left Camp at Six oClock. Camped at Antelope Creek [Spring] at Ten. Nothing occurred on the Road anywhere the Station has been burned down within a few days. We laid by during the day expecting to see the Emigrants come along but as they did not come, We started back at Sundown. And Camped in Spring Valley at Ten OClock p.m. distance traveled today Thirty Miles.

August 17, 1860 Left Lieutenant Good's party in Spring Valley at Ten Oclock and relieved his detachment at Shell Creek. At Twelve where we camped. Distance Eight miles.

August 18, 1860 Left Camp at Half past Eleven OClock. Leaving six men behind to protect the Station. Camped at Egan Canon at half past two. Distance Twenty miles.

August 19, 1860 Left Camp at Half past Six leaving Six men at the Station. Camped in Ruby Valley at Half past four. Distance Forty two miles.

August 20, 1860 All hands busy drawing clothes. Washing etc.

August 21, 1860 Laid over to have the horses shod.

AUGUST 22, 1860 The Company numbering Twenty two left Ruby at a Quarter past Six. Camped at Egan Canon at a Quarter past four. Distance. Thirty Two miles.

AUGUST 23, 1860 Left the Canon at a Quarter past Nine. Camped in Spring Valley at a Quarter past Three. Distance Thirty miles. Left two more men at Egan and Three joined us at Shell Creek making our number Twenty three enlisted men, including two Teamsters.

AUGUST 24, 1860 Left Spring Valley at Eight OClock. Saw a few Indian tracks at Antelope. We excorted the Mail as far as Antelope. Camped in Deep Creek Valley at Five OClock. Distance Forty miles. The Road was very dusty but a shower of Rain that Came up about Four OClock laid the dust and at the same time gave us a good drenching.

AUGUST 25, 1860 Proceeded to Deep Creek Station where our horses had grain and Hay fed to them. Workman and Six Men went back to our last Camp to protect the Emigrants that are waiting for an escort. Distance 6 miles.

AUGUST 26, 1860 We waited all day yesterday expecting the reinforcements to arrive but as it is we are waiting again today.

AUGUST 27, 1860 The Reinforcement arrived today numbering Thirty Men from the different Companies at Camp Floyd. Under Command of Lieutenant Murray 10th Infantry.

AUGUST 28, 1860 Moved down to the Six Mile Spring[29] and laid by all day. At Eleven OClock at Night Saddled up and under direction of a guide started for Pleasant Valley.[30]

During the next month, Scott's detachment patrolled back and forth along the Central Overland Trail, experiencing nothing of any consequence.

[29]This spring is six miles north of the town of Callao and is now the site of Six-Mile Ranch.

[30]Between August 28 and September 28, Scott's detachment traveled to Pleasant Valley, then back to Ruby Valley, then back to Deep Creek.

SEPTEMBER 30, 1860 Left Camp at Seven o clock. Camped at Fish Springs at Twelve o clock. Distance Twenty five miles Got a sketch of the Station. Plenty of forage here for our horses. Left Camp again at half past Eleven O clock to cross the desert.

OCTOBER 1, 1860 Got to Dugway a little before daylight. Two of the Mule teams ran off the road and down the embankment into the ravine. Santinger making a narrow escape with his life, halted at the Dugaway, fed and gave the Animals a little water that we brought along for them. Resumed our journey and camped at Indian Springs[31] at 3 oclock, all the animals very much fatigued and worn out. Plenty of water, wood, and grass. Distance from Fish Springs 45 miles. This Camp is off from the main road, and is only resorted to by migrants who desire to rest their cattle previous to crossing the Desert. Nicolai took a fine sketch.

OCTOBER 2, 1860 Laid by until four P.M. and then went up to Simpson's Springs and camped at Sundown. Distance 7 miles.

OCTOBER 3, 1860 Started at six. Camped in Rush Valley at one. Distance 28 miles. A storm of wind and rain the whole night, so that our last night out is some what similar to our first one.

OCTOBER 4, 1860 Started at six and arrived in Camp Floyd at eleven; quite different in appearance to what we were on the day of

[31]Scott did not mention Indian Spring during his westward journey, and it is probably safe to assume his detachment did not stop there. What prompted them to go to Indian Spring rather than Simpson Springs during their return trip is uncertain. This spring is located on the western slope of the Simpson Mountains, well off the stage road and about eight miles south and a little east of Simpson Springs. (See map 3.) Unlike Simpson Springs, this area had an almost unlimited supply of both water and grass, and beginning in 1860, most emigrant parties spent from one to three days here before starting across the Great Salt Lake Desert. It is not known who discovered this spring, but Private Scott is the first of our diarists to mention it. Prior to 1862, the only way for wagons to get to Indian Spring was to follow the stage road to Simpson Springs, then leave the stage road and continue south along the western base of the Simpson Mountains for about four miles, then turn back east into the mountain for another three miles. In October 1862, when Col. Patrick Conner was leading a contingent of California Volunteers to Salt Lake City, he had his soldiers construct a road going east from Indian Spring, across the ridge of the Simpson Mountains, and down Lee's Canyon into southern Skull Valley (Rogers, *Soldiers of the Overland*, 40). This road is still marked on some maps as "Government Road" and is probably the source of the names "Government Creek" and "Government Spring."

our departure. Captain John Gibbon, (our new Capt.) had the Quarters in first rate trim for us. The Results of our campaign may be summed up as follows. Gave protection to a large train of Mormon emigrants, who made affidavits that they would have been attacked by Many disguised as Indians had it not been for our presence. Kept a Mail route 600 miles long open for travel, and by our activity gave protection to the Stations. Travelled ourselves, over 2000 miles, mostly through a barren and unhabited country. Fought one Battle with the Indians and killed during the Summer about thirty, and wounded as many more Indians, so that they will be apt to remain quiet for some time to come. The only white man killed on the route was Conly and the two men of our Company who were wounded at the same time, have nearly recovered. The only Animal we lost is a horse that was shot in the fetlock joint at Shell Creek and had to be condemned and left there. We had one horse to give out on the Desert, but went back with water, and got him into Simpson's Springs where he will recruit up and be sent into Camp.

CHAPTER 9

Delia Thompson Brown

1860

WHAT LITTLE WE KNOW about Delia Brown is that she and her husband John and several children left Huntley, Illinois, and traveled by covered wagon to California, following the Central Overland Trail through Utah and Nevada. Delia's diary is quite short on details such as mileage traveled and landmarks passed, but is full of delightful comments about everyday life on the trail. She also had a disconcerting habit of writing about events that happened on previous days, so the reader must pay attention to keep from becoming confused. The Browns left their home in Illinois on May 7 and arrived in Salt Lake City on July 17.

A transcribed copy of Brown's diary was obtained from the Nevada Historical Society. When the editor contacted the society to obtain permission to publish it, the person he spoke with indicated that the diary had been donated to the society in 1992 by "the Waltenspiel Family," which might be in possession of the original diary. The editor was able to contact George Waltenspiel of Reno, Nevada, who graciously granted permission to publish.

July 17, 1860 We had a love of a road this morning. In the first place we had to climb a hill about 2 miles. It was very warm and I almost gave out, but when we commenced going down I felt better; I walked nearly all the way to the City for the team did not overtake me. I paddled in the brook just like any other girl. Mal went ahead and got a ride again with Mac. We had a fine view of the city as we came down from the mountain. We found letters here from home.

July 18, 1860 Very warm last night—somebody wanted to borrow our horses but Lyman was on guard and sent him off. He did not have his revolver or he would have shot. We started to go and view the city last night, but it was too late so we did not see the sight. Oh this has been a very warm day and I have been so lonesome—can't tell the reason why but for some reason I feel lonely. I heard from home yesterday but it makes me feel sad every time I think of them. Oh well there is a place where there are no separations never to come—may we all meet there, but I do want to see the children. We are now calculating to stay here until tomorrow morning. A train has just come here that has 92 horses.

July 19, 1860 Oh what warm weather and snow in sight too on the mountains. O well I went around the City some last night. I think it a very pretty place. The streets are straight and wide and nice shade trees and flower yards in front of the houses and the houses so neat and comfortable looking. I would like living here I think, if we were in some business that would justify our stopping. We went round Brigham's premises some, but there is such a high wall you can't see much unless you get permission to go inside, and I hate to go among strangers so I did not urge the matter. We passed under the arched gateway leading to his residence over which is a large spread eagle. Over one of the doors, on the door cap I think, is a large bronze lion which is all grand and I suppose he is rich. Wonder if he is happy or don't riches always bring happiness? I think not. I don't know but we shall have trouble the rest of our journey on account of the Indians, but we hope for the best. The mail from the west came in yesterday, the first for two months, so I think the way will be open for us. We will have a large Company and keep good watch and trust the great Protector of all for our safe journey.

July 20, 1860 We left the city yesterday about noon and drove nearly ten miles before finding feed. We passed some nice looking field of grain but 'tis so dry where they have not plenty of water for irrigating—the land is not very productive. Well this morning we had a long consultation and finally decided to go back to town and take the central route as they tell so many big bear stories about the troubles with the Indians.[1] Well perhaps 'tis all for the best. Night and we have traveled until sundown and not stopped to feed or have dinner yet. We crossed the river Jordan and took some of the water to make our tea for supper.[2]

July 21, 1860 Camp near Black Rock and on the bank of Salt Lake.[3] This looks beautiful from here and there are 2 or 3 large rocky mounds of Islands just in sight. They are boiling salt near here. Oh this is such warm weather; yesterday I got so tired and had the headache too, a very uncommon thing for me. Harlow had a severe headache and he don't feel well this morning—hope it is nothing very serious. We have been highly favored so far, but no more cool weather, I am afraid, for us.

July 22, 1860 Here we are at the foot of a mountain in plain sight of the Salt Lake. We only came about five miles yesterday morning and camped here where is a large company, so we shall not have to go alone.[4] There is good feed here and good water and so they let the horses rest a few days. Here we have a fine view of the Lake and it is a nice sight too. I believe there are 46 wagons here and I don't know

---

[1]When the Brown party first left Salt Lake City, they headed north with the intent of following the Salt Lake Cutoff and then the California Trail. For some reason, they stopped, held a meeting, and decided to return to the city and turn west to follow the Central Overland Trail. It appears that someone convinced them that the Indian danger would be less on the central route.

[2]The Browns crossed the river on the old North Temple bridge. This bridge was located on what is now North Temple Street. It may have been the only wagon bridge over the Jordan River in the Salt Lake Valley during the emigrant years. Twelve of our diarists used this bridge. Six mentioned the crossing, and one stated that he had to pay a toll.

[3]They were at the southeast shore of the lake. (See map 2.) Brown was the first of our diarists to take the route past the lake and through Tooele Valley. Their reason for following this route is unclear, since Camp Floyd was still in operation and the stage road still went through it.

[4]If Delia's distance of five miles was accurate, they would have been near the settlement of E. T. City, which was the first settlement that travelers would come to after passing the southeastern shore of the Great Salt Lake. This town got its name from Erza Taft Benson, who was among its first settlers. The name was changed to Lake Point in the 1920s.

how many horses or persons either, but I think a sight of this train will be sufficient to frighten most any company of Indians or Mormons either. I don't like to travel where there are so many horses, for when we come to where feed and water are scarce some of the horses will suffer. I had much rather travel with our own little company for I don't just fancy some of the crowd, but never mind, it's nothing to me. I am only a passenger. Oh well they had a little dance last night, but I think from the sound they had some noisy ones. I like to see people free and sociable but such boisterous outbreaks and forwardness I don't admire but it takes well with some; so you see opinions differ—well of course they do and that is all.

JULY 23, 1860 Oh what warm weather this is and we are here yet on this same camp ground. There is so much talk about the Indians and other trouble that it almost makes cowards of some. For my part I had rather start just with our company who have been together so long than to have such a pack of cowards along. One large train started from here this morning and I was glad we were not a part of it as they took so long to get started in a military manner. Well they finally got away. We talk of leaving tomorrow and I shall be glad. I don't like to stop so long in one place. They think of getting to a stopping place in 4 or 5 weeks and I am not sorry to hear it I am sure. Yesterday was a long day, Sunday you know and very warm and I hardly knew what to do, and then I am so indolent and feel so little like exerting myself. Well may hap I shall be smarter when I get old enough.

JULY 24, 1860 We are now about to start again on our perilous journey. Old Tom is sicker and we fear he will never see California.[5] Maybe some of the rest will not either. Well we must take the bad with the good I suppose and not complain. This is the day the Mormons have their 4th and it is just 13 years today since they first arrived in this Valley and I suppose they date their independence from that day. We had a female fight in our camp yesterday between two grass Widders—I think it is time we left. The girls climb a high mountain yesterday or at least tried to. It tired them very much of course it is such hard work; I hope they may never see harder times than they do now.

---

[5]In a later entry, Delia indicates that "Old Tom" is one of their favorite horses.

JULY 25, 1860 Noon Here we are and about ready to start. Yesterday we had very good roads but Oh how warm and how sleepy I did get. We passed through a small city of Mormons[6] and here too they were celebrating the 24th—all looked very neat and tidy. Pink seems to be the prevailing color; pink shirts for the little boys and blue 'Demmin' pants and the little girls with pink dresses or white trimmed with pink. I would have been glad to hear the discourse but could not. Well we found some water and stopped for dinner. There was not much grass so we did not stay long but drove on a few miles for dinner. There was not much grass so we did not stay long but drove on a few miles farther and found plenty of water and grass.[7] Just as we stopped there came up a sudden shower and this was very strange as they never have any rain here. Oh how thick the crickets are—they climb up the spears of grass and they are fairly black.

JULY 26, 1860 Oh dear what a time we had last night. It rained yesterday just as we had our dinner cleared away and that made the roads very bad indeed. We had a long drive in the forenoon and then did not find good grass or we should have staid over night. Of more bad luck—old Tom has been sick ever so long and last night breathed his last and has gone where all good horses go. We shall get used to bad luck I guess before we get across the desert. We talk some of staying here until noon and then going on a few miles and rest again before starting on the desert. I hope we shall have no very serious trouble. All I feel bad abut is the poor horses, if they live it will be a hard life at best. There were 3 or 4 companies camped here last night—some of them have gone on this morning. They are very much afraid of the Indians, but I don't fear them as much as I do starving the horses.

JULY 27, 1860 Who can tell in the morning what the events of the day may be ere it close? I have been led to ask myself this question by a sad accident that occurred yesterday. We started yesterday afternoon for a short drive all in health and high spirits—fondly anticipating I suppose a good time at night around the camp fire. But alas for human

---

[6] This was the town of Tooele, an early Mormon settlement located about twelve miles south of the southern shore of the Great Salt Lake.

[7] They had reached Faust Creek, probably just a short distance downstream from the Faust stage station.

calculations. We had not gone far ere a thunder shower came up and soon we saw a man coming back on horseback at the highest speed and brought the sad intelligence that lightening had killed a man and 2 horses. What shock to us all and all hurried forward in hopes that life might not be quite extinct, but too late for human aid. The young man has no friends or relatives in the crowd. He was going through with Mr. MacClellan and he had no acquaintance with him previous to the starting. Since he has no friends to weep for him all nature mourns. I never saw a harder shower than we had soon after starting forward with the corpse. We camped last night in a pleasant little valley and here made his grave.[8] All things were done decently and in order and all the camp nearly followed him to his lonely resting place. This morning is beautiful and we have just returned from the burial where "Earth to earth, dust to dust, has been consigned in calm and holy trust," here to wait until the resurrection morn. With what different feelings shall we proceed on our journey and how differently shall we view these things, and even a lonely grave will give rise to new thoughts and feelings. Here we are in the road after a few miles travel waiting on account of another accident. Mr. McClellan had the misfortune to break one of his axletrees and here in this desert country 'tis no small affair. He has to put his load on other wagons and try and tie his up so it will hold until we reach the next mail station. I guess he will think he is getting some pay as he proceeds. Oh how warm and no water for 18 miles from where we started this morning.

JULY 28, 1860 We got here to these good springs[9] about 6 o'clock, but Oh what a time it was so very warm and then no water for the horses. We did find a well with muddy water and they gave the horses some and we went on until we came to the station, and here we got a little more water and we took a luncheon and went on.[10] Our road

[8]This unfortunate incident must have occurred somewhere near Lookout Pass. The camp and the grave may have been at Point Lookout. See ch. 3, n8.

[9]They were at Indian Spring, which had the last water and grass before emigrants entered the forty-mile desert. (See map 3.) Even though it was off the main route, stopping at Indian Spring gave the emigrants the opportunity to water and feed their livestock before crossing the desert. See ch. 8, n31.

[10]In this sentence, Brown is describing what had occurred the previous day while they were on their way to Indian Spring. The station was the Simpson Springs stage station. See ch. 7, n6.

the rest of the way was Oh so rough and stony; I never got more tired, but we found a treat in good cold spring water and plenty of grass.

JULY 29, 1860 Well we are to leave here this afternoon at 4 o'clock so says our Capt., who by the way is J. P. Brown.[11] Well I hope our teams will stand it across the desert, but don't know. Two large teams trains ahead of us and more ready to go. 40 miles without water and not much then nor much grass, but we must trust in Him who ordered all things well.

JULY 30, 1860 Oh did anyone ever see such warm weather and Oh how dusty, yes, and we had such bad luck at our camp yesterday. You see we were going to be ready to start at 4 o'clock and travel all night as we would have no grass nor water for the horses. About noon the alarm was given that some men were driving the horses away, and so all hands started—they got all but 2, and those were Moo's—I think he has his share of bad luck. The boys followed after the Indians and 4 of them came near being shot; one ball went near Harlow's head and one near the head of another boy, and Lyman had a ball go between his arm and body; close call I think. This hindered us so we did not get started until late but we had a lovely night to ride; thought of Indians some but did not fear them much. We stopped in the morning and made us a cup of tea and traveled on until noon. Oh we had such a warm dry ride, and the poor horses wanted some water so much, and then just before we got to a stopping place they got in a mud hole and that was worse than all the travel. I don't know but we shall have trouble with the Indians but hope not and do not think much about it, but we will hope for the best.

JULY 31, 1860 Well we have come a long hard drive today across the sandy desert I tell you. I am afraid some of the horses will have to stop. Where we stayed last night the water was so salty it did not quench thirst much and it made us all feel rather dull.[12] Oh how hot the wind was—burned like fire most. We have good water here and middling good feed.[13]

---

[11]It is not known for certain, but one can surmise that this was Delia's husband John.

[12]Brown is talking about Fish Springs. See ch. 6, n4.

[13]They were at Willow Springs. See ch. 7, n9.

August 1, 1860 Oh how time flies and we are not at our journey's end yet, and a long drive before us today without any water; there seems to be a division in the minds of the people about going this morning or not until night. Our teams need rest, can't tell how the affair will be managed.

August 2, 1860 After many times changing their minds we finally started on the 30 mile trip without water and not much feed. We had quite an accident in our camp; just as we were ready to start John Frantz shot his wrist with a rifle, but I guess tis nothing very serious. We did not reach camp until nearly ten o'clock last night.[14] There were many campers already on the place. Oh this is a nice pleasant place, good water and good grass, so clean and nice. Last night was a lovely night; came through a deep canyon[15] and up a hill and when we reached the summit the sun was just setting; Oh it was a glorious sight—I was perfectly charmed. Could not have a thought of Indians though we were told we would have trouble. The moon shone bright and beautiful and I would have been willing to ride all night if the horses had not been tired. Don't know how long we will stay here, but long enough to let the horses rest well.

August 3, 1860 A bright beautiful morning and Oh such a glorious sunrise. The air is so bracing and pure but some complain of cold. It just suits me—so much better than the valley climate we have had. Well some of our crowd went yesterday and now we are going this morning. Travel 12 miles today, then 25 tomorrow. We shall have long drives now most of the way till we reach Carson Valley. I hope none of the horses will fail. We had a little dance last night—some green horns here too. Well never mind—they serve to make fun for the rest of us.

August 4, 1860 Oh well we came 12 miles yesterday and that was all. We started in the morning and came about 4 miles to a station[16] and there the stories about feed conflicted so we hardly knew what to do but finally they drove off the road about two miles but found neither good feed nor water. Here we took our dinner and then drove back to

[14]This camp was at Deep Creek, now Ibapah. See ch. 7, n11.

[15]Overland Canyon, between Callao and Clifton Flat.

[16]This was probably Spring Station, which was replaced two or three years later by Eight-Mile Station.

the station and watered and then on to camp. John had a balky colt in his team and he stopped to trade Polly for a Spanish horse and Lime drove the team and we had a grand time with the pony. John traded Polly for a wild pony—I don't know but we shall be sorry but she could not work. Wash traded Bob for a wild horse in the morning and it got away and he went after it; Harlow went with him and did not overtake us until last evening. Lime and Wash are both back but we are not in a place to wait for them. They will come on with an ox team I guess. Oh we came about 25 miles and Oh so dusty. I never had a more unpleasant ride. We staid at Antelope Springs[17] and here the Indians have been so troublesome that white men have abandoned the station. Feed was scarce but water plenty and so we staid over night, and they took the horses about three miles and let them feed until bed time and then tied them up at the wagons. This morning we got up early (This is Sunday by the way) and drove out here to the feed before breakfast, and now having had our grub while the horses eat I write. 13 weeks tomorrow since we left home; it seems long in one sense and yet time passes quick.

August 5, 1860 And here we are at Spring Valley and a nice pleasant place. We have found much better fare in our travel today than we expected this morning. Found feed and water at noon, a thing we have not done lately. We passed through a very bad canyon this forenoon, up hill all the way and so rocky some of the way. We started this morning before sunrise from Antelope Springs, and as I know no other name I shall call these mountains and this canyon Antelope Mts. and Canyon.[18] This they say is the most dangerous pass on the route on account of Indians. The men are looking for trouble tonight. Here is where the expressman has been shot. Well we will not borrow trouble but let it come as it will. 20 miles today. I have no accurate account of distances and have not been very particular.[19]

---

[17]See ch. 7, n13.

[18]Brown was right about the name of the mountain range. As for the canyon, the editor has been unable to learn its name, but it leads to Rock Springs Pass. Brown's comment makes it clear that her party followed the Pony Express route across the mountains by way of Rock Spring Pass rather than the stage road around the southern end of the Antelope Mountains. See ch. 8, n10.

[19]Brown was usually not very good with her mileage estimates, but in this case, she was right. It is almost exactly twenty miles from Antelope Spring to the Schell Creek station and the Browns' next camp.

August 6, 1860 Well here we are at Shell creek and a good place for Indians too I suppose. There is a station here but the people have been driven away by the Indians several times and the men now here have been here only two weeks. We staid at Spring Valley until noon today waiting for Wash and Lime to come up—they came all right about nine in the morning. There was a horse shot from under a man coming through Antelope Canyon soon after the boys came along. We have been fortunate thus far in not seeing any of the scamp, but today coming through Shell creek Mts. I kept a sharp look out expecting to see these dusky forms rising on the ridge, but saw none and I suppose they were watching us too. There were 4 wagons and a number of horses left us this morning and there came an Indian to three wagons and wanted ammunition. I think they should have shot him but perhaps that would not have been policy. Oh dear, the nice pony John got for Polly I am afraid has got her neck so badly hurt she can never hold up her head.

August 7, 1860 Just 3 months tonight since we left home and camped for the first time. Well, we are used to camp life now and I enjoy it especially when all the folks are pleasant. We came 16 miles yesterday, level road most of the way. We camp 2 miles through Egan Canyon[20]—I think it pretty but a good place for Indians. We have seen none yet but cannot tell how soon we may. We came 2 miles in the morning and then found good grass, so let the horses eat awhile. Some are so afraid of the grass they would not unhitch at all. Mrs. Webster has a great deal to say—I motion she is put in as Capt. Oh that makes me think, last night the wolves howled around and the ladies in Mr. Webster's tent routed them out to fight the Indians; I never saw such folks to get freightened at nothing.

August 8, 1860 A lovely morning but cool. We have very cool mornings and nights here in the mountains. We must drive 18 miles

[20]It appears as if Brown had gotten a little confused about on which day they did what when she said they "came 16 miles yesterday, level road most of the way." She is writing this on the evening of August 7th, but on the 6th, they had climbed over the Schell Creek Mountains, which would not have been a level road. During the day of the 7th, they would have been crossing Steptoe Valley, where there would have been a level road. The camp on the night of the 7th was about two miles west of the west end of Egan Canyon. (See map 5.)

today before we find water. I shall be glad when we reach Carson Valley. It is all bustle and activity in the camp when morning comes First very early with the first streak of dawn the men take their horses to feed and then by sunrise all hands are stiring, the babies squalling, larger children playing and the rest getting breakfast and getting ready for a start again. Wed. night: here we are at Butts Station. After coming 18 miles without water we are glad to get some and to find feed for the horses.[21] Our horses got very tired, one in particular but rest will make them right I guess. Some of the rest are worse off. We tried to drive our new pony today but it will not hold its head up. We came through another Canyon this morning up hill but not very bad—I walked quite a ways today.

August 9, 1860 Well we are undecided yet whether to go or stay here today; a rest would do the horses good but tis such a dirty place. I wish people especially of one family could agree on as much as one point, but this continual contradiction does annoy me so much. Evening and we have staid in this delightful place all day and are to leave early tomorrow morning. The sun has set, to us at least, or it is over the mountains, but I suppose it is quite high yet to those on the other side of the ridge. Oh well I tell you there are some strange specimans of humanity in this train we are traveling with now. It is quite a study for me and yet I can't fathom the mystery that surrounds some of them. I have many strange conjectures. One a widow (or at least so she pretends) is traveling in company with a gentleman who has left his wife in the states. She is a speciman—rather smart and has received a splendid education but she is so strange. Yesterday morning one of Mr. Cornell's horses was gone so they staid behind and came up with us this afternoon and now she wont get the men any supper. Oh I can't begin to tell of the squabbles that company have had—enough of this. Well John took his book this afternoon and I my sewing and we went up on the hill under the shade of a mountain Cedar and there we had a nice cozy chat. It seemed so good to get away from the noise and be alone. Oh well I wish I was as good as I want to be but the old nature

[21]Because they had access to water and grass, we can be certain that the Browns were camped at the station near Pony Spring. See ch. 8, n12.

will come up occasionally and I do what I am sorry for. I hope to do better for the future and now, my journal, good night.

August 10, 1860 And we have stopped by the roadside to let the horses eat and to take our own luncheon. We started early this morning and have come about 12 miles over the Butes Mountains most of the way—crossed one small valley.[22] Have 10 miles to go this P.M. and then we reach Ruby Valley just half way from Salt Lake City to Carson Valley. We have the hardest part of our journey to go now I suppose, that is as far as the horses are concerned. We saw several Indians round Butes Station—they seem very friendly. We are now out of the Goshute tribe who are hostile to the whites and have sworn vengeance on them. Oh how warm and I must climb some more hills so as to favor the horses all it is possible. Fri. Night and here we are camped at Ruby Valley.[23] It is a nice place, plenty of grass and nice good spring water. Two or three cattle trains are camped here. Oh just as we drive in camp (you see we were the last ones) we saw a fight in progress. Some of the men from the cattle train came over to whip the horse train, meaning ours. On account of hearing some of our men said they sold the powder and lead to the Indians who got Mac's horses and it made them mad—but they got whipped.

August 11, 1860 Here we are at the foot of a mountain and good grass and water. We have come 18 miles this afternoon. Has been very dusty and unpleasant. John went to the station this morning to enquire about the roads. He wanted to go the Humboldt route and Lyman has been in favor of that route until now he is opposed to it, so it is all the time so much opposition it sickens me.[24] Lyman had some wagon tire to set and we thought to wait until noon but some of the rest started early, and so I did not care to get up with them again, but nothing would do but we must go, ready or not, so we bundled up our

[22] Long Valley.

[23] See ch. 6, n8.

[24] For the Browns to get to the Humboldt River from the southwest foot of the Ruby Mountains, they could have followed either the Hastings Road or the Chorpenning mail route, which would have taken them to Gravelly Ford. Whatever Delia's husband's plan had been, he now acceded to the desires of the other members of the party, and they continued to follow the Central Overland Trail.

duds and started and went a few miles and then stopped and had our dinner. You see we were going to have a pot pie and I did not like to leave it. We had a nice good dinner and came on rejoicing, only were anxious to have some good water to drink but we are alright now.

August 12, 1860 We are not going to travel today for a wonder. Those of the company who were not willing to wait for us to fix our wagon yesterday morning are now ready to stop. This is a lovely morning and 14 weeks ago this day we were at Ruth's and were getting ready to start on this trip. Times flies Oh so swiftly and yet it seems a long time. Oh when will we get through? Oh there are some of the worst looking Indians round here I ever saw.

August 13, 1860 Camp at Diamond Springs. This morning as usual some wanted to stay and some wanted to go and as the majority rules we came. We started from Camp this morning on foot and came nearly the 9 miles before the train came up. O such a hard hill as we had to come up[25]—every woman and nearly every man walked up and then the horses had hard enough time. The coming down was nearly as bad. We expected to go on 9 or 10 miles farther this afternoon but the word now is there is no water nor feed for 30 miles.[26] Well so it goes—two or three 30-mile distances will tell on our teams but I guess they will go it with good care. Ah me how many things to try ones patience; if I could only always use gentle words and never wound the feelings of others I would be so glad.

August 14, 1860 Well we started last night at 12 o'clock. It was very pleasant riding. We crossed a plain 16 miles wide and then thought to get our breakfast but found no grass. Nearly all the teams were a long ways ahead and so we tried to follow but when we had gone 5 or 6 miles we thought to have some breakfast and feed and water the horses, so we did. After we had started and gone up a little rise we saw the balance of the train just ready to go on and lots of Indians there too. Night and here we are at Roberts Creek. When we got to the

---

[25]This was the Overland Pass in the Diamond Mountains. See ch. 8, n14.

[26]In most instances, the next stop for water and feed was Sulphur Spring on the west side of Diamond Valley, which was only thirteen miles from Diamond Springs. One has to wonder why they were told that it would be thirty miles to water.

station we had to go 4 miles up the creek to find feed for the horses. This seemed all lost travel, but we have a very good place. A man at the station wanted the use of a wagon to go 35 miles on our road; would draw the load and take 2 of the boys with his own team and board them till we came up, so John let our big wagon go and Hendrick and Johnny went with him so we will have quite a help.

August 15, 1860 We have gone 20 miles today, had a good easy drive mostly down hill and we had six horses so there was not much occasion for walking. I did not leave the wagon until we arrived here at the Wells.[27] Our road has been over a sandy plain. covered with sage brush and no water, but we carried water enough for our horses and had our luncheon when half way and then went on rejoicing. Our drive tomorrow is 20 miles again.

August 16, 1860 And here we are at Deep Creek[28] having come 20 miles over a sandy low country. We have not a very clean place but never mind—we are near a station and the man John let have his wagon gave us a nice piece of beef to pay for the use of it—quite generous to what some are. I have lots of baking to do tonight, don't feel very well either, but hope to feel better in the morning.

August 17, 1860 I had a high fever and was very restless all night. Had a hard time of it but was up early this morning and got breakfast ready so as to start early and just as breakfast was ready Mr. Walker came and said his wife was too sick to go today, so all the train waited and I have been sick abed all day for the first since I left home. I expect it is mountain fever—it is very much like ague.

August 18, 1860 Another week has passed and we find ourselves camped at Simpson's Park having come 25 miles and Oh such stony roads as it was most of the way. I did not feel much like walking but some of the way was so rough I could not ride.[29] We had one new pony on the lead today and it went first rate; had one kicking scrape. We came through a very rough Canyon and we looked some for trouble with the Indians but saw none. Harlow's birthday—22 years.

---

[27] This place was usually known as Grubb's Wells. There was an Overland stage station here, but it was only fourteen miles from Roberts Creek.

[28] Brown was mistaken about the name—it was Dry Creek.

[29] The Browns probably followed the route that went past Eagle Butte. See ch. 8, n15. (See map 6.)

AUGUST 19, 1860 And we have traveled 15 miles up hill and down but a very good road for all. We passed the cattle train again that tried to pick a quarrel with our company; they act fully as mean as ever. Well let them work their own way. We are to go 5 or 6 miles farther today and that is all; 'twill be a very easy day for the teams as they have good feed. This is Reese River,[30] a small stream of good water. Night and we have come 5 or 6 miles farther and got a mean dirty place and poor feed and no water—but no matter.

AUGUST 20, 1860 Camp near Station on Smith Creek but no feed within 2 or 3 miles. This afternoon we came over a sandy sage plain and had a wind and sand storm—crossed a level place hard and smooth as ice nearly; looked like a lake frozen over.[31] We had some very rough road.

AUGUST 21, 1860 Oh if any one ever saw such a rough road as we have come this afternoon and Harlow and Mal and Martha are all 3 sick abed. A hard ride they have. Our road was up hill mostly and so stony.[32] We are stopping now to feed our horses and take a lunch our own selves and then drive on a few miles and stop and prepare to cross the desert. We have no more of Indian troubles ahead of us but through the canyons we have passed there has been lots of trouble.

AUGUST 22, 1860 Well here we are yet. Staid here on account of the girls being sick. All three of them down and oh such grunting—well I suppose they can't help it. Harlow is some better today. We had the roughest road yesterday entirely and for sick ones 'twas awful.

AUGUST 23, 1860 We have come 14 miles over a very rough road and a long up hill. I tried to walk to the top but it was so far I did not make out too. We are now at Cold Springs and shall stay until tomorrow and then on the Middle Gate 12 miles farther and perhaps stay over night; shall if there is good water and feed. Mr. MacClelland had another horse die last night, which makes five he has lost since

[30]See ch. 3, n38.

[31]A little to the east of the center of Smith Creek Valley are two large and usually dry playas that are remarkably level and smooth and completely devoid of vegetation. The Overland Trail travels diagonally across the northern one. The distance across the playa is about a mile. (See map 7.)

[32]This was in Smith Creek and Edwards Creek Canyons. They probably made camp somewhere on Edwards Creek, possibly near the mouth of the canyon. See ch. 3, n40.

leaving Omaha. It rains now and I can't work until the shower is over. I don't care much—I shall do but very little any how.

AUGUST 24, 1860 At Middle Gate[33] and stopped to feed and take a lunch; some of our company staid behind today, I suppose to get good and ready for crossing the desert. Don't you believe I shall be glad when we get over? well you better believe it. We have so many storms I hardly know what kind of road it is, but hope tis better than we expect. If our horses don't give out we are all right. Have come 12 miles today and it is now 20 or 27 to the next water and not very good at that. Well we will trust Providence for a good time and not fret. We have some rough road again today—shall have some sand before we get through.

AUGUST 25, 1860 Here we are at Sand Springs[34] and rightly named they are too. But such Springs only holes in the sand bank and poor water at that. We get water at the station to cook with but it tastes of Sulphur. When we got to Middle Gate the water was not first rate and neither was there any grass, so we had our dinner and started on again. Traveled until sundown and then found some very good grass and so turned out the horses and let them eat and we had our supper and then drove on again. We had an alkali plain to go over[35]—this looks like ice by moonlight and it is a good road. We then had a long hill to go up;[36] walked nearly all the way. We got here at this place about 2 o'clock in the morning and then the grass was 2 miles away so we tied the horses to the wagons and gave them some grass and

---

[33] See ch. 3, n42.

[34] See ch. 3, n43.

[35] Here Brown is writing about the trail they had traveled earlier in the day when they had crossed Labou Flat, in Fairview Valley. None of our diarists felt inclined to include much description of this section of desert, but Samuel Clemens (Mark Twain) traveled this section of the Central Overland Trail in 1861, just two summers after it had been opened, and described it thus: "From one extremity of this desert to the other, the road was white with the bones of oxen and horses. It would hardly be an exaggeration to say that we could have walked the forty miles and set our feet on a bone at every step! The desert was one prodigious graveyard. And the log chains, wagon tires, and rotting wrecks of vehicles were almost as thick as the bones. I think we saw log chains enough rusting there in the desert to reach across any state in the Union. Do not these relics suggest something of an idea of the suffering and privation the early emigrants to California endured?" (Twain, *Roughing It*, 121).

[36] The eastern approach to Sand Springs Pass.

we took our blankets and laid out on the sand. I camped out for the first time. Mal and Martha slept in one wagon and Pauline and Fanny Hartwell in the other and John and I slept in the open air. I slept first rate and very sound. We came about 27 miles yesterday and now we shall start again this afternoon and try to reach the sink of the Carson. We have some heavy sand to go over. Some of our Company are back yet and some got in a hurry and went on, so you see there has been a sort of a division.

AUGUST 26, 1860 Here we are in Carson Valley near the Lake.[37] We started from Sand Springs yesterday afternoon and came 20 miles; our road was at first a little sandy, then over an alkali plain and one bad place to cross, but we had no trouble and then we came to a deep heavy sand and up hill at that. We stopped about sundown and fed and took our lunch and then on again; the horses stood it well. It was 4 miles to the top of the hill and then down it was very steep for a ways, but we had a good time.[38] Wash took off his leaders but John drove right down with his. We drove on awhile further and not finding good water concluded to tie up the horses and wait until morning. We did so but they ate nearly everything there was. They ate my sunbonnet up for one thing and so I must wear my hood. We started this morning and came on to the station and Oh such a place—no wood and no good water but we stopped and got breakfast and now are going to stay to do a little baking and start on tomorrow. Indians plenty here and will get you wood and water for something to "eat em." 'Tis a funny Sunday but will soon be done, this riding and cooking and all these things.

AUGUST 27, 1860 We have come I don't know how many miles today but one thing I know I took "Foot and Walkers Line" for the most part of it. We had an alkali flat to go over the first thing and then sand and then such a hill, long steep and rocky.[39] Wash's pony took

[37]The Browns were somewhere along the southwest shore of the lake, probably at or near the Carson Sink station. See ch. 3, n45. (See map 8.)

[38]This description of their route makes it clear that Brown's party had followed the stage road over Simpson Pass. See ch. 3, n44.

[39]Directly to the west of the Carson Sink Station is a flat area about two miles in width, which the trail crossed and then began to climb into the Dead Camel Mountains, most definitely a long, steep, and rocky road. See ch. 3, n46.

a notion not to pull up the hill so they put John in and come the rest of the way. Bye the bye John tired out the other evening coming to the Sand Springs but I guess he will live yet. It makes Harlow rather blue. Oh what a time we had yesterday at our camp—there came up a shower just as we had set the tent and got Martha a bed made but it did not wet much, only made it a little sticky, but after the shower awhile the water came running down from the hills and soon we were afloat—bed, stove and all. Had to take up the bed and raise the stove—you see I had bread baking and the fire went out. Finally we had to move the whole arrangement to higher and drier ground—so that was all got along with and we had our supper and done our work and went to bed. In the night the remainder of our train came up; they had a love of a time coming from Sand Springs and now we are here altogether again. Guess we shall remain so until we reach Carson River any way and there will come a separation and we many not meet again "For earth has many ways."

August 28, 1860 Yesterday we traveled 25 miles and the hardest days travel for the teams that we have had. In the first place we had to cross an alkali flat which the rain of the previous day had made very sticky—then came sand—and then such a hill—so long and steep our horses had a hard pull, but came up all right. We drove a short distance and then stopped for dinner. We had good grass but no water, only a little we brought along with us. In the afternoon we had very sandy road most of the way and the last part of the road hung on so long. We came in sight of trees on Carson River and felt a great degree of satisfaction on account of having a good place for the horses and ourselves too.[40] The moon shone bright when we came to the river and the noble cotton woods were a grand sight to us who have seen nothing but sage brush and grease wood for so long a time, and then it was such a luxury to have plenty of water. This has been a very pleasant day and all have enjoyed it.

[40]The Browns' party came to the Carson River somewhere near Bucklands Station, located about where the river is now crossed by U.S. Highway 95A (Townley, *Pony Express Guidebook*, 24). (See map 9.) They remained here for the next three weeks while Delia's husband and sons attempted to find employment in the area between Fort Churchill and Carson City.

August 29, 1860 Last night they came down from the station and took all who chose to go up to a dance.[41] The emigrant boys did not have a very good chance but the girls were in good demand. The station boys worked it cute. Well Lyman has started over the mountain and will be gone a week or ten days. We are going a few miles farther and then wait until he comes back. The boys are going to look for work—I hope they will get it soon so we can get rid of some of our work. Mr. Mac had a horse get in the mire last night; it seems as though evil luck is after him. Oh dear, such queer folks as some of our company are—but never mind we shall soon lose all trace of them.

August 30, 1860 Yesterday we moved our camp a mile up the river and on the opposite side to a lovely place and a grand place for the horses. Just after the boys had unharnessed the horses a man came and said the place was taken and the man who claimed it did not want emigrants to stop here. This made Mr. Webster's women fidget so much that he drove on and so Mr. MacClelland went of course, so we are here alone and in undisturbed possession of our camping ground. Oh these trees look so good. We are to stay here several days—I can't tell how many. The boys are going to work at something. John has gone on an exploring expedition and will be gone 2 or 3 days—shall be awfully lonesome but must not whine for we must do something. This is my birthday 33 years old. It hardly seems possible I don't feel so old. Memory is busy with the past and I contrast my circumstances today with those of other times. Eleven years ago today my eldest sister was married and started for Ill. How time flies and what changes it brings to us all. But "We will not deplore them the days that are past, The gleam of misfortune is over them cast, They ware sullied by sorrow and lengthened by care, Their griefs were too many, their joys were to rare."

August 31, 1860 Nothing of particular importance has occurred today. The wind has blown very hard and it has been very quiet, especially the forepart of the day. At noon a gentleman called an acquaintance of Lyman's and he brought a line from Lyman to John. Quite an agreeable young man and we had a very pleasant social chat. Just about

[41]Brown was apparently referring to the stage station that had been established at Bucklands.

the same time another train camped near us and some of the ladies called and then some of the gents, so put it altogether the afternoon has passed rather pleasantly. This train came through the Humbolt Route and had good grass and water all the way; only one 50-mile desert, and the way we came has been desert all the way from Salt Lake. It is rather provoking though both we and our horses have lived. O dear, well John has not got home yet and I fear he will not tonight. It is very lonely for me when he is gone. The girls were out to a dance last night and Mal has slept most of the time today and Martha and Pauline never talk and Judd and Harlow are working and the rest were gone so no wonder we had a quiet time.

SEPTEMBER, 1, 1860 And John has not returned yet—I do hope he will come tonight, it is so lonesome. Guess Harlow will be home too, have not seen him since Thursday Morning and Judd too is at work. Wash left us this morning, went with Mr. Walker's folks—don't know that he will go further than Virginia City. He had hard work to tear himself away and Pauline has drooped like a sick Pigeon ever since. Oh well she will survive I guess at least I hope so. Oh something funny today, a lady asked Martha if I was her Mother, now I feel imposed upon to be thought Mother to such an old grandmother of a thing as Martha. Well never mind I am only 3 years the oldest and feel more than a dozen younger, but I suppose the old lady thought where there was girls there must be a Mother of course and gave me credit for more than I am worth.

SEPTEMBER 2, 1860 A bright lovely day although a cool morning and last evening it was cold. Harlow and Judd came home again. John came home this morning about ½ half past eleven o'clock. A young stranger came with him and staid to dinner. Soon after their arrival 3 or 4 gentlemen came up on horseback and made quite a visit. One of them was in pursuit of a girl to do housework so Mal concluded to go and try it—a week for six dollars. One of the gents name was Mr. Brown, a great <u>pussy</u> man, but very social and pleasant. After they left we had our dinner and just as I commenced washing dishes several ladies and gentlemen called so the day passed. The gents seem to be a free and easy sort of fellows but what I have seen conduct themselves with great propriety. They say however they nearly all gamble and I don't doubt it. This is a lovely night but cold.

SEPTEMBER 3, 1860 Well last night in the night Wash got home again; had been gone 2 days and 1 night. He swapped ponies while here and when on his way to Silver City was taken for a horse thief, so he had to come back to prove to the contrary and get his own pony—this he did without trouble and went off with Flora Temple all right. Mal sprained her ankle yesterday so she could not go to work and Pauline took her place. She rode down with Wash and I expect it helped her a great deal—don't know how she will get along but I hope well. Can't tell yet what we shall do but hope something soon. A warm bright day and the wind don't blow.

SEPTEMBER 4, 1860 John went to cutting hay today and Hendrick and Henderson with him, so us girls had the camp to ourselves. Mr. Smith's folks left this morning so our train are all gone but us. They wanted Mal to go with them and she almost made up her mind to go with them but finally thought it would not be using Lyman well and so did not. About noon Harlow and Judd came home being out of work again; Harlow is undecided what to do I wish we were all going to have work near together but we must do as we can, not as would be most pleasing always.

SEPTEMBER 5, 1860 Bright and beautiful. Well Harlow took his pack on his back this morning and started for Carson City and I don't know how much farther. He had to go there to get his pay for the work he had done. I am sorry he cannot remain near us so I can take care of his clothes; but we are undecided yet where we shall be, maybe we shall be near each other after all before winter. When Lyman gets back we shall know a little better what to do.

SEPTEMBER 6, 1860 O how the wind does blow and it did yesterday afternoon. I can't work much, it is so bad having the stove out doors in the wind. Our boys are getting yet no chance to work for good wages. Hope Lyman will be home soon. Yesterday we had several calls one man by the name of Brown, a great whisky bloat, just about as much form to as there would be to a barrel set up on posts. I guess there are lots of mean fellows round here but they won't hurt me any I think.

SEPTEMBER 7, 1860 A fine day, the wind does not blow. I can't tell how long we shall stay here. We look for Lyman today. I hope he will come and bring us some letters. The boys are still getting hay.

SEPTEMBER 8, 1860 Lyman did get home last night after we were all in bed, but had not been to sleep. He found things all right at Indian Valley. He don't know whether it is best for us to go over the mountains or not; if we did not want to raise money to pay debts with we could do well enough anywhere. Night and the girls have been horseback riding Martha got throwed and so did Lyman and Mal too; quite a time they had. In the evening they went to a dance in another camp but did not stay late.

SEPTEMBER 9, 1860 Such a lovely day. 4 months we have been gone from home and Oh how I long to see the folks or even hear from them. Lyman brought me a letter from Amelia, but Oh she don't write much. But Abbie, dear girl, has gone and we never more shall see her or hear her sweet merry voice—but she is free from care and sorrow and pain and why wish her back. Her family may well shed tears for much will they miss her, but for me I cannot shed tears Ah no for now she is happy, may ours be the same happy lot. But why could I not hear from home and how they are all doing, but I must wait patiently and sometime I will get a letter. Once more the sacred day dawns on us and we are yet in an unsettled state, hardly knowing what to do. The boys, three of them have got work at the fort for a while and Lyman and John are going to draw hay. I suppose Lyman and the girls will go over the mountains anyway and John thinks he can do best here on this side. As for me I have no idea what is best but I am willing to do all I can to help along. Night and we have had a very quiet pleasant day; and some pleasant calls—some rather pleasant gentlemen. Mr. and Mrs. Geness and a Miss Reed called here but would not alight from their horses and as I had never seen them I did not take the trouble to speak to them. The girls were acquainted and that done as well.

SEPTEMBER 10, 1860 A very pleasant forenoon but Oh so windy in the afternoon, we could hardly work at all. The boys had great times drawing hay—not many calls today. Martha had a horseback ride Sunday night and is so lame today she can hardly walk; we have all laughed at her a little—poor thing, she takes it hard.

SEPTEMBER 11, 1860 This has been a very windy day and fire blew from the stove into a bundle of dirty clothes and burned them nearly up before we discovered it. One new calico dress and a pair of stockings for Pauline and four shirts for the boys, one towel and one pair of socks for John. No very great amount but it will amount to something to get them here again. At noon today I thought we were about to find a place where we could begin to make money but at night heard to the contrary. The reason I shall not tell even to you, my journal.

SEPTEMBER 12, 1860 This has been a very pleasant day, not quite so windy as yesterday. Pauline washed and I cooked and the rest sewed and done what else they chose. The boys drew hay. This afternoon we have all been sewing and had quite a gay time considering. Things you know will keep happening sometimes to please one so much they will laugh in spite of themselves, so it is with us.

SEPTEMBER 13, 1860 Here we are yet but the prospect is we shall leave tomorrow or next day sure. Shall go as far as Virginia City anyway and Lyman and the girls will go over the mountain. I shall be glad to get to work at something. Judd goes with Lyman. Hendrick and Henderson are at work at the fort. I wish I could hear from Harlow but must wait patiently.

SEPTEMBER 14, 1860 Well Harlow got home last night and we were glad to see him. I guess if we go over the mountain he will go with us. This has been a very pleasant day, not much wind.

SEPTEMBER 15, 1860 Here we are camped on Carson River, 4 miles above the Fort.[42] Lyman had his colt hitched up by the side of Bony so as to break it to drive. We had two little runaway scraps but not much damage done. I suppose our folks will separate tomorrow. Sure I shall be glad to get settled. Martha stays with us.

SEPTEMBER 16, 1860 Camp near Telegraph Station. We came about 12 miles today.[43] Left Hendrick and Henderson who are going to continue working at the Fort awhile longer. And so our mes . . . are going to separate. One after the other of the train that traveled with us have gone and now we too part "when to meet again."

---

[42] They finally moved their camp, but only about six miles. They had been camped in the Bucklands area, about two miles east of Fort Churchill. Now they were four miles west of the fort.

[43] This would have put them about four miles to the northeast of Dayton.

SEPTEMBER 17, 1860 Well here we are near to China Town. We parted with Lyman and the girls this morning as their course leads in another direction and so we are alone, Martha, Harlow and myself. John has gone to Carson City to get some money—will be home soon. You see I call it home where ever the horses are turned and we stop awhile. We had a view of Virginia City as we came along yesterday. It lies high up in the mountains, rather a rough looking view in the distance, but they say the Hills are rich in gold quartz. I do not know yet what our destiny will be. John was quite in favor of purchasing the Telegraph Station; I like the location very well and if we could have it without going in debt too much would not care. Then we should have a home of our own and that would just suit me, however humble.

SEPTEMBER 18, 1860 Well John got back last night and today Harlow and he have gone to Virginia City and Silver City. Martha and I are alone and have very quiet times though she is uncommonly talkative for her, but still tis rather lonely.

SEPTEMBER 19, 1860 Well when John got home last night said he had made arrangements for living at Silver City this winter.[44] Some gentlemen there had given him liberty to build on their lot and so today we are to go. Oh I am so glad there is a prospect of living again and in our own home too and now as soon as we have had our breakfast and can get ready we shall be off for Silver City.

---

[44]Silver City was a small mining town on the southeastern slope of the Virginia Mountains, about three and a half miles south of Virginia City. To get to this location, they would have left the Central Overland Trail near the town of Dayton, probably going up Six-Mile Canyon.

CHAPTER 10

Mary Karchner

1862

In 1862, Mary Karchner, her husband Nicholas, and a son named Harry left their home in Hessville, Ohio, and traveled to Auburn, California. Mary kept her diary faithfully, and even though she had some problems with spelling, she gives us a good description of where she went and her experiences along the trail. The Karchners began their journey on April 3 and arrived at Salt Lake City on July 10.

By using the interlibrary loan system, the editor was able to borrow a transcribed copy of the Karchner diary from the California State Library, which also granted permission to publish it (California History Room, California State Library, Sacramento, California, F593.K32).

JULY 10, 1862 left camp at 6, O, and had the highest hills to go over, we have had since we left home, drove 12 miles and stopped for noon on the side of a hill, feed very poor left there at 1, O, and landed in the great City at night can see Salt lake from the City. hadent hardly got in camp till we were surrounded with people trying to sell vegatables

JULY 11, 1862 morning clear and very warm. done my baking and cooking through the day got done quite early, and had a nice ride through . . . town also out to the warm springs,[1] which is as nice a sight as I ever seen

JULY 12, 1862 clear and warm, also very dusty . . . on account of so many train camping here my forenoons work is to wash, which I am going to take to a house to save carrying water. Well washing done and dinner over, and I am now ready to take a walk through town. received a nice preasant from Harry

JULY 13, 1862 morning fair and very warm. 1/2 past 9, work done and am most ready to go to church, which is at 10, O, church over, it done very well for the kind. had it in a nice . . . bowry in side of the temple wall, which is very nice and . . . high. noon we are in camp getting ready to leave traveled 12 miles, stopped for night had to hire pasture. had the good luck to get . . . close to a mountain stream.[2] . . .

JULY 14, 1862 left camp at ½ past 6, O, had very good roads most of the way. weather very very warm crossed Jordon river at noon in a ferry[3] toll $1.50 drove two miles further and stopped to feed. we got over among the first teems, but dident get off till most 4, O, on account of its taking so long to get them all over the ferry. only drove five miles and stopped for night near Jordan bay[4] feed quite good but water none of the best it is a small mountain stream but it has come moste to far to be good distance come 23 miles

JULY 15, 1862 left camp at 7, O, had good roads but very dusty passed through Camp Floyd at 10, O,[5] and watered and filled our kegs then drove out 4 miles and fed them drove 16 miles and stopped for night on a small creek near a ranch.[6] Camp Floyd is or has been a very nice place but the Soldiers have all left and the mormons have taken possession of it and are tareing the houses down and hauling them to the City[7]

JULY 16, 1862 left camp at 7, O, had fine weather and very good

---

[1]See ch. 3, n1.

[2]This was probably Little Cottonwood Creek.

[3]There was a well-established ford at this location, but this is the only reference to a ferry at this location of which the editor is aware. See ch. 2, n5.

[4]Karchner's "Jordan bay" would have been the northern tip of Utah Lake, where the Jordan River leaves the lake. This spot is almost exactly five miles from the site of the river crossing. (See map 2.)

[5]See ch. 2, n6.

[6]The camp for this night was on Faust Creek, somewhere near the Faust stage station. See ch. 8, n2.

[7]The last contingent of soldiers had pulled out of Camp Floyd on July 27, 1861, eleven months before the Karchners passed through.

roads with the exceptions of being pretty hilly scenery very pretty. stopped for noon 12 miles from where we started fed and watered close to a station[8] left there at three, O, traveled till most dark then turned the horses out and fed them got supper then started on and traveled till two O, had very bad roads in the night that is very rough, traveled 38 miles and reached Simpson springs[9]

JULY 17, 1862 morning fair and warm. are going to stay here a day or too to prepare for the next desert[10]

JULY 18, 1862 are washing and baking so we wont have to cook while on the desert. 3, O, and we are ready to start. traveled till dark, where we fed and got supper, then started on and drove till 3, O, in the night, where they fed and watered again, then traveled till 11 in the forenoon when we reached fish springs 45 miles from Simpson springs. left there at 1, O, and traveled 34 miles till dark Saturday night reached there with very tired horses place rather pleasant and water good feed nothing extra[11]

JULY, 20, 1862 are laying over at Willow springs to rest the teams, which need it very much

JULY 21, 1862 left camp at 6, O, weather fine and warm. traveled till 1, O, had good grass but no water, left there at 3, O, had a very heavy rain just before we started which wet in the wagon considerable went to deep creek[12] till night, 10 miles, had quite a rain after we stopped, camping ground very good, but grass very poor, traveled 22 miles

JULY 22, 1862 left camp at 7, O, traveled 10 miles and stopped for the rest of the day on account of grass and water being too far to reach without driving very hard[13] camping and water middling good but grass poor.

---

[8]Karchner's mileage figures are quite unreliable. The station near which they nooned would have been the Point Lookout stage station, which is only eight and a half miles from Faust Creek. See ch. 3, n8. (See map 3.)

[9]Simpson Springs is only twenty-five miles from Faust Creek. See ch. 7, n6.

[10]Karchner was the only one of our diarists whose party stopped to recruit at Simpson Springs.

[11]They now were at what was then known as Willow Springs and is now the town of Callao. See ch. 7, n9. (See map 4.)

[12]See ch. 7, n11.

[13]They were near Eight-Mile stage station, about eight miles southwest of present-day Ibapah. This station was sometimes called "Prairie Gate," which came from the name of a steep-sided and very narrow canyon, now known as The Narrows, a few miles to the west. Eight-Mile later became known as the Georgetta ranch and is now a part of the Goshute Indian reservation.

JULY 23, 1862 left camp at 4, O, weather clear and very warm, roads very good traveled 22 miles and stopped for noon where there was no grass or water gave the horses what grass and water we carried and started on. reached antelope springs[14] in two miles water the best kind then traveled 6 miles up hill, to another spring[15] water and grass of the very best kind and plenty of it think of laying over a few days to rest the teams and feed them up as they have had poor grass for several days

JULY 24, 1862 morning clear and pleasant have a very pretty place to stop, scenery the nicest kind. The . . . Canien is just wide enough to be cool and pleasant and is surrounded with magnificent mountains. beautifully decorated with Cedar and Pine. there is also splendid spring running out of a hill close to camp water very cold and clear a very nice place to harbor lazy folks in and it is well blest with them today, for they are . . . laying asleep in all directions. Well the day is most spent, and I am getting hair shingled to finish up with it

JULY 25, 1862 morning clear and quite warm not as much breeze as there was yesterday but all seem to enjoy the day, but Harry and he is not able to be around, caught a very bad cold and it settled in his . . . teeth, which ache pretty badly—

JULY 26, 1862 morning clear and warm, and we are doing our washing and baking to be ready to start in the morning. Harry is some better and the rest of the camp . . . are all merry and pleasant

JULY 27, 1862 left camp at 7, O, had good roads and pleasant weather but a little to much Alkali dust for pleasant traveling went 18 miles mostly through a canien surrounded by mountains of the nices kind they are very high with a gradual slope to the top and well shaded with evergreens there is also a warm spring pouring out of the side of a hill that produces water enough to turn a mill. there was a nice little mountain stream through the canien with plenty of

---

[14]See ch. 7, n13.

[15]This was Rock Springs on the northwestern slope of the Antelope Mountains. From Antelope Spring, the Karchner party followed the Pony Express route across the mountains through Rock Springs pass. See ch. 8, n10.

currant bushes on both sides, and a bountiful supply of fruit to give the trains a treat which come very exceptable in this wild country.[16]

JULY 28, 1862 morning finds us again prepareing . . . for our journey westward 8, O, and we are moveing roads for a few miles are very rough, but soon leave the mountain for a more even path. an alkali flat of a half a days drive which brought us to another range of mountains. found a rather a narrow canien with pretty rough roads but two miles brought our days journey to a close, with tired horses and people we gladly welcomed the station as our resting place[17] the mountain are very high and pretty all around traveled 18 miles

JULY 29, 1862 Tuesday left camp at 7, O, with rested horses and people we are trying the winding road of another range of mountains which in six miles brings us to another alkali flat of 10 miles. took dinner at the foot of the hill noon finds the train with some pretty sick folks which were taken very severe ti's supposed their sickness was caused by eating too many mountain currants the night before Crossed the flat and drove a mile or two in another mountain before we found water camped for the night close to a station also close to a very nice spring[18] mountain very high and well covered with evergreens feed very poor

JULY 30, 1862 morning finds the most of our sick a little better. left camp at 6, O, drove over a very high hill of four miles which brought us to a small hill of fine grass where we turned them out for an hour to make up for the deficiency of the morning stopped there till the rest of the train come that grazed their horses before they left camp then drove to the next station where they fed and took dinner. scenery grand . . . mountain very high, and beautifully decorated with evergreens. from thence we pursued our winding way through a deep but descending canien which brought us to Ruby valley[19] where we

---

[16]Karchner is probably describing Schell Creek Canyon on the western slope of the Schell Creek Mountains.

[17]During this day's travels, they crossed Steptoe Valley and made their way through Egan Canyon, stopping near the Egan stage station. See ch. 7, n14.

[18]They were at Pony Spring on the southeast slope of the Butte Mountains. See ch. 8, n31. (See map 5.)

[19]The camp was near Station Spring in Ruby Valley.

found plenty of Alkali dust and a good breeze to keep it in circulation drove to the station and camped for night. sick folks all better. camping ground good with a good spring close to it. traveled 22 miles

July 31, 1862 left camp at 8, O, had rather rough roads, through mountains weather clear and warm in the middle of the day but cold in the morning, & evening, drove 9 miles and stopped for dinner had a very pretty to stop close to a small spring left there quite early and drove till late before we found feed and water. had pretty good roads in the afternoon decending most of the way, camping ground not very good right between two hills, but feed and water excellent which is the all important thing sought after now a days.[20] distance come 23 miles

August 1, 1862 morning clear and warm, are staying in camp till noon to wait on a part of the train that staid back to get their wagons repaired. had a very pleasant place to stop good spring water and plenty of grass by going some distance for it the first half mile was up a high hill where they were compelled to double teams only drove six miles but through a very rough canien, stopped at a station, had a nice level place to camp on. plenty of water and grass, a range of hills back of us which are very pretty and a broad flat before us[21]

August 2, 1862 Morning fair and very warm. 7, O, again finds us leaveing camp (with the exception of one family, who by duty are compelled to stay a week or two with their teams) Come across an Alkali flat of twelve miles[22] which brought us to a station,[23] where we stopped to feed and take dinner. Dinner over and train are prepareing to start all but two teams ours and Mr Tiffany's It was real lonesome

[20]During the morning, they traveled all the way from Station Spring to the Overland Pass in the Diamond Mountains. That afternoon, they descended part way down Telegraph Canyon and set up camp while still in the canyon, rather than continuing on to Diamond Springs as most emigrants did. See ch. 8, n14.

[21]This entry is somewhat confusing, but Mary seems to be referring to another group of wagons that had been traveling with the Karchners' train when she described how they had to double the teams to get across Overland Pass. After the other wagons caught up with the Karchners, they all continued to the bottom of Telegraph Canyon and camped near Diamond Spring.

[22]The alkali flat was Diamond Valley.

[23]This was the site of the Sulphur Spring Pony Express and Overland Stage stations. It was on the western edge of Diamond Valley, at the base of the Sulphur Spring Mountains.

till they come back from their grazing their teams which was about 4, O, then had our supper and went out where feed was more plenty I with the rest took a horse back ride which was much more pleasant than staying alone

AUGUST 3, 1862 Morning fair and pleasant, left station at 7, O, had very rough hilly roads traveled 17 miles and caught up to the rest of the train which were waiting for us, found good feed and water, so put up for the rest of the day. scenery for the day very pretty camping ground very good, close to Roberts creek Station

AUGUST 4, 1862 left Station quite early went fourteen miles and arrived at the next Station,[24] where they fed and watered dident turn out their teams as they all had grass with them Took dinner and started on as soon as possible, all but Mr. Tiffanys &, us. we had Indians out after grass. and he was quite sick so we were obliged to stay till 3, O, had to make an 18 miles drive for water which took us till 10, O, traveled 32 miles and camped at the third from that left in the morning.[25] roads very good most of the way, which was quite an accommodation to the sick and there is quite a number of them in camp and I with the rest am not able to work any

AUGUST 5, 1862 Morning fair and warm . . . left station pretty early as there was no grass within some miles of it, so hiched up and drove out a few miles and found grass & water stopped and give the horses a good feed, then proceeded. Had very rough roads also a hill that we had to double teams on,[26] and the decent was much worse than the assent stopped at the foot of the hill for noon. had water but no grass, then within two miles of the Station and stopped for night right in the hills[27] I for one was very glad to stop as I felt very badly

AUGUST 6, 1862 left camp at 7, O, had very rough roads, but warm pleasant weather drove till noon and stopped at the foot of the hill grass and water good left there at 2 O, had a very

---

[24]The next station was Grubb's Wells.

[25]What Karchner meant by "the third from the left" is unknown, but their camp was almost certainly on Dry Creek.

[26]Karchner's comment indicates that her party followed the Eagle Butte route between Dry Creek and Simpson Park Canyon. See ch. 8, n15. (See map 6.)

[27]The camp was near the upper end of Simpson Park Canyon.

rough afternoons drive, and camped for night on the bank of green creek,[28] had a nice place to camp but poor feed sick folks not very well. traveled 22 miles

AUGUST 7, 1862 left camp at 7, O, weather fine.[29]

AUGUST 8, 1862 Morning clear and warm are laying in camp to rest the sick and graze their teams which are very much in need of it

AUGUST 9, 1862 left camp quite early had very rough roads drove till noon stopped near a small creek in a narrow canien[30] had good mountain clover left there at 2, O, and drove till most night got in camp the last ones had a very nice camping ground but a long way to feed. took their horses out 4 miles and kept them there till 3, O, in the morning drive 30 miles.[31] went through some very pretty places and some that were not so pleasant.

AUGUST 10, 1862 left camp at 8, O, day fine and warm had a flat to cross, very dusty but not very rough. drove 4 or 5 miles and come to nice bunch grass. turned teams out to graze an hour while they cut a lot of it for places where grass is scarce then drove to Middle gate[32] till noon where they camped for the rest of the day had to take their teams out 2 miles to grass where they found it plenty and very good. Place rather pleasant but I dident [feel] well enough to enjoy it much. Some of the train had a little trouble with the Indians which I hear is going to end in making the whole train trouble, distance come 10 miles

AUGUST 11, 1862 left camp a little earlier than usual as they had their teams on grass all night they brought them in at day light. drove till noon and stopped to graze one mile on this side of the Station[33] close to an Alkali flat, had good grass but no water. gave them what water we carried and drove on as soon as possible to Sand

[28]Karchner's "green creek" must have been the Reese River. See ch. 3, n38. (See map 7.)

[29]Karchner gives no indication of the location of this night's camp, but most emigrants made it from Reese River to Smith Creek in one day.

[30]The narrow canyon was Edwards Creek Canyon on the north slope of the Desatoya Mountains. See ch. 3, n40.

[31]Traveling for about thirty miles would have put them in the area of Cold Springs.

[32]See ch. 3, n42.

[33]This station may have been located in the middle of Fairview Valley near the site that later became known as Frenchmans.

Springs[34] where we found very poor water and feed a long way from camp camping ground very bad deep sand and very dry. Was here warned that if we went farther we would have trouble with the Indians. so sent a man back to Middle Gate to telegraph on to the Soldiers for help from Middle G. to Sand S. 27 miles

August 12, 1862 are laying over at Sand Springs weather warm and pleasant The men have not yet returned from Middle Gate so are ignorant of the future 5, O, men here and bring the news that the Soldiers are comeing

August 13, 1862 left Sand Springs at 7, O, had pretty good roads, with the exceptions of plenty of Alkali dust, had to make a drive of 20 miles for water and grass. found plenty of water but little or no grass. went 8 miles further and found grass & water stop for night have a very good place to camp[35] drove 28 miles. the Soldiers dident come, but the Indians have not troubled us yet

August 14, 1862 left camp at half past 5, O, which was 8 mile on this side of Carson river drove till 7, O, then had to ferry a branch of the Carson river. went on five miles and turned out had the best kind of bunch grass stayed till 2, O. day very warm and roads very sandy and hard traveling. drove to the next station where we put up for night as the teams were quite tired. camped right in front of Busbee Station. place very pleasant and folks kind. Lady of the house called to us, which to us seemed quite a compliment on this dreary road Drove 19 miles[36]

August 15, 1862 lef Station at 5, O, had pretty hard roads, very sandy most of the way but weather clear and very warm drove 14 miles come to good grass and are not going to start from here till 5, O, then drive in the night when it is cooler. dident get off till most 6, O, had it very cool and pleasant traveling drove till 11, O, then fed and drove on till 4, O, in the morning, where we took breakfast

---

[34]See ch. 3, n43.

[35]The Karchners' route between Sand Springs and Carson Lake remains uncertain, but Mary's next entry indicates that they went past Bisby's Station. (See map 8.) To get to Bisby's, they would have come to the Carson River somewhere near Ragtown. See ch. 3, n44 and n46.

[36]Mary's "Busbee Station" is undoubtedly Bisby's Station, located on the north side of the Carson River, about a mile and a half east of present-day Lahontan Dam.

and rested our tired horses then drove on till noon. fed and watered at a public house also cooked a warm dinner left at 2, O, and passed through Empire City 4, O, and from there to Carson City which finished up our days drive[37] stopped in one of their large Coralls and had a good place for our horses also a very good place for our wagons Quite a business place for a small town

August 17, 1862 left Carson City at 10, O, had hard sandy roads most of the way. day very fine and cool. stopped for dinner in lone Jack valley right in front of a public house 7 miles from the City. left there at 2, O, and drove to the foot of the hill and put [up] for night at a public house. had a very good camping ground close to a beautiful mountain stream[38]

---

[37]Going west from Bisby's station, travelers could follow the Carson River all the way to Dayton, or they could take the straighter, and somewhat shorter, but waterless route across the Twenty-Six Mile Desert. (See map 9.) Karchner's comments about the sandy roads and lack of grass for fourteen miles seem to imply that they took the desert route.

[38]This would have put them in the vicinity of Genoa. Mary Karchner was one of only five of the diarists who traveled the entire Central Overland Trail from Salt Lake City to Genoa.

CHAPTER 11

Albert Jefferson Young

1862

VERY LITTLE IS KNOWN about the background of this diarist other than he left his home in Missouri on May 27, 1862, and arrived in Salt Lake City on July 31.

Jim Hall found Young's handwritten diary in the Bancroft Library, where he transcribed the portion that covers Young's journey from Salt Lake City to Carson Lake. Young's handwriting was quite difficult to decipher, and words that Hall was uncertain about appear in brackets. Words and phrases that Hall could not read at all are indicated by ellipses.

AUGUST 6, 1862 This morning we rolled out of Salt Lake City. Our next destination being Carson City. Went up the Jordan River about 2 miles and crossed on a bridge.[1] Here we nooned. And [in] the evening drove over a good road through dust to salt [spring]. Water very salty good grass. Here we camped for the night.[2]

[1]The old North Temple bridge. See ch. 9, n2. (See map 2.)

[2]From the bridge, Young and his party headed west until they reached the northern tip of the Oquirrh Mountains, where there were several springs at that time. This area is now covered by a massive pile of waste from the Bingham Canyon copper mines.

August 7, 1862 Drove on this morning until we reached the shores of the Great Salt Lake. The water here is salty as . . . and appears to be [perfectly] green, though it is so clear when we are near it. Traveled along the shore [four] miles. Went . . . through the mountains up a Valley to . . . Found a nice [stream] of fresh water, nooned. In the afternoon drove to Tooele city. Half a mile beyond and camped.[3] Good water, grass and wood.

August 8, 1862 Reached to Rush Valley at nine o'clock in the morning. Drove into the valley [10] miles and nooned. Good water. After dinner drove 10 miles farther and camped.[4] Good water and grass. For fuel sage.

August 9, 1862 Struck stage road in 5 miles.[5] Good water here. Drove on to the summit of Point Lookout. Here we nooned and drove 1 mile farther to water and camped.[6]

August 10, 1862 Hooked up and drove to Simpson Springs[7] 16 miles and nooned. . . . water good but very [scarce] . . . some water to drink and use for camp purposes and for stock. Drove 8 miles farther over a very rough road to Indian Springs.[8] There are plenty of good [bunch] grass, good water and abundance of wood.

August 11, 1862 Stay here today until five o'clock. Preparation to crossing the desert of 45 miles. Started at six o'clock, and drove all night. Beautiful, moonlight and cold enough to frost. Had a good road all the way until reaching Dugway. There is a [very] steep ascent and descent. From there, though, road good . . . Fish Springs[9] at 11 o'clock. Will stay here until morning. Water and grass abundant, though brackish. Our stock last night, did not suffer in the least for water.

August 12, 1862 Left camp at [seven] o'clock. Drove on to first

---

[3]The camp would have been just south of the city of Tooele. The exact location is unknown, but it was also used by several other Central Overland Trail diarists. See ch. 9, n6.

[4]At this point, Young's party was on Faust Creek, about ten miles north of Vernon.

[5]The stage road traveled east and west across Rush Valley. Young was traveling south and would have come to the stage road about a mile east of the Faust stage station.

[6]This camp was at the large level area three-quarters of a mile to the west of Lookout Pass. See ch. 3, n8. (See map 3.)

[7]See ch. 7, n6.

[8]See ch. 8, n30.

[9]See ch. 6, n4.

station and nooned. No water till Willow Springs. Reached Willow Springs[10] about five o'clock. Plenty of good water and grass.

AUGUST 13, 1862 Stay here all day to do washing.[11]

AUGUST 15, 1862 Left camp early. 6 miles [to a spring].[12] Water for stock. Little grass. Drove on to [canyon station] and nooned. After dinner drove 9 miles to Deep Creek.[13] Camped 4 miles below station. Grass and water, little wood 3 miles before arriving at Creek.

AUGUST 16, 1862 Had to make a drive of 32 miles today. Left camp seven o'clock . . .Raining. [Eight] miles west of station a large . . .[14] Good grass. Water good. . . . to stop here and make the drive in two days. Drove [15] miles to station and nooned. Good [bunch] grass [to right of road]. . . . Reached Antelope Springs after dark.[15] Plenty of good water but no grass. Grass 2 miles beyond station.

AUGUST 17, 1862 Started from camp at 11 o'clock. . . . Quite a steep mountain to ascend 4 miles from the station.[16] Drove 7 miles farther to Spring Valley. Here found plenty of good grass and water, fuel sage brush.

AUGUST 18, 1862 Laid at Spring Valley all day.

AUGUST 19, 1862 Drove this morning to Schell Creek, where we nooned. . . . In the afternoon drove 16 miles to Egan Canyon.[17] Water 6 miles. . . . At the canyon. . . . Plenty water, wood, grass [two] miles off.

AUGUST 20, 1862 Drove [10] miles out from station and nooned. No water, but the mountain grass, at foot of mountain. Took left-hand road down to Butte station.[18] 15 miles and camped. Grass, wood and water abundant.

---

[10]See ch. 7, n9.

[11]The fact that the next entry in Young's diary was made on the 15th indicates that they remained at Willow Springs for another day.

[12]The spring was at present-day Six-Mile Ranch.

[13]The camp was about a mile south of the town of Ibapah. See ch. 7, n11.

[14]At eight miles to the west of the Deep Creek station, Young would have come to Eight-Mile station, sometimes called Prairie Gate station. (See map 4.)

[15]Young would have camped somewhere near the stage station. See ch. 7, n13.

[16]Because of Young's comment about the steep mountain, we can be quite certain that he took the Rock Springs route. See ch. 8, n10.

[17]Young probably camped at the west end of the canyon near the stage station.

[18]By taking the left-hand road, Young would have followed the Simpson trail past the Butte stations and would not have gone to Pony Spring. See ch. 8, n12. (See map 5.)

AUGUST 21, 1862 Left camp, and Butte station, 12 miles to Mountain Springs. Grass and water plenty. Afternoon, drive 10 miles to Ruby Valley.[19] Good grass and water . . . miles before getting to station.

AUGUST 22, 1862 . . . lost their [horses] last night. Suspects them to be stolen. Spent the day here looking for them.

AUGUST 23, 1862 Stay here to day looking for the horses but all in vain.

AUGUST 26, 1862 Out very early and got started by daylight. Road very good over an [alkali flat] for 12 miles to Sulfur Springs. Plenty of good water. Well at station. Struck the hills again . . . miles farther . . . some mountain grass on the left of road . . . afternoon drove to Robert's Creek. A nice clean mountain [stream at] station. Some wheat grass, but . . . by going off into the hills on the right find plenty of bunch grass. Fuel sage.

AUGUST 27, 1862 Left Robert's Creek station at seven o'clock. Drove on 12 miles to large field of wheat grass on left of the road. Water a mile and a half from road. [Went] a mile farther to station and camped.[20] Plenty of water and . . . good . . . to left of the road.

AUGUST 28, 1862 Drove from [Grubb's] Station to Dry Creek. 20 miles. No water or grass but a splendid road Here we met the California Regiment of volunteers bound for Salt Lake[21] Simpson's Park . . . over the mountain 14 miles . . . we took the [right] and camped 2 miles above the station. Pretty good grass to left of road[22] . . .

AUGUST 29, 1862 Found the mountains rather steep to go into, but the descent was worse still.[23] The . . . about 5 miles long and at the summit very steep, but we made it without difficulty and [arrived at] Simpson's Park camped 2 miles from the station, where we found plenty of grass. . . . is a kind of a . . . [place]. Fresh beef and . . . Camped for the night. Road today very . . .

---

[19]See ch. 6, n8.

[20]This camp was at Grubb's Well.

[21]Young was referring to the Third California Volunteers under the command of Col. Patrick Edward Connor, which was on its way to Salt Lake City.

[22]Although much of this very long entry is illegible, it appears that Young was camped at the mouth of Dry Creek Canyon and was writing about the route to Simpson Park, which he would be taking the next day. (See map 6.)

[23]This entry indicates that Young took the Pony Express route past Eagle Butte. See ch. 8, n15.

AUGUST 30, 1862 Started this morning at seven o'clock. At 2 miles out there is abundant mountain grass and a nice . . . 2 miles farther reach the summit of the hill.[24] From here, the road is descending to Reese River.[25] Camped 6 miles above the station. Good grass.

AUGUST 31, 1862 . . . Reese . . . the left, passed by the old [Jacobsville] Station. . . . Good [roads] from here to Smith's Creek, reached camp at five o'clock.[26] Wheat grass, fuel sage. Distance 21 miles.

SEPTEMBER 1, 1862 Followed into Smith's Creek 4 miles and struck Edwards Creek[27]and camped. Grass and plenty of good water.

SEPTEMBER 2, 1862 [The road] from Edwards Creek to Cold Spring station is 14 miles. Plenty of water . . . Middle gate where we camped. Good water at station for . . . Grass scarce.

SEPTEMBER 3, 1862 Middle Gate to Sand Spring is 25 miles. Road is very good. Here a large obelisk of [sand is found].[28] water is from some . . . in the hills.

SEPTEMBER 4, 1862 [Kept to] the right and strike the North side of Carson Sink [16] miles.[29] Plenty of good water.

We must end Young's diary at this point. Jim Hall found that he was unable to decipher any of the words in the few remaining entries.

---

[24]Emigrant Pass, at the ridge of the Toiyabe Mountains, about two and a half miles northeast of the town of Austin.

[25]See ch. 3, n38.

[26]This camp was on Smith Creek, near the center of Smith Creek Valley. (See map 7.)

[27]Young and his party would have followed Smith Creek upstream into the Desatoya Mountains, crossed Basque Summit, and dropped down about three quarters of a mile to Edwards Creek, where they camped. See ch. 3, n40.

[28]They were at Sand Springs. See ch. 3, n43. (See map 8.)

[29]From Sand Springs, Young and his party followed Simpson's outbound route to the northern end of Carson Lake (Simpson, *Report of Explorations*, 85). William Pennebaker's diary indicates that he found a bridge across the lake's outlet in 1868. Perhaps Young's party used this same bridge. See ch. 3, n44.

CHAPTER 12

B. P. Lewis

1863

B. P. LEWIS LEFT Henry County, Illinois, on April 13, 1863, and traveled to Placerville, California. It appears that he traveled with a group composed mostly of young men of about his same age. He arrived in Salt Lake City on June 18, 1863.

To the best of the editor's knowledge, there is no transcribed copy of Lewis's diary, but a copy of the handwritten diary was obtained from the California State Library, which also granted permission to publish (California History Room, California State Library, Sacramento, California).

JUNE 18, 1863 Left camp early in the morning bound for Salt Lake City. during the afternoon we traveled down hill principally all the time. Passed through Parley's Canon. Reached the city about seven Oclock. The soldiers in Camp Douglas (situated three miles east of here) have given us all an invitation to attend a grand ball, a great number of them have gone and while I am now writing letters home they are engaged in the marzy dance.

June 19, 1863 In the city all day. Visited the new Temple & Tabernacle which they are now building President Youngs residence. Theater . . . and the city generally. Streets wide neat & level. We laid in our supplies for the remainder of our journey. Brigham visited us in the evening & made a few remarks with which we were very well pleased.

June 20, 1863 Packed our wagons and left the City about twelve Oclock. Crossed the Jordan River about two miles west of the City.[1] Traveled about fifteen miles and camped near the bank of the lake. We have had a little rain this evening.

June 21, 1863 Traveled about twenty five miles passing the lake valley and the last Mormon settlement.[2] Are camped in Rush Valley[3] A little rain in the evening

June 22, 1863 The road to day has been level but part of the way very muddy then traveled in Rush Valley and we camped near a stage station with good accommodations[4]

June 23, 1863 Some of our horses strayed away this morning and we did not leave camp until quite late. The roads have been hilly & rough Are in camp near Government Springs.[5] Found very good feed & water. A part of two companies of soldiers are camped near us

June 24, 1863 Did not leave camp until afternoon Traveled ten miles over the roughest road I ever saw and are now camped near Indian Springs[6] in full view of the Desert lying before us. We visited the

---

[1]Lewis crossed the Jordan River on the old North Temple bridge. See ch. 9, n2. (See map 2.)

[2]In 1863, the last settlement on the road going south from the Great Salt Lake was Tooele. Stockton is south of Tooele, but it was not founded until a year later (Madsen, *Glory Hunter*, 113). See ch. 9, n6.

[3]The most likely place for them to have camped would have been somewhere near Rush Lake.

[4]This was Faust station. See ch. 8, n2.

[5]Lewis is the first of the diarists to mention Government Spring. This source of water was not used by emigrants prior to October 1862, when soldiers of the California Volunteers constructed a new road from Indian Spring across the ridge of the Simpson Mountains and into the southern part of Skull Valley. See ch. 8, n31. This new road passed right by Government Spring, making it a convenient camping place. Beginning in 1863, almost all of the diarists made camp, or at least made a short stop, at Government Spring. Although the exact location of Government Spring is uncertain, the editor believes that it was next to the now usually dry streambed of Government Creek, and about two and a half miles south of Pony Express Road. Five of the twelve diarists who wrote about Government Spring mentioned that it was part of or next to a flowing stream. (See map 3.)

[6]See ch. 8, n31.

battlefield between Indians & soldiers Saw the boddies of five Indians.[7] This is about halfway between Indian and Government Springs.

JUNE 25, 1863 We spent a part of to day making the necessary arrangements for crossing the Desert. Started about four Oclock. Distance across the Desert forty miles. A beautiful moon accompanied us on our journey the fore part of the night after which we wended our way by star light. are now across the Desert camped at Deep Springs.[8]

JUNE 26, 1863 We have now another Desert to cross twenty six miles wide and are going again to night. The water here is very poor. Left Camp about four Oclock P.M.

JUNE 27, 1863 Reached camp about two Oclock this morning found good water & grass. camp at Willow Springs[9] Have spent the day principally in sleeping

JUNE 28, 1863 Started from camp early this morning. The road has been good Passed the ground upon which three soldiers were killed by Indians.[10] They were killed last Wednesday. Are camped on Deep Creek.[11] A nice shower of rain passed over us this evening.

JUNE 29, 1863 The morning was clear and pleasant. Passed through Deep Creek station and camped six miles above to wait until evening Have good grass & water but no wood. We have Twenty six miles to travel without water[12]

JUNE 30, 1863 Arrived in camp about three Oclock A.M. Found good water but no grass. This is at Antelope Spring[13] After taking breakfast we started on our journey. Found the road rather rough and stony. Camped about one Oclock in Spring valley. Our guard

[7]The details are very sketchy, but according to James F. Varley, "On the twentieth [June 1863] Captain Smith and his cavalry surprised and killed ten Indians in a camp near Government Springs" (Varley, *Brigham and the Brigadier*, 146). If Lewis's and Varley's statements are correct, the bodies of the Indians had been lying where they had fallen for four days when Lewis encountered them.

[8]Lewis was at Fish Springs. The editor is unaware of any other use of the name "Deep Springs" for this place. None of the other Central Overland Trail diarists used this name. See ch. 6, n4.

[9]See ch. 7, n9.

[10]According to James Varley, this incident occurred on June 23, 1863 at Canyon Station in Overland Canyon. The Indians attacked the station and killed two soldiers who were stationed there to protect the Overland Mail (Varley, *Brigham and the Brigadier*, 147).

[11]See ch. 7, n11.

[12]This camp was near Eight-Mile station. (See map 4.)

[13]See ch. 7, n13.

Mr Jackman accidently shot himself this evening in the calf of his leg The wound is not dangerous if properly attended to. I am watching with him to night

July 1, 1863 Started from camp early. Passed through Shell Creek & Egan Canons. Camped at Egan canon station traveling twenty six miles[14]

July 2, 1863 Left camp about three Oclock A.M. Traveled three miles and camped to take breakfast and feed our animals. Found good grass. We were soon on our way again & twenty six miles ahead to water Found the road good reached water about two Oclock and camped for the night.[15]

July 3, 1863 Started from camp rather late this morning. Traveled to Mountain Springs, Sixteen miles without water. Fed our horses there and from there to Ruby Valley[16] where we are now camped with good accommodations. This is a beautiful valley. One company of soldiers are quartered in the valley,[17] and quite a town is situated near our camp furnishing one very good store. there is a P.O. here. The young emigrants (Ladies & Gentlemen) are having a dance here this evening. While they enjoy it I will write a letter home

July 4, 1863 I was awakened this morning by the sound of the booming canon at the Fort. At first I thought I was at home once more, but soon I remembered I was far from there The Soldiers are going to celebrate the day We have all been invited to attend. They are also going to give us a free dinner

July 5, 1863 The morning was clear & pleasant We were all obliged to take the oath of allegiance to the Constitution & Abe Lincolns Administration. Have traveled eighteen miles to day and are camped one mile from the road and good grass and near good water.[18] The road to day has been good

---

[14]See ch. 7, n14.

[15]This camp must have been at Pony Spring. See ch. 8, n12.

[16]The stage station and the old Pony Express station were next to Station Spring. See ch. 6, n8.

[17]The soldiers were a part of Col. Patrick Connor's California Volunteers and were stationed at Fort Ruby, which was about two miles west of Station Spring, where Lewis was camped.

[18]This camp would have been in the Connor Creek area, at the eastern base of the Diamond Mountains.

July 6, 1863 The morning was clear and warm Left camp early. Crossed Diamond Mountains[19] Found the steepest hill we have had to climb yet. Are now camped at Sulpher Springs without wood and very poor water and grass.

July 7, 1863 Traveled fifteen miles and camped on Roberts Creek. Three miles from the road found good grass and water. Are not going out until tomorrow eve The Indians are our constant visitors And we all dread to see them

July 8, 1863 The fore part of the day was spent in making preparations for traveling through the night. We left camp about three Oclock and traveled over a splendid road eighteen miles to Growls [Grubb's] Wells Reached here about nine Oclock P.M. and camped for the night

July 9, 1863 Started from camp this morning at two Oclock. Reached Dry Creek Station twenty miles distant abut nine Oclock A.M. The road to Dry Creek was good, after leaving there we had a very hard road to travel.[20] We are camped near Simpsons Park with good water but no grass.

July 10, 1863 Left camp early anxious to find grass for our hungry animals. Found good grass at Simpsons Park three miles ahead and camped for the remainder of the day. We were told to day that wages were five dollars per day in Reese River Silver mines. My-self and some others are going to stop if such wages are paid

July 11, 1863 The morning was clear and very warm. We made a halt at the mines.[21] Found wages good but no employment. We are camped on Reese River about twenty miles from the mines. This is a small stream. We have good grass

---

[19]This was the Overland Pass in the Diamond Mountains. See ch. 8, n14.

[20]Because Lewis mentioned that they traveled a "very hard road," it seems likely that he followed the Pony Express route past Eagle Butte. See ch. 8, n15. (See map 6.)

[21]The mining town of Austin came into existence in late 1862 and within a year, it had a population of 10,000. For the first two years of Austin's existence, travelers had to cross Emigrant Pass, then go south along the western base of the mountain, then turn back east and go up Pony Canyon. In 1865, a new road was opened from the east that went through Blackbird Canyon and crossed Austin Summit (Townley, *The Overland Stage*, 251). Although Lewis's route into Austin is not certain, he was the first of our diarists to stop at this newly established mining town. After that, all of our diarists made a stop at Austin.

July 12, 1863 The morning was clear and very warm. Last eve about ten Oclock our horses became frightened stampeded and ran away. We did not start in pursuit until this morning. They were found about ten miles from camp. After traveling twenty two miles we [reached] Smiths Creek on which we are now camped.[22] This is a small crooked stream. Affords good water. Grass is very poor here

July 13, 1863 Left camp early. Traveled up Smiths Creek about seven miles[,] crossed the summit of the mountain and came to Roberts Creek.[23] Traveled about four miles down creek and camped for the night with good grass and water.

July 14, 1863 The morning was indeed beautiful The showers which we had yesterday made the morning air cool & refreshing The road to day has been very stony and dusty. Traveled eighteen miles without water then to Cold Springs & thence to Middle Gate[24] 12 miles, where we are now camped without grass or wood and very poor water

July 15, 1863 The morning was clear and very warm Passed through West Gate seven miles from Middle Gate found the water very poor. from there to Sand Springs[25] where the water was still poorer. Went seven miles farther to Sulphur Springs[26] found splendid grass but miserable water. We have traveled thirty four miles to day. Are now ten miles from the Sink of the Carson

July 16, 1863 The morning was very warm Our first six miles was over a heavy sand hill.[27] We all suffered very much from the heat while crossing. Reached the sink about noon traveled along the bank about four miles and camped for dinner.[28] after taking dinner we started for

---

[22]Lewis's party would have followed the Reese River upstream for a short distance, then crossed the Shoshone Mountains via Smith Creek Summit, then camped on Smith Creek somewhere near the middle of Smith Creek Valley. (See map 7.)

[23]Lewis used the wrong name for the stream; it was Edwards Creek. See ch. 3, n40.

[24]See ch. 3, n42.

[25]See ch. 3, n43.

[26]What Lewis called "Sulphur Springs" is marked as Rock Springs on present-day maps. It is located on the western edge of Eight-Mile Flat. The Simpson expedition stopped here briefly during their return journey on June 29, 1859 (Simpson, *Report of Explorations*, 105). (See map 8.)

[27]The "sand hill" was Simpson Pass, which the stage road used to cross the Cocoon Mountains. See ch. 3, n44.

[28]This was probably somewhere near the Carson Sink station. See ch. 3, n45.

Desert Wells fifteen miles distant.[29] Reached the Wells late in the evening Found good water and grass

JULY 17, 1863 It was decided last night that we should not leave camp until noon consequently we did not arise very early this morning. Our horses all returned to camp about eleven Oclock and we were soon on our way for Fort Churchill Camped about five Oclock in a beautiful place.[30] Three of our boys hired out here to make hay at fifty dollars per month.

JULY 18, 1863 After bidding good bye to the boys we started for Carson City, thirty five miles distant. Passed through Dayton, Empire City & reached Carson City about sun set. During the eve I went up to the P.O. and rec'd a welcome letter from home

JULY 19, 1863 Took breakfast this morning rather late being in the city and wishing to conform with City-Styles. Triplett stopped there leaving me the only one to go through with Mr. . . . Left the City about noon and camped near Genoa.[31]

---

[29]Lewis would have had to cross the Dead Camel Mountains to get to the Desert Wells station, which was near the western base of the mountains. See ch. 3, n46.

[30]They would have crossed the Carson River, traveled past Fort Churchill, and camped somewhere along the river. (See map 9.)

[31]Lewis had now reached the western end of the Central Overland Trail. He was one of only five of our diarists who traveled the entire trail between Salt Lake City and Genoa.

CHAPTER 13

Flora Isabelle Bender

1863

FIFTEEN-YEAR-OLD Flora Isabelle Bender and several members of her family joined a wagon train that left Bell Creek, Iowa, in May 1863. The family seems to have consisted of Flora's parents, a boy named Charlie, and three girls, Clara, Nellie, and Flora. Also traveling with them was someone named John who may have been a hired hand. In the last entry of Flora's diary, we learn that three older brothers had preceded the rest of the family and were living in Virginia City. The Bender family began their trip on May 7 and arrived in Salt Lake City on June 27.

This diary was published in the Nevada Historical Society Quarterly *in 1958. The notes section of the* Quarterly *indicates that the diary was donated to the Historical Society by Mrs. Jay A. Carpenter and Mrs. George Worn, who were nieces of Flora Bender.*

JUNE 27, 1863 Rolled out this morning at 6 A.M. in order to reach the city in good season. Came through the Echo Canon, winding around mountains from two to three thousand feet high. Roads good but rocky in places. Found no grass but plenty of nice cold water. A great deal of travel on this road—Mormons hauling wood from the mountains. At 4 P.M. we left the Rocky Mountains and came down into Salt Lake Valley. After passing through Ft. Douglas came into the city at half past four, and are camped in Davis' corrall, right in the midst of the city. Six or seven trains are camped here. Stock put in a corrall—hay, grain and wood to buy. No sooner were we camped till the Mormons were flocking around, with vegetables to sell or trade. I can scarcely realize that we are in this Great Salt Lake City. It is a delightful looking place—the streets are all shaded with large trees and flowers just in bloom. It is great to us "Hemegrants" (as the Mormons say) to see such things, though I am sorry the peaches are not ripe. Whether warm and roads dusty.

JUNE 28, 1863 This morning before we had got "dressed up" a stiff looking little gent came to our tent and enquired if there was a family in our train named Bender. We acknowledged our relationship to that family, and he told us he was a Telegraph operator and my brother in Virginia had told him to hunt us up. He invited us very strongly to come up to the office and telegraph the boys. Ma, Nellie, Mrs. Holland and I thought we would go to the Mormon Church. We bolted into the walls of the Bowery, where service was held. A large congregation were assembled. The sermon was Mormonism—music splendid. What exertions they do make in order to have the ruling power over the United States—but they can't come it. Some old ladies looked quite suspicious at us when we laughed at some of Heeber Kimbal's outrageous expressions. How can people be fooled by that nonsense is a mystery to me. Old Brigham was not there, but we saw some of his wives,—they are very good looking ladies. This afternoon we went up to the Office and were introduced to three or four gentlemen. One of them—a Mr. Pratt—is well acquainted with Mr. Powell in De Soto. Nellie sent a long dispatch to the boys. This eve Nancy Brown and I went and took a walk around the city. Brigham Young has some handsome dwelling houses and indeed there are a great many all over the city—beautiful yards, adorned with shrubbery and flowers of all kinds. On each side of every street a stream of water flows along, also leads into the yards to irrigate them. I wish I could describe this city to advantage, but as I cannot I must only hope that our friends will one day see it for themselves.

June 29, 1863 Today all are preparing for the rest of the journey. I wrote letters to Flora Rhodes, Martha and others. We rec'd only one from Nellie C. and the boys. Those gentlemen came down to bid us good bye. Tonight we had a dance. The Mormons swarmed around like flies. Quite warm today.

June 30, 1863 This morning pulled up stakes and moved off about five miles from the city to a pasture where we are going to stay two or three days to recruit the stock. Splendid grass but poor water—the River Jordon and it is only fit for Mormons to drink. Today we cleaned house or wagon rather. It has been very warm.

July 1, 1863 Been baking and cooking all day preparing to start, and this evening what was our surprise to see Capt. Marvin come in. We went right up to see Mary and it was like meeting old friends to see her. She said they only had to stay at Laramie five days, when they released them. I hope we can be together now till we get through. We had a little dance tonight "by the light of the moon."

July 2, 1863 This morning was spent in lounging about. At noon, four or five wagons rolled out, leaving the rest behind as they were not yet ready. We went back to the city and took a cutoff. Crossed the River Jordon on a nice bridge.[1] We have passed the Devil's Gate and crossed the River Jordon—and if we are not in the "Happy Land of Canaan" we surely ought to be. After traveling 17 miles we camped at Salt Springs near a public house. Grass poor—had to buy hay. Miserable salty water. Good Roads. Watered twice till camped.[2]

July 3, 1863 Travelling four miles—find water to the right of the road. Driving 9 miles stopped at noon in a village called. . . . Watered and fed grain—no grass. This afternoon no water till camped, for ten miles, and tonight we are in sight of the Great Salt Lake. Passed through three or four settlements. Roads good. Grass short and poor. Our John left us here and went with another train.[3]

---

[1]The old North Temple bridge. See ch. 9, n2. (See map 2.)

[2]The Benders traveled southwest across the Salt Lake Valley and camped near the northern tip of the Oquirrh Mountains. At one time there were springs in this area, but they are now covered by an immense mine waste dump.

[3]It appears that they traveled nine miles in the morning and ten miles in the afternoon, a total of nineteen miles for the day. The unnamed village would have been E. T. City, which is now the town of Lake Point. See ch. 9, n9. The camp for the night was just south of Tooele, from where the Great Salt Lake could still be seen.

JULY 4, 1863 This evening finds us camped in a large valley near a small stream,[4] 60 miles from Salt Lake and 37 east of the great sandy desert. No water for 18 miles, only what we carried. Today is the Fourth of July. How many are enjoying themselves, while we are spending the anniversary of the Declaration of Independence in travelling the lonely plains. We are corralled with the yellow backs tonight. Good grass. Wheather pleasant, but roads dusty—very.

JULY 5, 1863 After travelling three miles came into the stage line. Watered at a station a mile further.[5] Here we saw the Captain of a Wisconsin train whom we got acquainted with back on the Platte. He was sick and his company had gone on and left him at this station. As there was no more water for 22 miles, we filled our kegs. Nooned at a Soldiers' Station.[6] No grass or water. During noon hour, we rec'd a call from a soldier. He took from his pocket an Indian's scalp what had been taken two weeks before. A number of soldiers were out on a hunting expedition. During the night ten Indians visited their camp. They were soon surrounded by the soldiers and guarded. When day broke, they were all killed but one squaw. They took her prisoner. She was kept a few days and then shot. These are of the Go Shoot tribe, hostile to soldiers and emigrants but friendly to the Mormons. Old Brigham gives them 300 pounds of flour for every soldier and 100 for every emigrant they kill. We are camped tonight on a small stream called Government Springs—seven miles from the sandy desert and near a Soldiers' Station.[7] We are off of the stage road, and the soldiers were sent here merely to protect the emigrants from the Indians. Poor camping place—had to take the stock a mile over the mountains to graze. Wheather warm. Roads awful dusty.

JULY 6, 1863 Laid over today to rest the stock for the desert. It has been very warm, and this eve five other trains came in, among them Mr.

---

[4]They were camped on Faust Creek, about eight miles north of Vernon. The term "yellow backs" refers to the wagons of a small party of emigrants that Flora had mentioned several times in the part of the diary that is not included in this book.

[5]The Bender family would have struck the Overland Stage road about a half mile east of Faust Station. See ch. 8, n2. (See map 3.)

[6]This may have been Point Lookout. See ch. 3, n8.

[7]Bender was the only diarist to mention that soldiers were stationed here. See ch. 12, n5.

Marvin's and the balance of our train that we left at Salt Lake. Nellie and I went down to see Mary. There is a lady in their train laying at the point of death. During the day, one of our company was sun struck.

JULY 7, 1863 This morning we rolled out, and went five miles. Stopped in a canon where there was good grass, and a splendid spring. Thinking we were within two miles of Indian Springs, where they prepare themselves with water, and after making all necessary preparations, at 3 P.M. we moved on, finding the roads much longer than we anticipated. Sun was nearly down when we got to the Springs.[8] Kegs and vessels were filled, horses fed, and we struck for the great desert. We went through a canon about 8 miles before coming to the desert. It was a horrid road and as it was pitch dark, it required careful driving. But after we struck the desert we found the roads excellent—no sand, but merely alkali dust, nearly as white as flour.[9] We fed and watered once during the night—a beautiful moonlight night and very pleasant.

JULY 8, 1863 Between daylight and sunrise, stopped at a stage station, where we fed and took breakfast.[10] After starting out passed over a few hills and then struck the flat desert. Splendid roads and the day warm. Are camped tonight at Salt Springs (or Fish Springs).[11] At 10 A.M. a little son was given to Mrs. Miller. She named it Johnny Desert Miller

JULY 9, 1863 After having 45 miles of a drive and it being a poor camping place, we rolled out a[t] 3 A.M. No water or grass for 28 miles. At 9 A.M. fed grain and watered out of our kegs. Twelve o'clock finds us camped at Willow Springs.[12] Roads good. Wheather pleasant. Good water, but not very good grass—low and marshy—great danger of stock getting mired. This evening Mr. Hopson's nice grey horse rec'd

---

[8] After 1862, most emigrant parties spent at least one or two days at Indian Spring, but the Benders stopped only briefly. See ch. 8, n31.

[9] The country between the Simpson Mountains and the Deep Creek Mountains was once covered by an inland sea, and the soil is a deep layer of silt. It is not really alkali, but the dust is very fine and almost white.

[10] The stage station was located in the bottom of an unusually wide ravine known as Old Riverbed.

[11] After leaving the Riverbed station, the Benders traveled about thirty-five miles before reaching Fish Springs, which most travelers considered a pleasant oasis. It seems that the Benders did not think much of this area. See ch. 6, n4.

[12] See ch. 7, n9.

a severe wound. A man, while taking some bedding out of a wagon, it caught on the trigger of a gun—it went off, passing through his wagon and hitting the horse between the ears. There is some hopes of its recovery, however.

JULY 10, 1863 Having traveled very hard for the last two days and nights, we thought it best to lay by a day, as there is plenty of grass and water. A number of trains have come in and all are in good spirits. There is a large station here, also a blacksmith shop. There are also a great number of soldiers come in from stations east—they are on their way to Deep Creek to fight the Indians.

JULY 11, 1863 Having 24 miles to go to the next camping place, without grass or water, we rolled out before daylight, in order to get through before the heat of the day. We also prepared ourselves with water before leaving. The first six or eight miles roads level and rocky, then came into a canon, roads on the ascend but good. At 9 A.M. stopped, fed and watered and soon after passed where, a few nights ago, a stage station was burned down by the Indians. The bones of one man and five horses were laying in the ashes. Three or four other soldiers were killed—they were taken to Willow Springs and buried. The Indians have not molested the emigrants, with the exception of one place. That was at Needle Rocks. They are very hostile towards the soldiers, having killed quite a number at stations, and they have been killed in return. 12 A.M. finds us camped in Deep Creek Valley[13] to the right of the main road. Good camping place, plenty of water and grass. Wheather warm.

JULY 12, 1863 Travelled but a short distance today, in order to prepare for the thirty-eight mile desert—are camped in Deep Creek below the station. Nice camping place, splendid water and the very best of grass.[14] At the station there are four or five log cabins, a blacksmith shop and Telegraph office. Nellie and I went in and sent a dispatch to the boys. This is a beautiful valley. The men have been mowing grass to carry along tomorrow.

---

[13]See ch. 7, n11.

[14]The station was about a mile and a half north of Ibapah. To remain near Deep Creek where there was plenty of water and grass, they could have moved no more than three or four miles at the most. (See map 4.)

July 13, 1863 After preparing ourselves with water for the day, and grass for both day and night, we rolled out at 8 o'clock—travelled across a beautiful desert—it was level and the roads splendid. Deep dust in places but very little sand. At noon, fed and watered. This afternoon had quite a little shower. Splendid day for traveling. This evening we are camped at Antelope Springs,[15] 25 miles from Deep Creek. There is a stage station and nice spring here, but no grass. Two other trains are camped here. Our mowed grass comes good.

July 14, 1863 Sixteen miles to grass and water. Leaving Antelope Springs at sunrise, 10 A.M. finds us camped at Spring Valley Station, to the left of the road.[16] Plenty of water but miserable grass. After resting two or three hours, Mr. Hollands, Eardleys and us rolled out from the yellow backs and resolved to stay out of that train henceforth and forever. After going 12 miles, we arrived at Shell Creek Station.[17] We passed plenty of good grass in a canon but, anxious to get to Shell Creek, we went on and left it—and found very poor grass here but excellent water. Rather poor camp ground—wet and marshy. This eve two soldiers came down and wanted Nellie and I to come up to the station, as they were going to have a dance. But we would not go, because all were strangers to us, and Mrs. Holland could not go. Several trains are camped around here. They have a splendid station at this point—a nice large garden, where all kinds of vegetables are growing. Pleasant day. Roads splendid.

July 15, 1863 This morning the men took the stock off a mile or more into the mountains to graze good bunch grass. Rolled out at 9 A.M.crossed an alkali desert 15 miles without water—one little spot of grass, where we stopped to graze. During the afternoon had a very hard storm of rain and hail which rendered the roads very bad for a few miles. After leaving the desert we entered a canon of two miles, a nice stream of water to the right of the road. We are now camped at Eagan Canon Station, on the range of mountains that divides the

---

[15]See ch. 7, n13.

[16]From Antelope Spring, the Benders took the stage road around the southern end of the Antelope Mountains, then northwest to Spring Valley. The station was located near present-day Stonehouse. See ch. 8, n10.

[17]Flora's Shell Creek Station was located at what is now known as the Schellbourne Ranch.

Go Shoot and Shoshone Indians[18] This eve a Beloit train came in, and on enquiring, Nellie found out that Mrs. Steele (a lady she know in Beloit) was in it. She was very glad to see her. We went over to another train where there was a crazy girl—they have to keep her tied all the time. Plenty of water here, though not very good grass. It rained quite hard this eve.

JULY 16, 1863 Having poor grass last night, we started early this morning, traveled three or four miles, and stopped at the edge of the mountains where there was splendid bunch grass, and let the stock out to graze, also cut grass to carry along. Have been travelling over a mountainous country today—crossed over a small valley. Roads good, considering the broken country. Had a very hard rain this afternoon. After travelling 18 miles without water or grass, we are now camped at Butte Springs[19] in the mountains. There are eight trains here, among them the Beloit, also a large freight train from Salt Lake. No grass close by—have to take the stock over the mountains, good water but scarce, on account of so much stock. Sharp lightening and thunder this evening. Merry times in camp, however—music by the band. We are now out of the dangerous Indian country—and have not seen one Indian all the way through it. They are not so hostile to the emigrants as they are to the soldiers and stage men.

JULY 17, 1863 21 miles from Butte Springs to Ruby Valley, one watering place called Mountain Springs, near a stage station.[20] 3 o'clock P.M. we camped two miles above the station in Ruby Valley,[21] two hundred and ninety miles from Virginia City. Today came over a mountainous country, until striking the Valley, where the roads were very good but dusty. Spent the balance of the day in cleaning house. A number of trains are here and are going to stay to recruit—miserable grass to recruit on. The Fort is about two miles to the right of the main road—good water here. We rec'd a letter from Wilse.

---

[18]The stage station was located at the western end of Egan Canyon. (See map 5.)

[19]This camp was at Pony Spring. See ch. 7, n12.

[20]The Mountain Spring Pony Express Station was located at the eastern base of the Maverick Spring Mountains, near the mouth of Murry Canyon, and about two and a half miles from the actual site of the spring. Bender's statement makes it quite clear that in 1863, a stage station was located at the spring.

[21]See ch. 6, n8.

JULY 18, 1863 The day was spent in washing and cooking. Wheather cloudy and windy. I wrote a letter to Wilse and Mrs. Castella. Nellie is not very well.

JULY 19, 1863 Nellie being worse, we called in the Physician—he thinks it an attack of Mountain fever. Ma is not well either. Several of our old trains came in this eve. I went to see them all—they are in good spirits. Creighton's girls called on us for the first time.

JULY 20, 1863 Nellie feeling better this morning, we concluded to go on. But after travelling two miles to the station, she found she could not stand it to ride, however soft the bed, so we had to stop. The merchant there kindly gave us one of his rooms to stay as long as we pleased, and we gratefully accepted it. I hope in two or three days we will be able to go on. Mr Hollands and Eardleys kindly stopped with us. It is keeping them back, but for friendship's sake, we want to keep together. How kind of them. And now we are domiciled in a nice large room, the first time in a house since we left home. There is also one lady of our old train lying here sick—no hope of her recovery. A lady who lives here called on us. During the day two hundred and eighty soldiers and three pieces of artillery arrived at the Fort, on their way to Salt Lake City. This morning all trains were visited by the officers, it being the law for all emigrants to take the oath of allegiance before leaving this place. Those who will not are taken to the Fort as prisoners, till they do, good for them!

JULY 21, 1863 A number of trains started this morning—how I dread being left behind. Reese River is our next point, one hundred and twenty miles. The day has been warm and lonely. I wrote a letter to Mary Etta Unthank. There is a Post Office, Telegraph office and Store here, besides a number of log cabins. Some stiff looking gentlemen, also. I went to see Mrs. R.—she is still very sick, poor thing. I expect she will never leave this place.

JULY 22, 1863 This morning, the sick being convalescent, we started once more, after telegraphing the boys that she was better. Went over an awful rough road, up one of the largest hills on the route, very steep and rocky, up and down.[22] Are camped tonight at Diamond Springs,

[22]The steep hill was the Overland Pass in the Diamond Mountains. See ch. 7, n14.

26 miles from Ruby. Good camping place and good bunch grass on the mountains. A number of Indians of the Shoshone nation are around camp, begging for biscuit. There is a Stage Station here. In a train near us, there is a very sick man—had to send back to Ruby for a Doctor.

JULY 23, 1863 After crossing a valley of 13 miles, we nooned at Sulphur Springs, taking the right hand road beyond the stage station. Plenty of water, both Sulphur and fresh, grass short, and alkali in abundance. After leaving this place, fifteen miles to water. When striking out cross a range of mountains, then a valley.[23] Travelling quite a distance came to Robert's station and watered. Leaving there we took a right hand road leading up to the mountains.[24] It was dark when we camped and our supper was soon prepared and eaten. The stock was taken into the mountains to graze all night. Drove about 30 miles today—good roads but dusty.

JULY 24, 1863 Having a hard day's drive yesterday, did not start this morning until nearly noon. Went 14 miles and are camped at a Station, name unknown.[25] Good well water—splendid roads and pleasant wheather.

JULY 25, 1863 Today have been travelling through Robert's Valley—roads very good and are camped tonight one mile and a half from Dry Creek Station. Leaving it, to the left, followed a canon up to the mountains. Good Camping place, splendid spring, and good bunch grass in the mountains.[26] Traveled 18 miles—no water or grass, only what we hauled. Pleasant wheather.

JULY 26, 1863 This eve finds us camped at Simpson's Park, 13 miles from Dry Creek and nine from Austin. Travelled an awful rough road, called a cut-off.[27] We would have done better had we kept the stage road, if there was no grass or water. There is a nice station and a family living here. Good grass in the mountains. Plenty of campers around,

---

[23]See ch. 10, n23. After leaving Sulphur Spring, they traveled through Garden Pass and then traveled along the southern base of Mount Hope.

[24]It appears that after crossing Roberts Creek, they left the main road and turned into the foothills of the Roberts Creek Mountains.

[25]Sometimes called Grubb's Station and sometimes Grubb's Well, this area is listed on modern maps as Grubb Flat.

[26]They were camped somewhere near present-day Dry Creek Ranch.

[27]The Benders followed the Eagle Butte route. See ch. 7, n15. (See map 6.)

among them a large freight train from California, with Government stores for the soldiers at Salt Lake.

JULY 27, 1863 After travelling 4 miles, came to some springs, and good grass. We are going to Clifton, but Mr. Hollands and Eardleys took a sudden notion to stop there in the canon, for fear they would find no feed at the town. Pa, anxious to move on, went on and left them. I hope they will not be offended, and overtake us in the morning, for we have been camping together so long now that I shouldn't like to be separated from them. We are camped tonight at Clifton. It is situated in a canon eight miles east of Reese River—it is a very pretty place and a curiosity to us—the houses are principally of canvas, with roofs made of cedar bushes—but very few wooden buildings. Austin lies up the canon about a mile.[28] It is much larger than Clifton, but both are flourishing little towns and ere long, this country will, I presume, be as rich as Washoe. The mines have just lately been discovered and are not wholly developed yet. For supper we had potatoes and onions, both 25 cents a pound—beef also 25 cents. This is a good place to get rid of your greenbacks, at a discount.

JULY 28, 1863 This morning we started on, without seeing Hollands—thought they would catch up with us at the river—but going about 15 miles we stopped on the river[29] to take dinner. Passed through Jacobsville, another enterprising little town. This afternoon we started out with the expectation of stopping at the next hay ranch, 15 or 16 miles. Came over a mountainous country but good roads.[30] Had some rain. We passed the haystack without seeing it as it was getting dark, and went on and on, finding no grass or water, till about 10 o'clock P.M. arrived at Smith River, about 35 miles from Reese.[31] No grass here, but plenty of water. We are all alone, not a single wagon but ours around and indeed we don't know whether we are on the right road or not. Pleasant moonlight eve.

---

[28]The little mining town of Clifton was in Pony Canyon, about a mile west of Austin. It appears that the Benders did not go quite into the town of Austin.

[29]Reese River. See ch. 3, n38. (See map 7.)

[30]The mountainous country was the Shoshone Mountains, which they would have crossed by way of Smith Creek Summit.

[31]The camp was on Smith Creek, near the center of Smith Creek Valley.

JULY 29, 1863 This morning started out, and after travelling a mile or two, came to a ranch. The man told us we were on the right road, and would find grass about 6 miles down the canon. Started on and arrived at Edwards Creek[32] about 11 A.M. Found campers here. Put the stock out to graze in a pasture kept by an old Frenchman. The remainder of the day was spent in washing, baking, etc., etc. Are camped in a nice spot—good water and plenty of bunch grass in the mountains.

JULY 30, 1863 Started early this morning and passed several nice ranches, before getting out on the desert. No water till we got to Cold Springs where we nooned—poor water. Proceeded on and after travelling over a sage brush country, arrived at dark at West Gate,[33] 28 miles from Edward's. Have to buy hay at 6 cts. a pound. Wheather very pleasant. This is a romantic looking spot—large mountains on either side, forming a gate way between them, hence the name West Gate.

JULY 31, 1863 After traveling 4 miles arrived at Middle Gate,[34] where we telegraphed to the boys. Supplying ourselves with water for the 22 mile desert, started on. Stopped at noon, watered and fed, and about five o'clock got to Sand Springs[35]—salty water and no grass. A miserable camping place. A family live at the station. Our road today lay over an alkali desert, strung with dead animals. We were invited in to dance this eve, but would not go.

AUGUST 1, 1863 Had a dreadful sandy road this morning,[36] nooned at a station at the Carson Sink.[37] Starting on this afternoon, we got

---

[32]The Benders went up Smith Creek Canyon, not down, as Flora indicates. After leaving this canyon, they crossed Basque Summit and then started down Edwards Creek Canyon. They could have made their camp at any of several places along the creek, but if the mileage she recorded the next day was correct, the camp would have been near the top of the canyon. See ch. 3, n40.

[33]Flora had her gates mixed up. Middlegate lies to the east of Westgate, and since they were traveling west, they would have arrived at Middlegate before they reached Westgate. See ch. 3, n42.

[34]Flora is still confused about the names of the gates. She is now at Westgate. Adding to the confusion is the fact that the telegraph station was at Middlegate.

[35]See ch. 3, n43.

[36]The stage road over Simpson Pass was notorious for its sand. Simpson had considered going through this pass during his return journey but his guide persuaded him not to because the sand would have caused problems for the wagons (Simpson, *Report of Explorations*, 105). Based on Flora's comment here, it is probably safe to assume that the Benders' party took this route. See ch. 3, n44.

[37]The station where they stopped for their noon break was the Carson Sink stage station, which had also been used by the Pony Express. It was located near the southwest corner of Carson Lake, commonly called Carson Sink at that time. (See map 8.)See ch. 3, n45.

on the wrong road, which took us to a hay ranch. We concluded to stop there as there was plenty of good grass and water. The lady of the house called on us. We also had a call from Mr. and Mrs. O'Neal, who were on their way to Reese River. The lady took supper with us. This is a delightful evening.

AUGUST 2, 1863 We got on the right road this morning and went over the most abominable ones, deep sand, along the Carson River.[38] At noon we stopped at a station, where we again overtook Clayton's, ten miles east of Ragtown.[39] This afternoon roads bad as ever—heavy freight teams stuck in the sand every few miles. At camping time got to Ragtown, which consists of one large house, at the junction of the Humboldt and Reese River roads. Passing that, we came two miles further, and stopped at a ranch on the Carson River—good grass—have to pay for it though. Wheather pleasant. Another train is camped here.

AUGUST 3, 1863 This morning came over a rough road, and noon brought us on the last desert, at the junction of the Honey Lake and direct stage route. We took the latter and at dark put up at a station, 16 miles from Virginia.[40] We expected to meet the boys here, but perhaps will meet them tomorrow. This is our last night on the plains. How happy we all are—to think that 1600 miles have come down to 16. I can scarcely realize that we are so near our destination. We hear awful stories about the sickness there, caused by using bad water. I guess it is more whiskey than water. Mary Ellen is not well this eve—had a hard chill.

AUGUST 4, 1863 Started early this morning, and at noon entered the 6 mile canon which leads into the city.[41] Going five miles we passed through a small town called Flowery, and then to the great Gould and Curry Mill. It is a handsome structure. Taking the right hand road, our longing eyes were soon gazing on the wonderful city. Coming up

[38]The Benders took the Ragtown route rather than going over the Dead Camel Mountains.

[39]The station to the east of Ragtown was known as the Old River station and was located in what is now the northern part of the city of Fallon (Townley, *The Overland Stage*, 259). The distance to Ragtown was about eight miles.

[40]This camp would have been somewhere near present-day Stagecoach. (See map 9.)

[41]They left the Central Overland Trail about six miles northeast of Dayton and traveled up Six Mile Canyon.

into the principal street, we found Wils. He said Almon had started to meet us, and Shaney went that morning before daylight, but he missed us by taking the road to Ft. Churchill. Wils conducted us to a house they had rented, and where we had a good view of the city. It would be useless to add how glad we were to see our dear brothers again. We are now ensconced in a nice little house, and rejoicing that we are "Hemegrants" no longer. We have travelled over a long, lonely and dangerous road—have been blessed with health, most of the way—found that savage race mostly harmless. And indeed, have had a pleasant trip across the plains—endured none of those hardships which we read of so often.

CHAPTER 14

George Harter

1864

George Harter and his family traveled from Cass County, Michigan, to California in 1864. Harter's route was somewhat unusual in that after following the Central Overland Trail to Austin, Nevada, he left it and turned northward along the Reese River, eventually getting onto the California Trail somewhere near the Humboldt Sink. Harter's diary does not take the typical day-by-day format, and he included very few dates in his account. Sometime during the year after his arrival in California, he rewrote his account to make it more understandable. In 1902, George worked on his account again—the editor hopes that he made only a few minor revisions. Excerpts from the 1865 revision have been published in the book Wagon Tracks: George Harter's 1864 Journey to California, *edited by Robert D. Harter (Tucson: Patrice Press, 2003). The 1902 version appears below.*

From the California State Library, the editor obtained a copy of a transcription made in 1957 by Doris Harter Chase. Permission to publish was granted by Loadel Harter Piner, a direct descendent of George Harter.

Camped after dark in the border of Salt lake valley, three miles from the City. Next morning drove in before breakfast. Turned our stock into a correl to hay. Bought some potatoes and vegetables and had a square meal. We soon dispatched a messenger to the P.O. as we were very anxious to hear from civilization. We received several very acceptable letters, but one brought the very sad news of the death of my father. It was not altogether unexpected though as is always the case very sad news.

It brought many vivid recollections of my youthful life and happy preveleges I had enjoyed under his care and proteaction. We stopped here on emigrant square[1] which is all the term implies and was occupied by a large number of weary wanderers from all quarters.

We offered the wagon that was purchased at Omaha for sale. It was soon taken. It was the best place to sell anything and old things of any description that I ever saw. Anything was in good demand and was not altogether safe laying around lose. We had to unload both wagons and see what we had and dispose of what we did not need in order to get the remainder all in one wagon. It was a very busy day with us. All of the company except myself and two children went to the theatre that night.

This is one of the Brighams individual institutions and is a fine building. There was a light show of rain in the evening and another in the morning which is uncommon here at this season. After dinner I saddled two mules and my wife and I took a ride through the City. (I forgot to say we got a good sidesaddle when Welshes unloaded and were going to leave one wagon and much of their plunder. When they stopped to leave our train their wagon and provisions and all other things that they would have were given back to them, but the sidesaddle they did not want.) The City is nicely located in a pleasant and fertile portion of the valley close by the eastern foothills.

---

[1]This was known as Emigrant Square, or sometimes Emigration Square. According to historian William Hartley, it was located on the block that now contains the Salt Lake City and County Building, bordered by 400 and 500 South, and State Street and 200 East (*Overland Journal* 11(4): 31). Eight of our diarists indicated that they camped here while they were in Salt Lake City.

The City is splendidly watered by a mountain stream conducted through all the principal streets and ditches for the purpose of irrigating gardens, etc., in the city and grain fields in the suburbs. The principal building recently erected are of brick. One stone front of gray granite. A large majority of the buildings are dobies. These are built of large square bricks dried in the sun laid up in walls from one to two feet thick. Brighams residence is a large fine looking mansion.

At his front gate is a very large spread eagle perched on the arch above and huge lion standing on each side. He had a square enclosed with a high brick wall which is his orchard and garden etc. Brigham had commenced erecting a temple which is all of gray granite and is procured in the mountains twelve miles distant. It is said to cost over a million dollars when completed but many think it never will be. This building is also enclosed by a high wall. In a very early day the City was encircled by a heavy earthen embankment for defense against Indians. In some places this wall still stands ten feet high. We rode two miles to the Warm Springs.[2] This water is clear but smells strong of Sulphur and tastes of salt and Sulphur. It comes out of a large mountain through a hole in the rock large enough for a man to crawl in and the stream is as large as my body. It empties into a large pool dug over three feet deep and enclosed by a high board fence for the use of visitors bathing in. In first stepping in it appears too hot but after being in a few moments is very comfortable. It is said to possess some powerful medicinal qualities, as some of our company experienced after bathing by getting so sick they could scarcely get back to camp.

From here we went two miles farther to the boiling springs. These are very similar to the former and so hot you cannot bear your hand in it at all. Along the way are numerous smaller springs coming out of the same mountain and all temperatures down to cold.

Going back to camp we were in rain from which my wife caught cold which troubled her seriously at times for over a month.

East of the City in the low hills is Camp Douglas. Here is stationed a regiment of California soldiers. They are very bold in expressing their

---

[2]See ch. 3, n1.

sentiments in opposition to Brigham and his institution generally for which I think they deserve great credit.

A large portion of this valley is comparatively worthless because of lack of water to irrigate to make cultivation profitable. Timber is very scarce. Fruit trees about the City look fine and were bearing full.

On Monday P.M. we hitched six mules to our wagons and drove out. This left more spare animals so we could cange and rest the weaker ones. We left in company with a two horse team we had traveled with a long time. It was over two weeks befor any of our company overtook us. About one mile west of the City is the river Jordan.[3] This is a deep and sluggish stream which is bridged here so we passed "over Jordan." For some days after we were at times singing, "Over Jordan into Glory." "We'll go on, We'll go on." It appears then was the first time that I really felt as though I was going to California.

We seldom looked farther in our guide book than to Salt lake which made it appear as if that was the end of the journey.

We were a little over three months from Omaha which was five weeks longer than we should have been had it not been for the Indians and scarcety of feed.

Our stock had gotten very poor, but we had fared so much better than many others in saving our lives and all our stock that we felt truly thankful and went on feeling encouraged and refreshed by our rest in the City.

According to our guide book we had to travel 1,142 miles from Omaha and had 679 miles before we reached Marysville, our destination.

Camped on salt grass which grows on flat land and is poor feed though our stock ate it readily. Some places it is so strong it tasts quite salty. This is the Bush road and said to be shorter than the stage road.[4] Next morning we were soon in sight of Salt Lake. The road is only a short distance from the shore. Along the waters edge are numerous

---

[3]The old North Temple bridge. See ch. 9, n2. (See map 2.)

[4]The Harters had reached Salt Lake City by following the stage road, but left it there to go through Tooele. They rejoined the stage road at Faust Station in Rush Valley. The editor has found no other mention of the name "Bush Road."

furnaces with pans to evaporate water for the manufacturing of salt. When dried is as white and nice as I ever saw.

There was at this time no work being done, but plenty of salt lying around. It is said that three pails of water make one pail of salt.

We had long promised ourselves a swim in Salt Lake. It was rather cool but this was our only chance so wife drove the team and the two boys and I each kept a mule to ride and had a fine bath and swim. The water is as clear as crystal. The bottom runs in very gradual slope and is a white pile stone or clay. The water is so heavy with salt a person can sit or lay full length without sinking. If there are any sore or raw spots on the body you can very easily locate them. After coming out and drying off we were covered with a coat of salt and our hair was perfectly white.

I do not know the size of the lake but in it is a very large mountain apparently a mile or more from the shore where we were. I was told that Brigham keeps this for his private grazing ground.

The lake has no outlet, but a number of good sized streams empty into it.

When we left the lake the wagon was a long way ahead. In the P.M. we had a hard wind with rain and hail. We passed through a small Mormon village called Tuella.[5] Drove two miles farther and camped alone. Drive the stock up a very steep mountain on a level bench and found good bunch grass.

Next day passed through Stockton a mining town just started, said to have fine prospects of rich silver ore. Next day overtook the two horse team we started with and camped together. Wife was feeling badly. Made a short drive next day to the stage road and stopped at a stage station[6] where we found a doctor camped and had him give wife some medicine. The boys took the stock three miles to a mountain but got little feed. Next morning wife was some better. Had quite a range of mountains to cross and but little water for animals. We were late getting into camp with those we were with the night before. This

[5]This was the Mormon settlement of Tooele. See ch. 9, n6.

[6]This was Faust Station. There was, and still is, a grassy meadow here that would have been a good place for emigrants to camp. See ch. 8, n2.

is Government Springs several miles off the main road but we had to go for water and it was also a fine place to lay over and recruit before starting on the desert.[7] We remained here over Sunday and Monday. Ike Banta and Lew Harter washed and baked bread.

We generally used light bread and when laying over baked and put in sacks enough to do about a week. Wife was not able to be out of the wagon, but felt quite comfortable.

I herded the stock a mile away on fine bunch grass and wrote a letter home and mailed it at the next station. Tuesday drove seven miles over another range of mountains some very rough and steep roads. Camped at Indian Springs.[8] Splendid water at mouth of canyon. Took the stock over a mile up some steep and narrow canyons to good feed. Here we lay until next day four o'clock P.M. then started on a forty mile desert. At midnight we stopped and I fed my mules some chopped wheat and gave them the water we had brought along in a ten gallon keg swung under the wagon for that purpose. Soon we came to quite a mountain and passed over.[9]

When the moon arose we were traveling near the foot of a mountain and so continued until nine o'clock when we came to fish springs[10] and camped. In the morning before we camped some of our mules got so tired and weak we had to walk and whip them to get them along. Lew Harter was sick all night from eating a mess of elder berries the day before. These springs are deep holes or pools of clear water with many nice fish in them but we could not get them to bite a bait at all. The grass is salt also the water is so it is not fit for tea at all.

This is a stage station and they were making arrangements to have a dance with some emigrants that were laying over here.

At five o'clock P.M. started on a twenty-one mile drive over very level roads. At sunup came to Willow Springs[11] and camped. This is quite an extensive valley. These springs are deep holes like wells and some

---

[7]In Harter's first draft of his account, he said they "were obliged to go there for water" (Harter, *Wagon Tracks*, 58). See ch. 12, n5. (See map 3.)

[8]See ch. 8, n31.

[9]This was Dugway Mountain, which they crossed by way of Dugway Pass.

[10]See ch. 6, n4.

[11]See ch. 7, n9.

so deep there can be no bottom found. Some run over, others stand level full. Every year some stock is lost here by drowning in these wells. Grass and water salt. At three P.M. we started to drive seven miles where we found good water and a little bunch grass.[12] Were here alone.

Next morning our stock had wandered several miles into the mountains in search of feed which they are very apt to do where feed is so scarce. Got started late. Drove sixteen miles over a range of mountains to a valley called Deep Creek[13] where we overtook the two horse team again.

Next P.M. drove five miles and camped on fairly good feed.[14] Next morning filled our kegs at stage station and started on a twenty-five mile drive. The ropes gave away by which the keg was swung under the wagon and it was lost so the animals had no water all day, but we had a two gallon keg we carried in the wagon for drinking and cooking purpose. The road to-day was perfectly hard and smooth and almost a water level.

Camped at Antelope Springs.[15] After supper Ike Banta and Lew Harter took blankets on mules and took the stock a couple of miles but found only a little feed. After leaving Fort Bridge [Bridger] we did not correl the stock any more but when they were taken some distance some of us would take blankets and stay with them and bring them in the morning.

Next day passed over another range of mountains and camped at Shell Creek.[16] But little feed. Next day drove five miles and found good feed and water near the summit of a range of mountains. To-night one of my mules left the band and came a mile to camp and was very sick caused I think by eating too much bunch grass which operates about the same as too much grain. By morning she was all right.

About nine o'clock the two companies we left at Salt Lake City caught up and we all drove fifteen miles to Egan canyon.[17] Here is

[12]This camp was at what is now known as Six-Mile Ranch. It is six miles north of Callao.

[13]See ch. 7, n11.

[14]This would have put them near the Eight-Mile stage station. (See map 4.)

[15]See ch. 7, n13.

[16]Harter climbed through the Antelope Mountains by way of Rock Springs Pass, but he had his creeks mixed up, calling Spring Creek "Shell Creek." See ch. 8, n10.

[17]On this day, the Harters drove down the western slope of the Schell Creek Mountains, crossed Steptoe Valley, and made camp somewhere near the eastern end of Egan Canyon.

another mining town just started, and quite a stirring place. Another dance with the emigrants here. Next day drove eighteen miles. About noon missed our dog. Isaac Banta took a mule and went back and found him where we had camped. He came in camp a while after dark. We had become attached to the dog because of his strict watchfulness while among the Indians.

They could not come around without him knowing it and they had to keep their hands off things. He was always the best guard in the camp. Here was the last we saw of the two horse team and the three Norwegians. They were good company and nice to travel with.

To-day we drove seventeen miles considerably hilly but good roads. Wife was quite sick again. Camped at Ruby Valley.[18] This is a military station in a nice valley with considerable agriculture. We lay over next day and wife was quite sick until towards evening. Here all of our company left us and we traveled alone to Austin, a distance of 115 miles. Next morning wife was better and very anxious to go on. We started and she continued to improve and we drove sixteen miles. When we got in camp I was very sick with cramp colic but soon got relief by some medicine we had along. This was the only sickness I had on the trip.[19] Drove eight miles next day over Diamond Mountain which was the steepest road we had found.[20] It was all our six weak animals could do to haul our load. Camped at Diamond Springs at the foot of the mountain. Plenty of pure water but warm. Soon after turned our stock loose. There were two men with three Dromedarys overtook us and camped with us. These animals frightened our mules very much, one of them was so poor he fell down when he tried to make a quick start to run and when he got up he was over his scare. These animals are used some here on the deserts and carry large burdens. They look and act and endure much the same as a Camel.[21]

---

[18]See ch. 6, n8.

[19]This would have put them in the Connor Creek area, near the eastern base of the Diamond Mountains.

[20]See ch. 8, n14.

[21]It is fairly well known that the army experimented with camels during the 1860s. Their use in commercial transportation is less well known. Six other Central Overland Trail diarists mention sightings of these animals.

Next day traveled twelve miles over a very level desert. There was a small band of Elks crossed the road not far ahead of us passing from one range of mountains to the other. Camped at Sulphur Springs with the Dromedaries. Poor feed. Made a long drive next day over a range of mountains and got in camp after dark alone. Poor feed and but little water. Next day drove nineteen miles over a level desert and camped at Dry Creek. Poor feed. Here we took fool's cut off which is well named.[22] Traveled four miles up a rough and steep mountain. Reached the sumit at noon. Turned out on good grass. After dinner hitched the wheel animals onto the wagon and started down. After going a little way we stopped and cut down a good sized pine tree and hitched it behind on the wagon and drove down about a mile to a spring and camped and drove the stock back where we had nooned. Without the tree behind I think the wagon would have run over the mules. Next day drove over some very rough roads and camped at a spring a regular camping ground three miles from Austin.[23] This is an important mining town built within the last two years. The ledges are rich in silver ore and there are two quartz mills running and others constructing. It is a hard looking place for a City as it will be in a few years. There are fine business houses here but all building timber has to come from the Sierra Nevada Mountains a distance of about two hundred miles and hauled on wagons. There are some valleys in this region of the country that produce hay and a few vegetables but grain for feed and all provisions and merchandise and machinery has to be brought by teams from the valleys and Cities in California taking from forty to fifty days for a trip.

We lay here ten days to recruit our stock. We had come so far over hard roads and much of the time scant food. We took them two miles into the mountains to good bunch grass and brought them down once a day to water. They picked up fine. We moved our cooking and beds into a vacant shanty that had a fire-place in it and dirt floor and took

---

[22]Harter followed the Eagle Butte route. See ch. 8, n15. (See map 6.)

[23]The editor has been unable to determine the exact location of this camping place, but it must have been somewhere along the eastern edge of the Reese River Valley. Several of our diarists probably used the same camping area.

the door for a table instead of taking a tin plate on our knees and sitting on the ground or stone so we lived quite at home and refined. Wife's health improved very fast here so she felt better when we started again. My wagon tire had gotten quite loose. I intended to have them set in Austin but they wanted $25.00 for the job. I concluded I could do better so I took the tires off and put one thickness of leather in each joint of the fella and also under the shoulders of the spokes next the rim of the wheel until all the joints came up tight. I heated the tire and put them on and the wheels would ring like new and they never got loose again while I owned the wagon. Several companys here adopted my plan. I did my mule shoeing here. We sold some chopped wheat here at 16ct. per lbb. Dried apples at 25ct. per lbb.

We heard from our train that had left us behind. Two wagons went on to Virginia City and one remained to recruit his stock and came to see us. From accounts from California and of several years drouth we concluded to go to the extreme northern part of the state to winter our stock.[24] Here we got acquainted with a nice family from Illinois by the name of Davidson who joined us and we arranged to start in a few days. We first came to Rose [Reese] river Valley and traveled twelve miles and camped on the bank of the river.[25]

---

[24]Ironically, at about this same time, the small emigrant party that included Reverend John Fackler was camped on the Humboldt River about ninety miles to the north, where someone persuaded them to leave the California Trail and head south to Austin. See Fackler's diary entry for September 5.

[25]See ch. 3, n38. When Harter's small party reached the Reese River, they left the Central Overland Trail and turned north. Thus, the Harter party began to follow the Reese River downstream toward Battle Mountain at about the same time that John Fackler and his party began to follow it upstream toward Austin. Neither Harter nor Fackler mention meeting anyone along the trail. Harter's account of the trip continues until well after he reached California, but because he was no longer following the Central Overland Trail, we end it here.

CHAPTER 15

Mary Warner

1864

Sometime in the spring of 1864, Mary Warner and her husband left DeKalb, Illinois, and headed west. In her diary, Mary referred to her husband as "Warner" or "A. L. Warner," but never included his first name. An unknown number of pages are missing from both the beginning and the end of Mary's diary, and the date when the Warners began their journey is unknown. We do know that they arrived in Salt Lake City on May 30, 1864.

A copy of a transcription of Warner's diary was obtained from the Bancroft Library, which granted permission to publish it (BANC MSS C–F 66).

May 30, 1864 Today finds us in Salt Lake. Last night after supper we women with C. H. Warner went up to the City. Passed Brigham Young's house where all of his wives live, with one store, printing office and his other offices all contained with in a large wall. The gates are not opened on Sunday so we could not enter. One of his houses is very nice. There is a large lion in front. From there we went around to the place of worship called the Bowery and then went to the new temple which is being built of stone with out the sound of hammer or chisel. Warner says it has not progressed much since he saw it in 1862. It is going to be very nice indeed when complete. This city lies in the wild territory of Utah is indeed very pretty place in the morning. Celia who was not able to go with us yesterday rode around town with me this morning in the buggy. I went in some of the stores. One can find every thing one can ask for but though it takes money to buy. For instance let me give you the price of some of them. They pay $15 per hundred for flour, sugar $100, Calaco 28cts and for a course combe they asked $1.00. Celia sold her crape shawl for $12.00. They gave us only half an hour to be gone in so we had to hurry very much (I must not forget to say there is a small stream for running water each side of the street which sounds so nice and pleasant on a warm day). After getting back found they were all ready to start so Celia got in to the wagon and she and the rest went on while I had to stay in town and hold the horses while Warner was getting some work done. They did not get started until nearly noon so we traveled only fourteen miles.[1] We found them just as they were setting down to supper. They gave me a letter from home which I can assure you I was most glad to get. Did not find myself as hungry as I thought I was after getting my letter. Celia allso had one from home.

MAY 31, 1864 Did not get an early start in the morning and traveled very slow all day. Our way lay by farmes owned by the Mormons. Passed through one town. Allso around the south side of the lake from which we had a very fine view. We camped at a small settlement.[2] Took the horses over the mountain for feed. After getting supper and things put to rights it was surely dark and I had retired as soon as we camped being very tired and most sick.

JUNE 1, 1864 It commenced raining about dark last night and rained all night. About 12 o'clock part of the guard came down to camp and told them the horses were restless. They would have to be brought down so they got up in the rain and secured the horses which ocupied them nearly two hours. Then they tried to get a little rest in their work clothes. I think about them. They all thought it was a hard

[1]Traveling in a slightly south of west direction from the center of Salt Lake City would have put the Warners at the northern base of the Oquirrh Mountains. (See map 2.)

[2]The settlement near which they camped was the town of Tooele. See ch. 9, n6.

road to travel. Breakfast was got in the rain and ate in the rain. I did not get out to get any not being well as hungry. Things were packed up and we were on our way at half past five. Went thirty miles and gave the horses grass four an hour[3] and so went five and camped for the day near a station of soldiers.[4] It cleared off and was quite pleasant.

JUNE 2, 1864 Started twenty minutes past eleven and went only twelve miles. I was quite sick all day and the Dr. says with the mountain fever. It hailed hard in the afternoon.

JUNE 3, 1864 Commenced our journey again early in the morning. Went twelve miles and stopped two hours to feed the horses. In the afternoon passed through a small cañon, allso Lookout Mountain so they told me but I did not look out all day.[5] Rode in the big wagon with Mary. Camped at night at government springs.[6] An Indian came in camp.

JUNE 4, 1864 Started quite late in the morning as we had only nine miles to travel to day. Went down some very steep hills and over very rough roads which made it hard for sick folks. Cora was taken sick to day and Mary is not very well. It was only twelve o'clock when we camped.[7] Mary Danwell and Celia done some washing for me in the afternoon and the rest of the women who were able done some cooking and made preparations to cross the Desert.

JUNE 8, 1864 I again take my pencil to resume my journal. While I was sick I did not write and did not know much that transpired around me. We crossed the desert in the night. Stopped one day on a small green spot in the desert[8] where we could rest the horses as they had brought grass along to feed with and the next night traveled again. On this day we were still scouting horses at a place called Willow Springs.[9] Though I took but little notice of the desert crossing it as we did, in the

---

[3]They stopped to feed the horses when they reached Faust Creek. They were about five miles north of the Faust stage station.

[4]This camp was near Faust station. See ch. 8, n2.

[5]There is no Lookout Mountain in this area, but Mary did cross Lookout Pass and go past Point Lookout. See ch. 3, n8. (See map 3.)

[6]See ch. 12, n5.

[7]This camp was at Indian Spring. See ch. 8, n31.

[8]This was Fish Springs. See ch. 6, n4.

[9]During the time that Warner was sick, the train had crossed the desert and set up camp at Willow Springs. See ch. 7, n9. (See map 4.)

night, it is one dreary waste of Alkali dust—not a green shrub or blade of grass in sight. The distance across they estimate at eighty miles. We arrived here yesterday and could have gone on to day if it had not been for our stampede last night—if it is possible to give a description of it with pencil, or of the feelings we had last night you shall have them. About the hour of one o'clock we were awakened by the rushing noise of the feet of some eighty head of horses, twenty of them belonging to another train camped with us. The men started on foot after them just as they were when first awakened, barefoot and partly dressed. On the frightened horses ran some four miles with the men pursuing and then entered the mountains. At that the men turned back unable to go further on foot as they were sore and bleeding. On getting back found they had of the eighty horses ten left. The guard told them the Indians frightened the horses which set them running. They dressed, saddled the horses left and got their revolvers ready and then started for the mountains. Imagine our feeling while alone (or nearly so) there at the midnight hour on this dreary land, our horses gone not knowing as we would ever see them again or the men alive and we who were only partly dressed keeping up camp fire so the men could see camp and listening at every sound and longing for the break of day but time. . . . Daylight came with her bright beams and at seven o'clock while straining our eyes on the distant mountain discovered them returning. They were so far off when we first saw them that when they got in camp it was nine, two hours. When they got back found they had got all of ours but only five of the other companys. It was nearly night when they found them and then found them in care of Indians.

JUNE 9, 1864 To day got started early in the morning. Drove five miles and then found a spring[10] where we will not find water again for twenty miles. Seven miles from the springs came to a station.[11] Met during the day a company of men returning from California to the States. Distance traveled during the day in all about 26 miles. At night

[10]Six-Mile Ranch.

[11]This was Canyon Station, sometimes called Round Station because of its circular construction. It was a replacement for an earlier station, also known as Canyon Station, that had been located farther north in Overland Canyon and had been burned by raiding Indians the previous year (Townley, *The Overland Stage*, 231).

we were surrounded by Indians. Celia and myself done some washing. We had a sick horse which the men set up and doctored nearly all night

JUNE 10, 1864 Will stay here all day at Deep Creek[12] on account of the sick horse. It is very warm weather. Georgia, I again send my journal so as to give you all something to read. I send the collar to mother. You can make you one if you like it. It was made about the time I was on the summit of the Rocky mountains, making myself one like it. Now do not do any thing only when we lay over as the weather is so very warm. Oh dear, how I wish I was through. I am getting so tired and sick of this way of living. We expect to get through in three weeks if nothing happens by the time you get this. Be sure and let me know if you get all of my journal and the collar. Love to all. Your sister, Mary.[13]

JUNE 11, 1864 As we could only go seven or eight miles and not care to get an early start and did not for just as we were thinking of starting it commenced raining and rained quite hard when the sun came out again. We found the mountains covered with snow which were but little way from us. We got started about two o'clock and it soon commenced raining again. We came to a station which was with in three miles from our last camp.[14] It was quite a town for this inclusure containing several houses. One store blacksmith shop and stage and telegraph office. We there mailed some letters bought some bread and milk from which I dined from in the buggy. As I said we had but few miles to travel when we came to the place where we were to camp.[15] Found four companys allready there. Plenty of neighbors you see. We had not been there long before our friends of the forest came to us. Several squaws came around our table and were quite surely till at length Warner took the horse whip to them at which one of them struck him. After I had retired some of the ladys came to our camp.

JUNE 12, 1864 Sunday we were aroused by the cry of the general at the early hour of one o'clock to get up and make preparations for going on. They got breakfast and ate it with the exception of the women

[12]See ch. 7, n11.

[13]This entry indicates that Warner was occasionally sending the completed parts of her diary to a sister named Georgia. That may account for the fact that some of it is missing.

[14]This was the settlement of Deep Creek, a couple miles north of present-day Ibapah.

[15]They were now at Eight-Mile Station.

folks who did not get [any] untill the late hour of ten, as the road was smooth and level so far. Slept well.[16] The rest of the way was up long high hills. After traveling thirty-five [miles] camped in the mountains near some springs.[17] One of the companys that was by us last night camped at the same place. In the eve some of our ladys returned the call they had the night before. I came near forgetting to mention that as usual an Indian and his family entered our camp and were very peacefull. Kelly came up from his camp and commenced cuffing and kicking them untill they went away. We thought it wrong for him to do so as it lay in their power to injure us. Back to one of the stations he had misused some of the Indians as he came through the cañon alone. His company having gone a head the Indians followed him and fired on him for which he is bound to pay every Indian—innocent or guilty. So far we have treated them well and they have us which I think the true way to get along with them. It rained and rained at spells all day. You may think it strange for us to have snow in this month but remember we are now very high up in the mountains where it is never very warm.

June 13, 1864 Last night we were camped at Deep Creek, a place which will remain in our memory owing to the associations connected with the place.[18] This morning as they were harnassing their horses A. L. Warner called on one of the boys to help them at which he made a fuss as if he would do more than his share (he is one they had some trouble with before). Warner had some words with him and he went up to Lord and he took his part. Then [Warner] refused to travel longer with them under such conditions. We had got harnessed and then we stood some two hours and had a great time quarreling. Then Lord took charge of the train for that day and then we went on four or five miles and turned out to wait. Staid an hour and half and the men talked the matter over again and concluded to divide. Lord to take his third of horses and everything else and we would leave them. We

---

[16]Sleeping in the wagons as they traveled was hardly typical behavior for emigrants. One has to wonder what circumstances prompted it on this occasion.

[17]This was Rock Springs, located on the northwestern slope of the Antelope Mountains.

[18]Warner was mistaken when she said they were camped at Deep Creek the previous night. This incident occurred at Rock Springs.

traveled seven miles further and camped for the night on shell creek.[19] There they commenced dividing the things or at least got them ready to divide in the morning. Mr. Lord was very sorry that things were so that we could not travel any longer together. Said it should never of been so if it had not been for his wife. She had him so very ugly all the way through. We thought as we were going to divide we would have to pay for her hack before we left. Struck for the night thinking that for the last time this family would all camp together.

JUNE 14, 1864 This morning arose very early. After breakfast the men commenced dividing the things. Did not get them all separated untill nearly eleven o'clock. Then harnassed and started—found only two of the men were to go with Warner's company. Those two or three that had got mad with Lord's wife hired the rest to go with them. So it leaves our company rather small. We went on a head passed through Egan Cañon. It is a small town built in the cañon on the side hill. They have discovered a silver mine there and are working it. The distance traveled that day in all amounts to some twenty one miles. At night Lord's train passed us while we were getting super so we got our supper and ate it, then packed up our things and went up in the mountains. Stopped about eight o'clock and let the horses feed untill one o'clock. Then harnessed and went on—over took Lord's train by a spring.[20] As we stopped for water Lord's train passed us again. They had traveled all night. They went up in to the mountains and got breakfast. They thought we would breakfast by the spring but we too commenced to get breakfast in the mountains so we passed them again. We got breakfast and the horses got what they wanted in an hour and a half so we went on. Traveled 42 miles through valey and over mountain and camped Wensday night at a stage station called only Valley.[21] This is allso a small town of half a dozen houses. While we were getting ready for sleep Lord's train came in sight—camped a little way from us. We had cooked our victuals for the next day. Had bread and milk for supper. We got the milk at this station. We

[19]This camp was on Schell Creek, near present-day Schellbourne Ranch.

[20]This was probably Pony Spring. See ch. 8, n12.

[21]Warner was in Ruby Valley. See ch. 6, n8.

camped in time for a late dinner that day. A very good dinner for one to get on the plains. It consisted of warm biscuit and butter sausages, coffee and dryed peaches and dryed apple pie. You see our family is so small we can afford to live better. When we divided the victuals we took two thirds so it left Lord a small share with all his hungry men.

JUNE 16, 1864 Started at seven in the morning—got breakfast. Just after day light in the mountains walked up the highest [hill] we have yet come to.[22] We found ourselves tired and very tired before we reached the summit. Just as we got up an Indian came up on the other side and told us we could get water up to his Wickiup which was just over the hill. The distance we went that day was 42 miles.[23]

JUNE 17, 1864 As usual this work started at the early hour of twelve. Got to Link's well and Lord's train passed us while we were getting breakfast[24] Stoped at noon in the mountains to rest the horses. Camped at night at Roberts Creek.

JUNE 18, 1864 Did not start untill nearly day light. Went to Diamond Spring and gave the horses water.[25] Then went on untill noon. Gave the horses feed in the mountains. Went on to a camping ground. I have forgot its name.[26] It was in a cañon by a small creek of willows. As Lord's train was a head and our men wished to get to Austin[27] first

[22]There seems to be something wrong with this entry. Warner noted that they started at seven in the morning, and then says that it was just after daylight when they came to the high hill, which was clearly the Overland Pass in the Diamond Mountains. Even though the clock settings may have been somewhat different from those used today, it must have been daylight well before 7 A.M. in the middle of June. Moreover, since they had to travel approximately twenty miles to reach Overland Pass, it must have taken them something like six hours. The most likely explanation for this discrepancy is that the seven o'clock time is wrong and should have been much earlier. In the next day's entry, Mary indicates that during this part of the journey, their usual time to get started was twelve, meaning midnight. See ch. 8, n14.

[23]This would have put them in the vicinity of the Sulphur Spring stage station. See ch. 10, n23. Forty-two miles is an unusually long distance for a day's travel and is another argument for a much earlier start than seven o'clock.

[24]This is the only reference to "Link's well" of which the editor is aware. The context indicates that it would have been somewhere between Sulphur Spring and the southern foothills of Mount Hope, possibly in the Garden Pass area.

[25]Warner was mistaken about the name of the spring where they watered their horses. It was not Diamond Springs, which was back about forty miles, but it could have been Grubb's Wells, which is about thirteen miles southwest of the Roberts Creek stage station.

[26]This was Dry Creek.

[27]See ch. 12, n21.

we started at ten in the evening. The men lay down for rest and an Indian guarded the horses for a while, while we women sat by the fire and kept camp guard untill the men were ready to start. We tried to get sleep but got little as the ground was very rough. We arrived two miles this side of town about five o'clock in the morning so you see we came out a head of the Lord's train which pleased us very much. We stayed here all day. The men all went up to town. The town is five thousand of only a year's growth. It is a mining town and everything is very high. Gold is the only money in use. Flour is $20 per hundred in gold, in green backs it would be nearly $90 per hundred. Warner bought a come [comb] for me and gave a dollar for it.[28]

[28] This ends the portion of Mary Warner's diary that is available. At this point, the transcriber has added a note that indicates that there were additional pages, but they are missing.

CHAPTER 16

Phebe Abbot Carleton

1864

In early 1864, William Carleton and his family left Illinois as part of a wagon train headed for California. The family consisted of William and his wife, Melissa Jane; son, William Edward; and daughters, Harriet and Phebe. Phebe, who was twenty-one years of age, kept a diary during the journey. The Carletons did not own a wagon or any livestock and were paying for their passage. The owner of the wagon they were traveling in was A. A. Beveridge, who was taking several wagons and a herd of horses to California. As a part of the arrangement, Mrs. Carleton and the two daughters were to do the cooking for the company. The Carletons' party departed from their home in Rockton, Illinois, on March 18 and arrived in Salt Lake City on June 21.

A copy of a transcription made in 1989 by Sally Thompson was obtained from the Washington State Historical Society, which granted permission to publish (Abbot, Phebe Carleton, diary, 1864 [MSSC60] Special Collections, Washington State Historical Society, Tacoma, Washington).

JUNE 21, 1864 Everyone was in haste to get started for the city. There was much haste and some running by. The lucky ones were those that do not have to stop to get wood. Nearly every wagon has a cooking stove attached to it that had to be supplied with fuel sufficient to last during our stay in the city or we should have to buy it at an exorbitant price. There is no wood within 12 miles of Salt Lake City. Mr. Quackenbush was first and Mr. Beveridge had followed him into the City. They were in two hours before the others. Our road lay for 20 miles through a very narrow canon. A beautiful clear stream flowed through its whole length. The road most of the way had been constructed upon the side of the mountain. In many places impossible for two teams to pass each other in the rest barely possible. It was descending grade all the way. About seven miles from the city we rose a long steep hill and there before us in the Great Basin lay the Morman City. It was not what would be called a large city in the states but its size is certainly remarkable when we consider its inland position. When we arrived we found Ed had engaged pasture for the horses and we were to camp on the public square[1] which like the same place in Rockton had nothing to distinguish it as a Public Square except that it is a square piece of ground. No sooner had we made our appearance up[on] the spot than men, women and children began to flock around us with garden sauce to sell. We had strawberries, lettuce and onions for supper and we relished it emmensely after our long diet of bread and bacon with now and then a few small potatoes or a little applesauce. The best of all was our letters from dear friends. It was like cold water to a thirsty soul.

JUNE 22, 1864 There is no grass on the square and we are camped all in the dust. I presume it has not rained here in a month. The wind blows hard and we are almost suffocated. Our camp has been thronged today by all classes and sizes from the City. They wish to buy everything you can think of even to old clothes. The boys have sold all but part of a chest of tea. In fact everything they can spare and some they can not. Joseph and Jimmie sold the wagon they owned jointly for $175. Joe put one span of horses on Henry Robinsons wagon and has the

[1]This campground was known as Emigrant Square. See ch. 14, n1.

privelege of partly loading it. Edward sold Ganny for $300. We had fish and green peas for dinner. For supper we had strawberry short cake. Mr. B furnished the berries and cream and Joe the butter. It was capital. The young folks went round town to see the curiosities. The Morman Temple not yet completed was the first and chief attraction. They have been eleven years at work on it and the foundation is not all laid yet. The design which we saw of it was very beautiful. The building is to be of grey marble, enclosed by a stone wall. Brigham's house we could not see as it was enclosed by a high wall. People said that he was not at home, we did not see him. There is not much life in the city, business I should think was not very exciting. The city is laid out in very large squares with wide streets and side walks. There are many very beautiful gardens, but few handsome houses. Every house is built of sun dried brick. No lumber in the place of any account. There are any amount of peach trees cultivated in and around the City but the fruit will not be ripe for six weeks. Mr. Fish is not going any farther with the boys, but he is going to Clifton City in Nevada with a man by the name of Lawrence in our train.

June 23, 1864 Ed sold Chief and Warrior for $300 each today. The boys bought their grain and provisions and loaded up today it has been a busy day for all. Still nearly all the young people feel like dancing I guess for they have all gone to Camp Douglass tonight for the purpose. The soldiers stationed there, invited all to come up to their quarters and spend the evening. They sent down an ambulance, as it is several miles up to the camp.

June 24, 1864 We left the city this morning after Ed had bought two more horses. We only went 17 miles[2] as some of the horses in the train are sick. We crossed the river Jordan as we came out of the city.[3] Ed has taken a man by the name of Meyers to board through to Washington. He is subject to fits every two or three weeks and is disagreeable otherwise. Ed told us yesterday he shouldn't take any more boarders and we did not know that he had taken this one till tonight

[2]Traveling seventeen miles in a slightly south of west direction would have put them near the southeastern shore of the Great Salt Lake. (See map 2.)

[3]The Carletons crossed the river on the old North Temple bridge. See ch. 6, n1.

when Ed brought him in to supper. It was discovered this afternoon that Dan Reyan, one of our train had not come out of the city and an irishman in our train reported that he was confined in the lockup for drunkenness and fined $12. Ed and Joe began to feel quite anxious as they have a mortgage on his team. They knew he had not money enough to pay the fine and they were afraid he would sell the horses and then not come any farther. Joseph and Mr. Ward started back on horse back about sundown to look after him.

June 25, 1864 When the boys went to get the horses to harness this morning. The two sorrels were not with the rest. Ed started out to look for them. Mr. Brown, a man owning considerable stock in the train took one [of] Mr. B's horses and rode off in another direction, he soon returned with the missing horses, some one fired [a gun] and Ed came back to camp and we started. We passed through a little village called Willy [Tooele] City, farther on we crossed quite a stream, here we filled our kegs with water[4] and went about two miles farther and camped for the night, here was some grass but no water. We used the water in the kegs to get supper with and they took the horses back to water them. Joe and Mr. Ward came into camp tonight with Mr. Reyan. We passed within a few rods of Salt lake, some drank of the water, they reported it as salt as brine.

June 26, 1864 The road was very level today but very dusty, this last though is getting to be an old story it is so every day, we can hardly tell the color of our clothes when we get into camp. We passed by two military stations and saw quite a number of soldiers.[5] We camped near a stage station[6] in a pretty place near to water but no grass. It looked very much like rain but not a drop reached us.

June 27, 1864 We started early this morning and after traveling 10 miles up hill and down over rocks and stones we came to good grass and turned out to bait as the horses had had nothing scarcely to eat

[4]The stream where they filled their kegs was Settlement Creek, which flowed out of Settlement Canyon, just south of the town of Tooele. See ch. 9, n2.

[5]Earlier that year, Gen. Patrick Conner had established a military camp on the east side of Rush Lake, near present-day Stockton. The Carletons would have passed by this camp (Varley, *Brigham and the Brigadier*, 177).

[6]The stage station was at Faust. See ch. 8, n2.

last night.[7] We stopped about two hours then hitched up and drove 13 miles. We camped a little off the main road by a small stream.[8] The grass was good—Some Indians came to our camp tonight, they were part Spanish, one of them had whiskers something I have never seen on an Indian's face before. Every one is talking of the desert which we are to start across day after tomorrow.

JUNE 28, 1864 We hitched up this morning and drove 4 miles over the mountains and camped by several springs,[9] the water was much better than we usually get here the grass is to be cut to take on to the desert, it is very good and everyone is busy with saythe [scythe] or sickle. Claude's horses balked coming up a very long steep hill today.[10] The Mason boys were driving and Claude had gone ahead, the boys don't know how to drive and they could'nt make them start a foot. Mr. B offered to put his on and drive it up that steep place, so they took Claud's off and put B's on and then drew it up the steepest part of the hill and although the road for some ways beyond was ascending they thought that Clauds horses could not balk again, so they took off Andrews and put them on again. Andrew got them started and gave the lines to one of the Mason boys and they soon balked again. Andrew thought he would not bother with them any longer, so he took his off and put them on Clauds wagon again and drew the load up to the top of the hill on level ground then they hitched on Claud's again and they went along. One of Ed's horses is sick tonight.

JUNE 29, 1864 We started this morning and came 6 miles up and down one of the steepest and longest hills we have experienced yet. We are in camp by the last water this side of the desert. It is a beautiful spring and the best water we have tasted for months.[11] Here we rest and the horses feed till 5 o'clock and then we start across the desert. There are some emigrants here that have just crossed the desert going back

---

[7]The place where they stopped to let the animals feed may have been Point Lookout. See ch. 3, n8. (See map 3.)

[8]Government Spring. See ch. 12, n5.

[9]Somewhere on Lee Creek.

[10]The hill where the horses balked would have been just above the mouth of Lee Canyon, on the eastern slope of the Simpson Mountains.

[11]Indian Spring. See ch. 8, n31.

to the states. They gave a very doleful account of the passage across the desert, but we are not discouraged. We are cooking up provisions to last a day or two and the men are cutting a little more grass and filling every available thing with water.

JUNE 30, 1864 Last night at five o'clock everything being in readiness we started across the American Desert. Ed and Joe having only a ten gallon keg in which to carry water for their 13 horses, had soaked up their cracker barrel and thought it would not leak, they filled it with water when they started but contrary to their expectations, they saw that the water was all leaking out soon after they started. The man that Ed has taken to board had a fit tonight. We had anticipated a very dusty, disagreeable time but the wind was favorable, and blew from one side of the wagons to the other and the air was cool enough for the stock to travel good and not too cool for the comfort of the people. Ed's sick horse seemed better and travelled off quite well Mr. Brown a man in the train having but one wagon and considerable loose stock wished Mr. B to carry some grass for him as he had plenty of room in his wagon. Mr. Brown was to let Mr. B drive a span of his horses half of the way. They harnessed Mr. Brown's horses to Mr. B's wagon for the first half of the way and Mr. B tied two of his behind the wagon. By the way Mr. Brown's horses happened to be somewhat balky and besides they had not had a harness on since they left Missouri early in the Spring. However they started them on level ground and everything went off smoothly till half past twelve when we came to a mountain, very difficult to ascend. Mr. . . . was driving, I was riding with him. We had ascended part way up the mountain when it became necessary to stop the horses in order to let them breathe. The wheels were blocked and the horses stood still but in attempting to start them again, they balked. Mr. Brown who was behind us in his own wagon came forward to assist as they were his horses, by taking hold of their heads he succeeded in getting them a little farther up and then he let them stop to breathe again, Mr. Brown now said he would get his whip and then he thought he could make them go. I did not feel safe in the wagon behind balky, high spirited [horses] and a man whipping them, besides the road, which we were endeavoring to follow in the darkness, in this place was barely wide enough for one wagon to pass along on one side, a bank rose several feet high on the other side it sunk down eight or ten feet perpendicular. It was rather a dangerous place and I insisted on getting out before they attempted to start again. Mr. B was holding the wheel to keep it from going downhill and Mr. Brown was holding the horses, so I helped myself out as quick as possible, and although they both kept telling me that I would fall down the bank I was in such haste to get out of the way and so dizzy from riding so long in the dark that the first thing I knew I was falling down the bank eight feet. I did not happen to strike a stone and did not hurt myself any to speak of as it was the circumstance only afforded us all much amusement afterwards. I scrambled up the bank as best I could neither of the two men could have assisted me if I had broken my neck, as they had their hands full to keep the horses and wagon from coming down after me. Mr. Brown started his horses again but instead of going forward they went the other way and crowded one of Mr. B's horses, which was tied behind the wagon, down the bank the horse struck on his back, he came onto his feet the next instant and we knew he was not dead. Mr. B cut his halter and Mr. Brown succeeded in stopping his horses before the wagon went over. Mr. Brown still wanted to make his horses draw the wagon up to the top but Mr. B thought it was risking too much, others by this time having arrived on the spot said the same and so they took off those horses and put Mr. B's on and then we all went on and arrived at the summit in safety. Going down was long a gradual descent on a wide smooth road.[12] About two o'clock most of the train stopped and baited their horses but some of us kept on till sunrise and then baited and had lunch, then we went on till 1 o'clock and all turned out again, baited the horses with the grass we brought and watered them from the kegs. We made a fire with a little wood which we brought along and had some tea and ate dinner. We were then within 25 miles of good water and grass. Most of the train thought best to remain where they were till 3 or 4 and then hitch up and go the 25 miles. Claude and two or three others were going 2 miles

[12]The party was climbing up the eastern approach to Dugway Pass when they had the problems with the balky horses.

farther and where there was some water and grass[13] and spend the night there, but the water and grass was very salty and but few were willing to keep their horses on it when there was good to be had within 25 miles. Only three wagons, Mr. Brown, Mr. b and one other thought best to go right on after baiting their horses. Those thought the horses would gain nothing by standing in hot sun all the afternoon with nothing but salt water to drink, as they had just given them the last they had brought in the Kegs. These three, myself with them had started at half past eleven in the morning. On we journeyed over the wold waste, a long 25 miles it seemed to us and our tired horses which had travelled 73 miles since last night. They did not seem to suffer much with thirst and hardly lagged a step. Just as the sun went down behind the hills, we who were ahead turned out upon the fresh green grass and stopped by the side of the clear cold springs in what is called Thousand Spring valley.[14] It looked a thousand times more beautiful in contrast to the barren tract we had just left. Mr. Brown's people have got supper and they invited Mr. B and myself to eat with them as none of the rest of our family have arrived yet.

July 1, 1864 The remainder of the train except what stayed at the salt spring with Claude came on at twelve last night. Today we are laying by, to recruit and rest. Ed's horse was not able to come on last night so he stayed with Claude and they came into camp about noon today. The horse is very sick and they think it will not live. Mrs. Otis is quite sick, Mother is doctoring her. All most every one is laid out asleep. It has been very warm.

July 2, 1864 We have travelled today 26 miles, it was after one o'clock when we came into camp.[15] Mrs. Otis is much better. Ed's horse was alive this morning and Joseph drove it along six miles and he was going to stay there by a spring and let it rest. He has not come up yet, but we did not expect he would overtake us tonight. Still we are feeling somewhat anxious about him as we heard after we came into

---

[13]Fish Springs. See ch. 6, n4.

[14]Carleton's "Thousand Spring valley" was Willow Springs, located within present-day Callao. The editor is unaware of anyone else using the Thousand Springs name for this area. See ch. 7, n9. (See map 4.)

[15]The campsite was somewhere near the Deep Creek stage station. See ch. 7, n11.

camp that a man belonging to another train was shot at by an Indian in the canyon through which Joseph will have to pass.[16] There are a good many Indians around here and there is no telling what they may take a notion to do. The grass tonight is very good, we [are] in Deep Creek Valley. The soil here is very good and there is a great amount of grain raised through the valley.

JULY 3, 1864 We travelled only 13 miles today, we could go no farther without going too far on account of water.[17] It does not seem at all like the Sabbath. Everyone is cutting hay to take along tomorrow as there is none within four miles of the water where we must camp. The grass and water are not together tomorrow. It was decided to stay by the water and take the hay. It is almost sundown and Joseph has not come yet. Ed has been telling that he was going to ride back a few miles and see if he could find anything of him but he has not started yet and I do not think he will, as he has just sent back eight miles to the station by another man that was going down to see if he had been seen or heard of there.

JULY 4, 1864 H. Robinson, Mr. Brown and Mr. B took horses last night about sundown and rode back to look after Joseph as he had not arrived. They met him after going two miles. He was all safe and the horse was no better. He and Ed have gone 8 miles back this morning to see if they can not dispose of him as he can go no farther. The rest of the train have gone on and we are having a quiet time by ourselves. Ed and Joseph returned to us at eleven o'clock, having sold the horse for fifty dollars. We ate dinner and then harnessed up and followed after the train. We were obliged to travel 23 miles without water, except what we carried with us. The wind blew a perfect gale directly in our faces. When we got into camp,[18] everything was gray with alkalii dust. We all looked as though we had been powdered. As we were traveling along, a pony came running towards us out of the mountain. The boys attempted to catch it but it seemed very wild and

[16]Joseph would have stopped at present-day Six-Mile Ranch with the sick horse. The canyon they thought would be risky was Overland Canyon.

[17]Carleton overestimated the distance. They could not have traveled any more than about nine miles. Had they gone any farther, they would no longer have been on Deep Creek, which was the only place where grass could be found. The camp was probably near the Eight-Mile stage station.

[18]Antelope Spring. See ch. 7, n13.

they let it be and it followed us all the way into camp and then went to eating some grass that Mr. B had thrown down by his wagon for his horses. There were some men camped there from California going to Salt Lake and they said they would take the pony back and see if they could find the owner. The boys told him that they themselves should keep it till the owner came for it. Then these men went to petting it and before our boys realized what they were doing they succeeded in getting it among their loose stock which they were about driving up the mountain to feed during the night. It was now dark and impossible to do anything, so it rests, but our boys are determined to get it in the morning. There are some soldiers stationed here and they give our boys encouragement that they will help them if necessary.

JULY 5, 1864 This morning early Joe and Claude started up the mountain after the said pony. They found it but before they could secure it the man that was up there with his stock caught it and rode it farther back into the mountain, leaving his own ponies and mules along, so Joe very coolly drives these down into camp and shuts them up in the corral, determined not to let them out till he has the pony safe. The man on the pony up in the mountain stays up there about half an hour when he discovers that we are not going to leave nor allow them to take their stock either, so down he comes still on the disputed pony and rides up to his wagon and buckles on a revolver, then riding out to the corral demands his stock but Joseph having previously put on his revolver makes a show of it and tells him that not one will go out of the corral until the pony is delivered up to him, many hot words ensue and then both parties agree to leave the whole matter to the decision of three soldiers. These after short consultation decide in favor of our train. Therefore we took the pony and immediately departed on our journey. After going 16 miles we thought we had arrived at our camp for the day but we found the flies so thick that we were fearful they would eat the horses up so after staying one hour and baiting the horses we pulled out and came 6 miles and here we rest.[19]

[19]Upon leaving Antelope Spring, the Carletons followed the stage road, which went around the southern tip of Antelope Mountain. After turning northwest at Twelve-Mile Summit, they came to Spring Valley, where they encountered the flies. See ch. 8, n10. After going north for three miles, they turned into Stage Canyon in the Schell Creek Mountains. The camp was probably at Schellbourne Spring.

JULY 6, 1864 After going four miles we came to a stage station where there was quite a large machine shop.[20] There we started across a level plain sixteen miles in extent,[21] the ground was white with alkaly. The wind blew in our faces the dust was suffocating. When we had passed over this we entered Egan Canon. This is interesting on account of the gold and silver which is supposed to lie hidden in its rocks, prospecters are busy at work digging and we saw stakes stuck up every 100 feet to denote the respective claims that have been made. There were also quite a number of little houses or cabins erected. It is supposed to be a very rich mine but as yet no quartz mill has arrived. At the head of the canon there has been a city laid out called Tiptoe.[22] The people at the canon invited our train to come to one of their houses and have a dance. The dancing part of the community went. There is no feed here for the horses so the boys let the Indians take them up in the mountains and watch them tonight and bring them back in the morning. They will do for some biscuit.

JULY 7, 1864 The Indians took the horses, up to the mountains but they did not bring them all back in the morning as agreed upon. When they had come down 17 were missing. The Indians said they would go back after them and it was two hours before they were all found. This made us very late starting. The road part of the way was very mountainous. We camped part way up a very high mountain at Pony Springs.[23] We were obliged to pitch our tent on a side hill in the dust, there was not a spear of grass to be seen. The wind blew a gale all the while we were preparing supper. I should think we all finished our peck of dirt this time if we never had before.

JULY 8, 1864 We reached Ruby Valley[24] today and camped near the station. There is a trading post here but everything fearfully dear.

---

[20]This was the Schell Creek stage station, later the site of Fort Schellbourne and now occupied by the Schellbourne Ranch.

[21]Steptoe Valley.

[22]Either Carleton or the transcriber misunderstood the name of the town. It was Steptoe, which was also mentioned by both Lucretia Epperson and George Bushnell. This short-lived mining camp is not to be confused with another town of the same name that was about 30 miles to the south.

[23]See ch. 8, n12.

[24]The Carletons traveled about twenty miles on this day and then stopped near Station Spring, where there was a stage station and a store.

Butter $1.50 per pound, Syrup $2.00 per quart. Claude and Mason got into a little trouble last night about the horses, Claude called Mason hard names and Mason picked up the ax and started at Claude. Claude caught M. and held him not injuring him in the least. Many hot words passed on both sides and Claude told Mason that he would not carry him any farther than Ruby, which is this place. Mason threatens to shoot Claude, before he gets through, he tried to borrow a revolver this afternoon for that purpose, but did not succeed in getting one. What will be done remains to be seen. There is a Fort near here[25] and a number of the soldiers are here in camp, one intoxicated just staggered past our door.

JULY 9, 1864 Most of the young people went up to the Fort to have a dance last night, they did not get back till sunrise this morning. They said they had a very nice time. We stopped about two hours to feed the horses after going eight miles. Then we came twelve miles and camped at the foot of a very high mountain by some springs.[26]

JULY 10, 1864 This morning we ascended the highest and most difficult mountain on the whole route.[27] It was a hard pull for the horses but everybody walked and thus lightened the loads. The horses were obliged to halt every two or three rods to breathe and rest and so at length we reached the top and then it was all the way down hill for two or three miles. At the foot we found water and grass and we all turned out and rested two hours. There was a stage station[28] and we found a young man, George Brown who lived in Rockton 10 years ago. He was very glad of an opportunity to inquire about Rockton people once more. Then we came 14 miles across the valley to the next range of mountains and stopped at their foot.[29] Claude will not let Mason go any farther with him, but he pays another man in the train for taking him through.

JULY 11, 1864 We traveled only 15 miles today and camped near

[25]Fort Ruby was about two miles west of the stage station.

[26]The camp may have been near Corta Spring, which is just below the Overland Pass in the Diamond Mountains.

[27]This was the Overland Pass in the Diamond Mountains. See ch. 8, n14.

[28]The Diamond Spring station.

[29]After crossing Diamond Valley, they camped near the Sulphur Spring station. See ch. 10, n23.

the stage station.[30] There was no grass at all hardly and they took the horses up in the mountains at night.

July 12, 1864 We started early and after going 8 miles we came to some good grass and water so we turned out and stayed three or four hours.[31] The horses had all they wished to eat and drink and were rested and the boys I suppose had a good time playing cards, for they played all the time. Though that is nothing unusual for they are at it every moment they can get and some they cant.

July 13, 1864 We came about 20 miles and stopped in the canon here. Claude expected to find enough grass to cut to carry with us across the desert but there is hardly any here.[32] There has been an Indian here wanting to buy the pony which came to us, he showed $24.00 in silver which he would give for him. It was all he had, but the boys would not sell him.

July 14, 1864 The first thing this morning we came up a very high mountain and from its top we looked down on the road by which we were to descend. It was very crooked sometimes almost doubling itself, very steep indeed it exceeded anything I ever saw for rockyness. None of the women were possessed of nerves steady enough to ride down so we all walked feeling safer on our own feet, though it was difficult to keep from going faster than prudence permitted. We passed by a house where a 'sicish' [secessionist] resided and he informed us with a great deal of animation that 38,000 rebels were within seven miles of Washington. Lizzie Parker had the audacity to tell him that she wished he was back in Ruby packing sand. That means carrying sixty pounds of sand on his back from sun up till sundown with a soldier holding a bayonet behind him lest he should slacken his pace or lay down his burden. We camped about three miles out of Austin.[33] The

[30] This day's journey would have taken them to Roberts Creek.

[31] Carleton describes where they stopped for a short time during the day, which may have been at Rutabaga Creek, but she says nothing about where they camped for the night, which must have been near the Dry Creek stage station.

[32] This camp was at Simpson Park, where there is usually a great deal of grass. The fact that there was very little in July 1864 may indicate that there had been a significant amount of emigrant traffic on the Central Overland Trail. Carleton's description of the crooked and steep road indicates that they followed the Pony Express route past Eagle Butte. (See map 6.)

[33] See ch. 12, n21.

grass and water are fine and there are a great many trains lying over here. Mr. Fish found his brother in Austin and brought him over to see us tonight.

July 15, 1864 Joseph and Mr. B went through Austin this morning to get some provisions the rest of us did not as it was farther that way.[34] We saw a great many places where claims had been made and shafts sunk, we passed through a little town called Jacobsville.[35] Then we came to Red [Reese] river[36] and after following it three or four miles camped.

July 16, 1864 Claude sent Ed ahead this morning and told him to go to the summit of the mountain and there camp. Our teams travel so fast that none of the others can keep in sight. We found no water at the summit so we kept on down a little distance and there found nice water and feed so we turned out and camped,[37] but none of the rest of the train came up to us they all stopped on the other side of the mountain. I think it much pleasanter being by ourselves.

July 17, 1864 We did not start as early as usual and the others had nearly caught up with us. We came 17 miles to Cold Springs. The boys have been up in the mountains trying to find grass, but did not succeed. Just now there was an Indian here and he said he would take the horses to good feed and guard them for $1.50 so the boys are going to trust to him, how well they will make out I do not know. Ed and Joseph have another horse that is not well he has been failing some time.

July 18, 1864 The boys had to go up to the mountains with the horses themselves and they said they had a time getting them up to feed and down again. Some of them came down on their hunches it was so steep. We started in search of grass and water. Claude thought he knew where it could be found so we followed him five miles over

[34]Joseph and Beveridge may have taken the Austin Summit route into Austin.

[35]Jacobsville was a short distance east of the Reese River, about one and three quarters of a mile downstream from where U.S. 50 now crosses the river. (See map 7.)

[36]The Carletons probably crossed the river just west of Jacobsville, and then followed its west bank upstream to the camp. See ch. 3, n38.

[37]They crossed the Shoshone Mountains by way of Smith Creek Summit, crossed Smith Creek Valley, climbed up Smith Creek Canyon, and dropped down into Edwards Creek Canyon about a half mile to Edwards Creek, where they stopped for the night. The distance covered during this day would have been about twenty-four miles. See ch. 3, n40.

the roughest road we have experienced, then we came to the mouth of canon[38] and there we stopped. There was a stream of water running through the canon but very little grass. There was a stone house here empty. It had a cooking stove in it and Claude immediately took possession and Mrs. Mason did her work there. The sun was burning hot, but in the house it was comfortable. The nights have so far been chilly after the sun went down but tonight it is as warm as any summer eve in Rockton.

JULY 19, 1864 Everybody is in possession of a cold this morning. The wind came up in the night and this morning before sunrise, it was cold enough. We started early and after coming 10 miles we reached a stage station where we could water the stock,[39] but the horses were very hungry not having much to eat last night. Two miles farther we came to some good grass and we and some others turned out to bait. We stopped three hours and then going two miles farther came to water again. Our horses drank four pails of water each and then were ready to go on, 10 miles to the next place.[40] We filled the kegs because at this place all the water we had we had to buy and give two bits per pailful. At this place we stopped one hour and a half cooked our supper baited the horses and then on again 13 miles to Sand Springs[41] here was water free and they tied the horses to the wagons and fed them the hay that they had brought.

JULY 20, 1864 The men were up at two o'clock and we shortly after 20 miles of hard traveling today and the prospect of a very warm day. It took hours to water all the stock, as it had to be drawn up by a bucket and we did not get off till half past four. It was 16 miles to the first water and that was salty. The sand was very heavy[42] and

---

[38]This was Eastgate, where there is always a good flow of water coming out of the canyon. For at least a part of its existence, the stage road traveled directly south from Cold Springs to Eastgate and then turned west to Middlegate. Only three other diarists mention going through Eastgate: John Fackler, who was traveling by stagecoach, the Colwell brothers, and Mary Jatta.

[39]This was the Middlegate stage station. See ch. 3, n42.

[40]This would have put the Carletons near the middle of Fairview Valley, somewhere near what would later become known as Frenchmans. See ch. 9, n35.

[41]See ch. 3, n43.

[42]It appears that from Sand Spring, the Carletons followed the stage route to the south shore of Carson Lake. (See map 8.)

the sun scorching hot. Claude was obliged to change horses, one of his was about done out, the sweat rolling off from him. We gave the horses one pail of water each and then came on 5 miles farther and reached Carson Slough.[43] There the water is not quite so salty, we camped here tonight, though there is scarcely any feed. We met a team from California loaded with green apples, the first we have seen. Mr. B and Jimmie bought some, giving 30 cts per pound. It took four to weigh one pound. They were very nice. We have had fresh meat since leaving Austin but just now we are subsisting on bread and molasses and barley coffee. I forgot to say that day before yesterday we found any quantity of wild currents along the creek where we camped We stewed and sweetened them and they were very good.

July 21, 1864 Some of the boys went out after the horses last night but they hunted for them till nine o'clock and then came back with out them. There are 12 gone. This morning we started with what horses we had and came six miles to good water and grass, three or four of the boys went to look for the lost horses. We had been in camp only a little while when they came with the horses all safe. Libbie Parker is quite sick. We have been here all day. There is a ranch near and we got some milk and butter. Two bachelors own the place and keep house for themselves and a number of men that they hire. It was a very nice place just as neat and clean as could be. Hattie and myself were invited to tea and we had everything nice.

July 22, 1864 Under the influence of the homeopathic medicine which we brought with us and administered by mother Libbie Parker was much better this morning and we broke camp again. After two miles travel we turned from the main road, passed through a ranch and came to Sand river[44] this we crossed and then filled our kegs as the people there told us it was 17 miles to water. Claude knew nothing about this road as he had never been this way but everyone said we

[43]Near the Carson Sink stage station. See ch. 3, n45.

[44]Carleton's "Sand river" may have been present-day Sam Springs Wash at the eastern base of the Dead Camel Mountains. It appears that at some point, they left the "main" road (presumably the stage road) and followed Simpson's return route through the Dead Camel Mountains. See ch. 3, n46.

should save from 20 to 50 miles by taking this cutoff. Claude supposed all in the train could see the track where we turned off the main road so we did not wait as some were half an hour behind us, but when we had been on the road several hours we discovered that about half the train were no where to be seen. No doubt they have taken the other road. We found the road today the hardest of any since we started, very heavy sand nearly all the way and instead of being 17 it was 25 miles, some of the horses in the train gave out and they had to change them. The day was very warm and the sweat poured off of some of the horses. We stopped and baited half way across and did not get into camp till five o'clock I hope never to see such a cross set of people again as we all were. They ranched the horses tonight and we camped under a large tree in the meadow.

JULY 23, 1864 We did not start out today till noon. We crossed the river on the toll bridge[45] and entered Fort Churchill. This is a very beautiful place—500 soldiers stationed here. The houses are alike and the streets neat and clean. The men had to take the Oath of Allegiance here. We saw the Major and talked with him he is a very fine man. We went about 2 miles out of the Fort and camped, we had not been there long when one of the soldiers came and ordered us from the Government Reserve, so we hitched up and went three miles farther and put the horses in a ranch.[46] We met R. Bly of Rockton today, he is staying with the boys tonight. Joseph bought a little meat for supper.

JULY 24, 1864 We started this beautiful morning for Virginia City. The road was very good except that the last six miles was up hill grade all the way.[47]

---

[45]This bridge crossed the Carson River a short distance east of where it is now crossed by U.S. 95 A. (See map 9.) The bridge was built by Samuel Buckland in late 1859 or early 1860 (Townley, *The Pony Express Guidebook*, 24).

[46]Their camp for the night was on the north bank of the Carson River, about five miles west of Fort Churchill.

[47]Although their exact route to Virginia City is uncertain, they probably left the Central Overland Trail about six miles northeast of Dayton and traveled up Six-Mile Canyon.

CHAPTER 17

Lucretia Epperson

1864

In April of 1864, Lucretia Lawson Epperson, with her husband, Brutus Clay Epperson, and their two-year-old son, Charles, left Illinois and began a journey to California. Lucretia faithfully kept a diary, but one thing that she failed to mention was that she was pregnant during the entire trip. The Eppersons began their journey on April 1, leaving from Brutus Epperson's mother's home in Coles County, Illinois. They arrived in Salt Lake City on July 1.

Epperson's diary was first transcribed and published in The History of Colusa County, California, *edited by Will S. Green in 1880. In 1983, the Arthur H. Clark Company published the diary in* Covered Wagon Women: Diaries and Letters from the Western Trails, 1840–1890, *compiled and edited by Kenneth L. Holmes. In 1989,* Covered Wagon Women *was reprinted by the University of Nebraska Press; in 1999, that press published it yet again in a Bison Books edition.*

July 1, 1864 Started early, all eager to reach Salt Lake City. We passed some neat little adobe houses, all having nice gardens. We found great quantities of mustard growing by the roadside. Mrs. Coleman and myself walked along and gathered enough to make a good mess for supper. This was quite a treat to us, who had been so long without vegetables. About ten o'clock came in sight of Fort Douglass, General Conner in command. His heavy guns covered Salt Lake City, in order to compel Brigham Young and his saints to respect the laws of the United States, and permit emigrants to pass unmolested. Uncle Sam does not intend to have the Mountain Meadow massacre repeated. Here I will say it is my belief that General Conner was the best man the Government ever sent out to look after Brigham Young and his followers. He will not be forgotten by the emigrants of 1864. Entered the city about noon. Mr. Epperson procured pasture near the city, and we turned our horses out to graze, but kept close watch over them, as Genner Conner told us they were looking for an outbreak among the Mormons, for which reason he held himself in readiness. He said there were a great many good, honest and well-meaning Mormons, who were subordinate to Brigham Young and his disciples. We received letters here, from friends in Illinois and Kentucky, also from C. C. Epperson, of Sutter county, California, informing us of the drouth and hard times there.

JULY 2, 1864 Mrs. Coleman and I rode through the city on horseback; stopped in front of Brigham's Lion house (so called in honor of a carved lion, couchant, in front of the building). We conversed with some of the guards at the gate, who invited us to enter and see Brigham's building inside the wall. Mrs. Coleman was afraid to enter; said they might close the gates upon us. After dinner Mr. Epperson went into the city to purchase flour for use until we arrived at Austin. Could get no flour or other necessaries, as the sale of such things by Mormons to emigrants was forbidden by the "high and mighty Brigham." They would sell milk, vegetables, butter and fresh meat. An elderly man saw Mr. Epperson when he was refused flour. He came to our wagon after dark, and said that he had plenty of flour, and if Mr. Epperson would go to his house between then and eleven o'clock, he would let him have what flour he wanted. Asked that Mr. Epperson would tell no one, as he was at the tender mercies of Brigham and his saints. Mr. Epperson paid the enormous sum of fourteen dollars per hundred pounds.

JULY 3, 1864 Started forward, crossed the river Jordan,[1] and camped on the south side of Great Salt Lake.[2]

JULY 4, 1864 Early in the morning Mr. Epperson took our son Charlie and a few of the men, and went to the lake to bathe. Mr. Epperson put Charlie on his back and swam out into the lake near a quarter of a mile; Charlie enjoyed it very much; the men said he looked like a large toad on his father's back. Charlie is two years old and very fleshy. We saw a number of Mormons at work making salt on a small scale.

JULY 5, 1864 Started early, passed a place where some of our predecessors had celebrated the Fourth of July. The programme of the day was written and placed upon a board, and nailed to a tree by the road side. We stopped, read it, and felt a little more patriotic. Found a good camping ground for the night.[3]

JULY 6, 1864 We now approach the great desert; at noon we found excellent grass for our stock.[4] Mr. Epperson ordered the men to cut some for feed while crossing the desert. The mountains are covered with good "bunch grass," the best we found so far. Encamped at the entrance of a beautiful canyon; had plenty of company. Quite a number had camped here upward of one week, in order to let the stock rest.[5]

JULY 7, 1864 Traveled until noon and then halted near a stream of clear, cold water.[6] The men are busy cutting grass with their knives and putting it into sacks. Our cook is baking and preparing food for use while crossing the desert.

JULY 8, 1864 Men still cutting grass; our cook filled the casks, kegs and jugs with water at eleven o'clock; at eleven o'clock dinner was ready, and we all took an extra cup of coffee, as this would be the last warm

---

[1]The Eppersons crossed the Jordan River on the old North Temple bridge. See ch. 9, n2. (See map 2.)

[2]This camp was near Black Rock, an isolated rock formation on the southeast shore of the lake.

[3]This campsite must have been somewhere in the northern part of Rush Valley.

[4]This was somewhere near the Faust stage station. See ch. 8, n2.

[5]Going west from Lookout Pass, the next camping spot for the emigrants was usually Government Spring, but this area is not at the entrance of a canyon. The Eppersons probably went past Government Spring and traveled another four miles before making camp near the mouth of Lee Canyon.

[6]Indian Spring. See ch. 8, n31.

meal until we arrived on the other side of the desert. Everything in readiness, we started and reached the desert at four o'clock. The sun shone bright and warm in our faces as we traveled westward, and the alkali dust filled the air like fog. Just before sunset we came to the foot of a mountain; here we took some grass and water from our wagons, gave some to each of our animals, and took a cold supper ourselves; after resting an hour we prepared to start. Our little boy fell asleep; I put him in bed and told Mr. Epperson I would walk forward with Mrs. Coleman. We proceeded up the mountain half a mile; perceived a trail which seemed to cut off quite a distance, and concluded to follow it. The wagons were behind us; we chatted and walked along, thinking we would soon come into the road again. It grew dark rapidly, and we were getting anxious to see the road. We hurried on, and very soon it was quite dark. We listened for the sound of the wagons as the wheels jolted over the rocky road, but could hear them no longer. Mrs. Coleman said, Mrs. Epperson, we are lost! We can never find the train, it is so dark. We shouted at the top of our voices, but received no answer. She proposed going back; I was unwilling; told her to follow me, I was going forward, as I felt certain we would come to the road soon. It was now so dark we could not see the trail. We continued on up the mountain side for some time; at last I stepped into the dust, and felt convinced we were on the road. We were almost exhausted I assure you. We were afraid the wagons were beyond the point where we came into the road. At last we heard sounds like the loose stock coming; so we sat down by the roadside and waited for the coming of the train, and meanwhile vowed we would not undertake to travel by "short cuts" again.[7] I was so fatigued, I went to bed in the wagon immediately and slept until we began to descend the mountain; the road was rough, I could not sleep, reached the foot of the mountain about two o'clock. Just before daylight we came to a stage stand,[8] could get no water for our stock; water had to be brought from a distance of sixteen miles for the stage horses.

---

[7]The getting lost incident must have occurred when they were crossing Dugway Mountain, the only mountain on the trail across the Great Salt Lake Desert. The distance that Epperson and Coleman traveled on foot could not have been any more than about three miles.

[8]Epperson must have been referring to the Black Rock station. Water for this station had to be hauled from Fish Springs, which was about nine miles away, not the sixteen that she indicated.

July 9, 1864 About nine o'clock we gave our horses water from the supply we carried with us. We partook of a slight repast ourselves and then drove on through heat and dust, arriving at another stage stand about two o'clock.[9] Here we found two ox teams,[10] some of the oxen almost worn out. The owner was trying to buy water from the man at the station. Soon after the man left, Mr. Epperson produced a flour sack containing some choice tobacco. This he passed among the station hands, who pronounced it excellent. One of the men who seemed to be manager, told Mr. Epperson to go into the shed where the water barrels were kept and give each of our animals a bucket of water. Mr. Epperson gave each man a good supply of tobacco, and we drove on our way. Just as the sun was sinking in the far west, we drove into Willow Springs.[11] Our stock looks tired and worn. The cook soon prepared a good hot supper, which we enjoyed more than any meal since leaving home.

July 10, 1864 Let our tired stock rest; had good feed; all day teams kept coming in; everything was in confusion; every train that arrived, everybody would rush to see who it was, and if they had met on the road. When night came I was as weary as if I had been riding all day

July 11, 1864 Started early. All feel this morning like the most difficult part of our journey was over. In camp on Deer creek.[12] Indians in camp asking for bread.

July 12, 1864 Drove eight miles and camped for the day.[13] Cut grass for our horses as we have to cross a desert twenty-two miles in width.

July 13, 1864 Drove across the desert by three o'clock; camped near stage stand. There was a little fort here and a few soldiers.[14] Some Indians came and wanted to take our horses a distance of two miles to graze. The soldiers said they were to be trusted, so we permitted

---

[9]Fish Springs. See ch. 6, n4. (See map 4.)

[10]Oxen were not common on the Central Overland Trail. Only four of our diarists mention them at all, and only Porter and Ringo indicate that they owned oxen and used them. Ringo used both oxen and mules.

[11]See ch. 7, n9.

[12]Either Epperson or the transcriber got the name wrong—they were now at Deep Creek. See ch. 7, n11.

[13]They were near Eight-Mile stage station, the last water before crossing Antelope Valley.

[14]This camp was somewhere near Antelope Spring. Phebe Carleton, one of our diarists, observed soldiers in this area, but only Epperson mentions a fort. See ch. 7, n13.

them to go with our stock. Some of the guards remarked that they would sleep well to-night.

JULY 14, 1864 Early this morning our horses were brought to camp. Mr. Epperson paid them for their work, gave them something to eat, and soon after we were on our way.[15]

JULY 15, 1864 Did not feel well this morning; drove only a few hours, and camped in a lovely canyon; found plenty of feed and mahogany wood.[16]

JULY 16, 1864 Started early; came to a little village, only five or six huts. The name of the village is Steptoe.[17] Passed into Egan canyon. Mr. Epperson found some California miners at work, tunneling the hill. They think it a rich mine. The soldiers told us to-day that Salt Lake City was under martial law.

JULY 17, 1864 Camped at Butte springs.[18] About twenty wagons left camp, intending to travel all night, it is so very warm during the day. A Californian trader pitched his tent here, with emigrant supplies. Only asked one dollar per pound for cheese, and one dollar and one-half for coffee, and everything else in proportion.

JULY 18, 1864 Traveled over a rough mountainous road and camped in Ruby valley.[19] Here we found quite a little settlement, grocery store and fort. The soldiers are going to give a dancing party to-night. They have a wagon in camp now, to take the ladies of our train to the ball. There are a great many camped in the valley. We have to make certain drives to obtain water and feed. This causes the camping place to be crowded. I am very tired to-night; will sleep soon, knowing we are in no danger.

JULY 19, 1864 Have a dusty drive before us to-day, but I console myself with the thought that every day brings us nearer home. How glad I will be when this toilsome journey is at an end. Had but little water for our stock to-day. Camped on Diamond mountain.[20]

---

[15]During this day's travel, they made their way to Spring Valley, but Epperson does not tell us which route they followed. See ch. 8, n10.

[16]This would have put them at the Schell Creek station, near present-day Schellbourne Ranch.

[17]See ch. 16, n22.

[18]See ch. 8, n12.

[19]See ch. 6, n8.

[20]They were somewhere on the eastern slope of the mountain, possibly at Corta Spring.

July 20, 1864 This is the steepest mountain we have encountered so far.[21] Met a number of teams on the road to Salt Lake. Camp at Diamond springs. I counted forty wagons near us. The stage has just passed. The sky is cloudy and everything has a gloomy appearance. Gave Charlie a bath, and covered him in bed. I am alone at the wagon, sitting on the tool-chest writing. Ponto, my dog, seeing me alone, came up, wagging his tail, as much as to say he was still on his way to California, and hoped to find a better country than we were now in.

July 21, 1864 There was so much noise in camp last night, I slept but little. Traveled all day, and camped near a mountain stream.[22] Thirty wagons near by, and enough of crying children to disturb a camp meeting. After it was quite dark, a wagon came into camp from Austin. Mr. Epperson went to the wagon, and found one of his old Californian friends, Thomas Andrews, former Sheriff of Nevada county, California. Mr. Epperson brought him to our camp. I soon prepared a good supper for him, and we all sat around a cheerful camp-fire until quite late. He was taking a mowing machine to Ruby valley, to cut his hay. He gave us a supply of sugar, our's being almost out.

July 22, 1864 The men came into camp with only three horses; said the others had wandered off, and they could not find them. Mr. Epperson sent two Indians to look for them. They soon found them and brought them to camp. Mr. Epperson gave them powder and caps for their trouble. The Indians here can be trusted to some extent; they are kept down by the soldiers. An old Indian is now walking around camp with an old plug hat on, which hat constitutes the principal part of his clothing. You can imagine how comical he looks.

July 23, 1864 We traveled alone today for the first time, the rest stopping to recruit their stock. I was thinking we would have a lonely camp, but by evening we came to a beautiful canyon, where we met a number with teams on their way to Austin. All camped together, and quite a joy crowd camped around the fire before retiring.[23]

July 24, 1864 When the men were bringing the horses to camp this morning, one of our mares started back on the road we traveled

---

[21]This was the Overland Pass in the Diamond Mountains. See ch. 8, n14.

[22]Roberts Creek.

[23]Dry Creek. (See map 6.)

yesterday. She was caught by some men at a stage stand eighteen miles from our present stopping place.[24] Mr. Epperson started immediately after her, and did not return until nearly night. It was a lonely day for me.

July 25, 1864 Started early. I rode horseback up the canyon. Looking down on the little valley below, I saw we had a very steep hill to descend,[25] I dismounted and walked. The men tied a tree to each of our wagons, to keep them from rolling forward too quickly. I was somewhat alarmed, but we arrived at the bottom safely. This afternoon we passed "Simpson's Park." It was enclosed by stretching strips of raw-hide from post to post. This was the first raw-hide fence I had ever seen. We met a man to-day looking for his wife; said he with his team started for Virginia City after provisions; while absent, his wife sold the ranch, purchased two horses and a wagon, and started for Illinois, her former home. He wished to know if she had been seen by us. After giving a description of her, we assured him we had met her over fifty miles from this place. He sighed and said "well, I will let her go, as I could not overtake her before reaching Salt Lake." I pitied him, but could not help laughing when he told his doleful story. He turned about and started westward. We camped at Emigrant springs,[26] the dustiest camp that we had during our journey; were obliged to drive the horses two miles to feed.

July 26, 1864 William Maran is herding the horses. Mr. Epperson and his men are gone to Austin, about four miles distant. There is a small party encamped near by, so I have company. Charlie and Ponto (my dog) are playing around our wagon. The mountains near are perfectly bare, no vegetation; those more distant have a few small pine and cedar. Mr. Epperson came into camp in the afternoon, bringing with him Mr. Gabriel Stickley, and old Californian friend. He told us that he owned a wood ranch about six miles from Austin, and at that place we would find good feed and water for our horses, and insisted

[24] The horse was at the Grubb's Well station.

[25] The Eppersons took the Eagle Butte route from Dry Creek to Simpson Park. See ch. 8, n15.

[26] The editor has been unable to identify an "Emigrant Springs" in this area, but this camp may have been at present-day Thorpe Spring, near Emigrant Pass in the Toiyabe Mountains.

that we take our stock there and camp as long as we wished; he also proposed to go with Mr. Epperson and show him the place. His kind offer was accepted with gratitude.

JULY 27, 1864 Mr. Epperson and his friend Mr. Stickley, started early on horseback to see the ranch. Another lonely day for me. I occupied myself by writing letters to friends at home. At intervals, teams pass whom we had met before on the road, and so the day passed. Mr. Epperson came to camp about dark, well pleased with the proposed change.

JULY 28, 1864 Started early for our new camping ground, arrived safely there about noon,[27] and soon after the men had a brush shanty made for me, which I occupied with great pleasure. The sun was very warm, and no shade but that made by the wagons. We turned the horses loose, thinking they would not stray off, but before dark the men went to drive them close to camp, and three were missing; and were not found to-night.

JULY 29, 1864 Bright and early our men started to find the missing horses. Soon after the men were gone the horses were driven into camp by a wood chopper, who camped near us. He was looking for some horses he had lost, when he came upon ours. In the afternoon, a gentleman rode into camp very much excited, and wished to know who owned those jennets branded with the letter "B" upon the jaw. Mr. Epperson replied, "they belong to me." And then he asked "where, and of whom did you buy them?" Mr. Epperson said, "I purchased them in Burbon county, Kentucky, of old uncle Ben Bedford, last February." When he heard that he jumped from his horse and shook hands with us all, as heartily as if he had known us for years. He told us Mr. Bedford was his uncle, and that he had left Kentucky before the commencement of the war, and had not heard from there for quite a length of time. Mr. Epperson told him of many changes that had taken place since he left his home. He stayed all the afternoon at our camp, made Mr. Epperson promise to take our little boy and myself to Austin, so that we might occupy one of his houses until we started

[27]Epperson does not give us enough information to determine the location of this "ranch." All that we really know is that it was within a few miles of Austin.

for California. He said we should have it free of charge. I thanked him very much for his kindness, and told him I had been in camp so long, I would as soon remain in camp for the short time we expected to remain. He would not listen to my refusal, but turned to Mr. Epperson and says, "I shall expect to see you in Austin to-morrow; will show you the house I wish you to occupy, as I shall be absent for three or four days after to-morrow." After bidding us good-bye he rode off, and I felt we had found a true friend, although an entire stranger. Be assured we appreciated his kindness. I was not feeling well. Had it been necessary for us to rent a house, we had not the means to pay rent, we had left but one dollar and fifty cents. Mr. Epperson had written to his brother, C. C. Epperson of Sutter county, California, to send us one hundred and fifty dollars. Mr. Epperson could not go to Austin to-day, as I was feeling very badly. Our stock seem contented and do not require such close watching.

JULY 31, 1864 Mr. Epperson started for Austin. William Maran stayed at camp and took charge of Charlie and prepared dinner. Our men are all off prospecting, hoping to discover a rich silver mine. It is amusing to see them coming into camp loaded with rock; never saw a silver mine until they went into Austin a few days ago; they would not know a valuable piece of ore if they should find one. We are in camp some distance from the road, and can see nothing but black hills, most of them entirely barren. Occasionally a raven may be seen flying overhead chattering a doleful tale.

AUGUST 1, 1864 Up early and hurrying around preparing to move into Austin.[28] William Maran went with us to take the horses back to camp; he will be alone in camp as the men have gone to work. Austin is quite a little place, everything stirring. Our house is made of adobe. We put our bed and trunks in the house, had lunch, and Mr. Maran started back to camp. He appeared somewhat lonely, but will have neighbors, as there are men only a short distance from our camp chopping wood.

AUGUST 2, 1864 After a good night's rest, I feel like preparing our breakfast, which I have not done for some time. Breakfast ready,

---

[28]See ch. 12, n21.

Mr. Epperson and I sit down along (our table is a pine board two feet wide and four feet long) for the first time since leaving our home in Illinois. One year ago to-day I was with my mother; I wish she could see me in my little mansion, dirt floor, bedstead made of pine posts, stools for chairs, and our trunks; these are all that our furniture consists of. Many of the houses are covered with canvass. Our friend Mr. Stickley called and wished us to go with him to Mrs. Hick's, where he boarded, and take super. I found Mrs. Hicks very pleasant. She had one room with plank floor, of which she was very proud, as but few could afford plank floors, lumber being very scarce, and worth two hundred and fifty dollars per thousand. Saw for the first time the Chinamen in their washhouses.

AUGUST 3, 1864 Mr. Epperson found quite a number of Californian friends and acquaintances in Austin to-day, among them was Mr. Robert C. Murdock, who is a resident of Colusa at this date. Also George W. Thomson, from Colusa county, a well known stock-raiser, but now interested in the hardware business in Santa Rosa, Sonoma county, California.

AUGUST 4, 1864 Mr. Epperson found another friend, Mr. James Rooker, formerly of Sutter county, California. He was engaged in the butcher business. Informed Mr. Epperson he had married since they last met, and had the biggest boy of his age in Nevada Territory. Mr. Epperson asked him the age of his boy. Said a little over two years old. Mr. Epperson told him he had also had married, and had a boy a few weeks younger than his, whom he would like to weight against his; and it followed that they weighed them next day.

AUGUST 5, 1864 After breakfast Mr. Epperson, with our Charlie, started for Mr. Rooker's shop, and quite a crowd gathered around to see the children weighed. Mr. Rooker's son weighed forty pounds, and Charlie forty-four. Those who witnessed the weighing told Mr. Rooker not to boast of his mammoth infant any longer. Charlie was brought home with his hands full of candies, very much pleased indeed.

AUGUST 6, 1864 Mr. Spurgeon and family drove into town and camped near our house. I was glad to meet them again. They had been delayed by sickness, and two members of his family not able to sit up at this time.

August 7, 1864 Mrs. Hicks spent the afternoon with me; together we called upon a sick man camped quite near; he is not expected to live.

August 8, 1864 Started to walk about the town and see some of the quartz mills, but soon tired and returned home.

August 9, 1864 Attended an exhibition given by the pupils of the public school. This was the first exhibition given in Austin. Nothing of interest transpired for the next nine days.

August 19, 1864 Wm. Mason and Mr. Stickley brought our stock to town, we loaded our wagons again and were soon in the Reese river valley.[29] Mr. A. C. Chalmers drove the loose stock. It was nine o'clock before we found a desirable place to camp for the night.[30] The wind blew extremely cold and chilly.

August 20, 1864 Had breakfast ready by the time the sun rose, anxious to get on our road early. I must confess I really enjoyed camping again. We crossed a barren alkali flat, that was so white when the sun shone upon it, that it was almost blinding.[31]

August 21, 1864 Camped in a deep canyon,[32] no feed near by; had to send the stock off about two miles to graze. Mr. Epperson and I are alone.

August 22, 1864 Camped in the greesewood,[33] bought feed for our animals, and had quite a shower which laid the dust.

August 23, 1864 Our horses strayed off into the woods which caused us some delay,[34] crossed the Carson desert, in going about

---

[29]Heading west from Austin, the Eppersons crossed the Reese River, probably just west of Jacobsville, then turned south and began following the river upstream. See ch. 3, n38. (See map 7.)

[30]The exact location of this camp is uncertain, but based on Epperson's entry for the following day, it was somewhere east of the barren playa in Smith Creek Valley.

[31]There are two very large playas in Smith Creek Valley; the emigrant road would have crossed the northern one. Epperson does not say anything about where they camped, but it was probably on Smith Creek.

[32]The trail went through two canyons immediately to the west of Smith Creek Valley—Smith Creek Canyon, and then Edwards Creek Canyon. If the Eppersons had traveled the average distance for a day's journey, they would have reached the latter, which is located on the northern slope of the Desatoya Mountains. See ch. 3, n40.

[33]Because they were at a place where they could purchase feed, it is quite certain that they had reached the Middlegate area, where there was a stage station. See ch. 3, n42.

[34]Considering the desolate and barren nature of this part of the country, it is difficult to imagine what Epperson was describing when she used the term "woods."

twenty-two miles I counted sixty-five head of dead horses and cattle; camped at Salt Wells.[35] Here we found the water very salt, our stock would not drink it. From the salt lake here, they make tons of salt, which is shipped in great quantities to Austin and Virginia City. The salt is used in the quartz mills. Saw several camels carrying packs of salt.[36] Several in camp to-night, are having a dancing party; made so much noise until midnight we could not sleep.

AUGUST 24, 1864 Camped in the sand; no wood, bad water, bought or hired pasture for our stock; every little oasis is claimed by some one; we have to pay dear for the grass we get.[37] This is the most desolate looking country we have yet seen. Now and then we pass a little hut, cannot imagine how the occupants exist. All the money in Nevada Territory would not induce me to live here.

AUGUST 25, 1864 In the afternoon came to a little ranch, where we saw a fine garden. Mr. Epperson bought vegetables, also a nice large watermelon. This place looked so inviting after traveling through such a dreary part of the country, we concluded to encamp here for the night. We are near the Carson river.[38]

AUGUST 26, 1864 Passed Ragtown this morning. The town resembles Truckee. We crossed a desert twenty-five miles in width to the Truckee river. This is altogether desolate. The ground looked as if a fire had passed over it. Near sunset we came near the Truckee river and were thankful for good drinking water.[39]

---

[35]There is now a Salt Wells about ten miles northwest of Sand Springs, but it is rather doubtful that Epperson was referring to this place. It is much more likely that the Eppersons were at Sand Springs. See ch. 3, n43. (See map 8.)

[36]Five other diaries in this collection mention sighting camels or dromedaries. See ch. 14, n21.

[37]This entry exemplifies one of the striking differences between the conditions experienced by the emigrants of earlier times and those of the 1860s. The Eppersons kept running into private property. As a general rule, earlier emigrants camped wherever they could find a satisfactory spot. The Eppersons found that the good places to camp had been claimed, and the occupiers were selling grass and other items to the emigrants who followed.

[38]The Epperson's route from Sand Springs cannot be certain, but Lucretia's comments on the 24th and 25th about ranches and farms leads the editor to suspect that they followed Simpson's outbound trail to the northern shore of Carson Lake, then turned west toward Ragtown. See ch. 3, n44 and n46.

[39]After passing Ragtown, they left the Central Overland Trail, followed the general route of present-day U.S. Highway 50A, and came to the Truckee River somewhere near the town of Wadsworth.

CHAPTER 18

John G. Fackler

1864

THE REVEREND JOHN G. FACKLER and his wife left their home in Buchanan County, Missouri, in May 1864. They were accompanied by at least two hired hands and three wagons. The first page of Fackler's journal tells us that there were "not less than one hundred souls" in the party they joined. At Salt Lake City, after some serious debate among the members of the party, the Facklers and a small but unspecified number of the original group decided to follow the Salt Lake Cutoff and the Humboldt River route. The larger portion of the party decided to continue west on what Fackler called the overland stage road. Fackler's journal is included in this collection because when his small party reached the vicinity of Battle Mountain, Nevada, it left the California Trail and followed the Reese River to Austin, where the group began to travel the Central Overland route. The Facklers left St. Joseph, Missouri, on May 19 and arrived in Salt Lake City on July 28.

A copy of Fackler's handwritten diary was obtained from the Missouri Historical Society, which granted permission to publish it (John G. Fackler Diary, Missouri History Museum Archives, St. Louis).

JULY 28, 1864 Ewing & myself ride in advance of the train. The road for the most part is down the canon & along mountain streams. In some places it is very narrow scarcely affording room for teams to pass. On our arrival near the . . . in the suburbs of Salt Lake City, we met Mr. Jones & Andrew . . . in a buggy coming out to meet us. The City as seen in the distance presents a handsome appearance. The trees in all the peripheral streets, are refreshing to the sight, exhibiting a singular contrast to the general barrenness of the valley in which the city is located. About 3 O,clock the whole train arrived and is camped in Emigration Square[1] in a dusty & filthy place, full of horses & waggons from the states & . . . In the evening a large number of old acquaintances came into our camp to congratulate us on our safe arrival. Mrs. Jones went at once to her boarding house, glad indeed to know that her journey was at an end. The Mormons crowd around us, anxious to sell their various commodities or to buy any thing we may have to dispose of. They ask exorbitant prices for what they have to sell. Retired greatly wearied & worn out by the day's labors & anxieties.

JULY 29, 1864 In the forenoon went out with my wife to call on some friends & see the city. Visited in company with Mr. Jones & his wife the Tabernacle, the Mormon Temple in the center of . . . & the business portion of the town. The evidences of prosperity on every hand are surprising. The merchants seem to be doing an active & profitable business. A great many strangers are here, gathering from the different states & territories. Met with a large number of persons, whom I have known in Missouri. The city is insufferably hot & dusty, & our situation in Emigrant Square unpleasant. In the afternoon a portion of our train went out about 20 miles to a canon in West Mountain.[2] Some of the mules gave out & we did not reach our camping ground until nearly midnight. Turned the stock loose in the dark, to take care of themselves. We are on a very small stream, three or four miles up the canon. Retired, weary & anxious.

---

[1]See ch. 14, n1.

[2]Fackler's west mountains were the Oquirrh Mountains, on the west side of Salt Lake Valley. They apparently camped somewhere between Bingham Canyon and Magna, possibly in either Coon Canyon or Harker Canyon. (See map 2.)

July 30. 1864 Found the stock this morning scattered about in different directions on the sides of the mountains near by. Bunch grass abundant, but hard for the mules to get at it. The stream is . . . dry & mill not afforded sufficient water. We must find a better place. Found an immense quantity of service berries in the canon. Will remain here till Monday.

July 31, 1864 From necessity Ewing & myself spent most of the day searching for a better camping ground. A day of . . . riding in the hot sun. I went up to what is termed the "Point" near West Mountain & a view of Salt Lake in the distance, and saw several very large & beautiful springs on the road there, but all of them are brackish.[3] Ewing went south in the direction of Bingham's Canon. He returned late in the afternoon & reported that he had found a fine camping ground, with abundance of good grass & water, about twelve miles from our present location. We have decided to move our teams there tomorrow.

August 1, 1864 Dispatched our teams to "Bingham's Canon," under the care of Clarence Chiles. Ewing & myself concluded to return to the city, with some articles for sale. Took my ambulance & small waggon with. Arrived in the city about 6 O,clock p.m. and camped on a private square, where I found Van Ausdale, Price, & others of our original party. Called in the evening with Mr. . . . to see Rev. Mr. Snow at the Salt Lake house. The ladies in the camp gave me an amusing account of their visit to the Tabernacle on Sabbath, & their impressions of Brigham Young

August 2, 1864 Spent the day in the city, disposing of various articles. Dined with Mrs. Jones & Mr. . . . at their boarding house. Enjoyed the occasion very much. After consultation with friends, most of our party have decided to take what is known as the Humboldt route. The overland stage road is said to be badly supplied with either water or grass. It is painful to have to separate from some of our friends who are compelled to go by Reese River. Bought a large quantity of shoes for our stock, as they must be shod before resuming our journey.

[3]Fackler was probably at the northern tip of the Oquirrh Mountains when he saw these springs. Today, a large portion of this area is covered by waste from the copper mine in Bingham Canyon.

AUGUST 3, 1864 Parted with my friends Van Ausdale, Price, Cochrane & their families, and went out to the canon where the teams are. The camp is near a very fine spring. The grazing is of the best quality. Have as my purpose to rest the remainder of the week & have all of the stock re-shod by a government blacksmith near by. A mile above us is a camp of U.S. soldiers, California Volunteers. The quiet & rest of this place is very refreshing.

AUGUST 4, 1864 A still quiet day. Our teamsters are somewhat excited by reports of a silver mine a few miles above us up the canon. They are also dissatisfied because we have decided to go the Humboldt road after leaving here. Some suggestion of insubordination. We must stand firm.

AUGUST 5, 1864 Spent most of the day in writing letters to friends in Missouri & elsewhere. In the evening had a talk with my drivers about their leaving. They claimed themselves now entirely satisfied to go on with us. Have enjoyed the rest. A number of Indians came into the camp.

AUGUST 6, 1864 Ewing & his wife returned to the city, where they will remain until we go in on Monday. Spent most of the day in having my stock shod. The weather warm & sultry. More Indians in camp. A party of Mormons passed up the canon going after berries.

AUGUST 7, 1864 Everything quiet & peaceful. Read my bible a good deal. Most of the men have taken another tramp up to the mines. A violent thunder storm & heavy rain in the evening. After we had retired for the night the creek rose very suddenly & rapidly giving us some concern, lest our camp might be submerged. The roar of the mountain torrent was terrible to the weak nerves of the ladies. We suffered no . . . however.

AUGUST 8, 1864 Broke camp about 8 O,clock & started for the city. About 10 O,clock encountered an immense swarm of flying ants. They followed us for several miles, literally covering the waggons & ambulance. I must have killed millions of them during the day. Met Ewing & his wife coming out to meet us. Camped in a meadow 3 miles from the city. Stock grazed half of the night. Grass very poor.

AUGUST 9, 1864 One of my mules is very sick & I fear she will not be able to travel. Passed through the city, stopping long enough to make a few purchases, & get some mail mailed from the post-office. Met with a number more of my old friends. Called to take our final leave of Mrs. Jones & Mrs. . . . who parted from us in tears. Employed a German to assist in cooking. Our route has been up the valley, through a very thick & thriving Mormon settlement. By irrigation the valley has been made to blossom like a garden. Saw some very remarkable warm & hot springs.[4] Camped in a meadow near Farmington, 14 miles from the city. Here we met with Dr. Fackler[5] & Mr. Ramage awaiting our arrival. The pasturage is good. At night my mule died. It is a heavy loss but as it is providential, I must bear it.

Fackler and his small party are now headed north following the Salt Lake Cutoff. His diary entries for this portion of the trip are interesting, but since they have nothing to do with the Central Overland Trail, we skip forward to when they reached the vicinity of Battle Mountain on the Humboldt River.

SEPTEMBER 5, 1864 Made a drive of 20 miles.[6] Passed during the day several hay ranches. When we stopped to noon, although no Indians were in sight, in a few minutes they came pouring out of the willows & sun flowers by dozens, & soon swarmed in our camp. They seem in suffering condition. We camped where a party of men were engaged in cutting hay. Here we found a large quantity of stock, a herd that had been driven east to this region from California. A gentleman came into our camp & advised to leave this route & strike south to Austin 80 miles distant.[7] The night was quiet.

[4]See ch. 3, n1.

[5]There were two individuals named John Fackler in this party, the writer of the journal, and Dr. John M. Fackler of Leavenworth, Kansas. Whether they were related is unknown.

[6]Fackler and his party were camped near Battle Mountain, where the Reese River comes into the Humboldt River from the south

[7]Unfortunately, Fackler fails to identify the man who came into their camp, and fails to explain why the man suggested that they leave the Humboldt route at this point.

SEPTEMBER 6, 1864 This morning Ewing & myself concluded to abandon the Humboldt route & go by Austin. All of the party agreed to go with us except Mr. Bushnell who joined himself to another train. We broke camp about 12 O,clock, striking south through the sage brush following a few waggons tracks for about 9 miles to a Hay Ranch. Took the stock off to a canon four miles distant. Good grass & water. Remained out all night.[8]

SEPTEMBER 7, 1864 One of the most fatiguing days we ever had. Our route of travel was through sage brush & dust with but little more than a trail for a road. Traveled until 9 O,clock at night when we came to a place known as Wilson's Ranch on Reese River—at the sink.[9] A number of the mules gave completely out during the drive. We came out less than 30 miles. The grazing rather indifferent & the water very poor.

SEPTEMBER 8, 1864 Remained in camp all day on account of our tired animals. The country around presents a singular appearance. Within a circuit of three miles, there are many very remarkable hot springs. This morning we could see the vapor rising from them like smoke from a furnace. In the afternoon I enjoyed a bath on one of these springs. The water possesses remarkable cleaning properties.

SEPTEMBER 9, 1864 Made a drive of 22 miles. The road is a great improvement over that of yesterday. We camped on a hay ranch in a beautiful natural meadow, nicely cut. During the night we had a partial stampede of the stock. By 2 O,clock in the morning it was all over and brought back to camp. These night interruptions after a weary day are not very pleasant.

---

[8]The Fackler party had turned south, following the streambed of the Reese River and present-day Nevada State Road 305. The distance between Battle Mountain and Austin is almost ninety miles. The editor is unaware of any other emigrant party that followed this route in this direction. However, at about this same time, George Harter and his small party was traveling it in the opposite direction. Harter commented, "This road from Austin to Humboldt is new and not improved."

[9]The editor has been unable to identify or locate Wilson's Ranch, but thirty-four miles south of Battle Mountain, there are several hot springs. This is Fackler's first mention of Reese River, but they had been traveling not far from its streambed for the past two days. Since he said they were at the river's sink, it is quite likely that there was no water in the streambed below this point. See ch. 3, n38.

September 10, 1864 Made an early start & traveled 20 miles, camping at the head of Boon's canon, near Krippen's Ranch. Here we found an abundance of wood, water & grazing. We are twenty miles from Austin. In the afternoon started in my ambulance, with Ewing, Dunlap & Compton for Austin, in the hope of being able to make arrangements to dispose of our waggons & C, in order to take the stage from there to California. We drove our weary mules until 9 O,clock at night when we reached Austin.[10] Slept in the ambulance. A cool night.

September 11, 1864 Sabbath. This morning walked down with to Clifton, where we found Van Ausdale, Sublette, Price, Cochrane & other friends which we had left at Salt Lake City. The joy at meeting was unbounded.[11] I spent a very quiet day & enjoyed the rest more than at any time since the beginning of the journey. Felt too weary to go to church.

September 12, 1864 Returned to camp & found all well. We have decided if possible to dispose of our outfit in Austin & take ~~the old~~ our light waggon for Ewing & myself. Will leave the stock on hand under the care of some of the men, to be driven through in the course of a month.

September 13, 1864 Returned to Austin. The whole party camped in Clifton. We reached town about 2 O,clock. Had a kind reception from our friends.

September 14, 1864 Spent most of the day in endeavoring to make sale of waggons & camp equipage. Sold my large wagon. Met a number of persons from Mo.

September 15, 1864 Ewing has not yet come in from the herd. In his absence, I hardly know what arrangements to make about the disposal of his wagons. Am thinking of selling both of my wagons & going through by stage. Sending the ambulance & four mules through with Edward.

September 16, 1864 Ewing came in to-day about 4 O,clock. We have finally concluded to sell out every thing & take a public

---

[10]See ch. 12, n21.

[11]Ironically, the Facklers arrived in Austin just one or two days after the arrival of the members of their original party, who had traveled the Central Overland Trail.

conveyance, leaving our stock, to be brought through in the course of a few weeks. Am a good deal fatigued in going up & down the hill to & from Austin.

SEPTEMBER 17, 1864 All our arrangements have been completed. We have decided to take what is termed the "Fast Freight line" through to Sacramento. Mr. Compton & family will go in the same mode of conveyance. Sold my other wagon, & all my camp equipment except what may be necessary for Edward & Mr. . . . who left in the afternoon with the ambulance. I am to preach tomorrow for the N. S. ministries Rev. Mr. Miller. After the fatigues of the past week, I certainly feel very little like preaching.

SEPTEMBER 18, 1864 Sabbath. Preached to day in the Court House to a good congregation. Had to decline an invitation to preach for Rev. Mr. Miller, a Methodist brother at night. Quite unwell all the afternoon.

SEPTEMBER 19, 1864 At 3 O,clock in the afternoon, the stage called at Clifton for our party. It already contained six or seven passengers. We protested earnestly against such crowding, but to no purpose. My self & wife, Ewing & wife, Mrs. Tyson & her son Willie, with our baggage, now added to the already overloaded stage. Mr. Dunlap concluded to wait longer & take the overland mail coach. A night of horror lies before our party. Bade farewell to our kind Clifton friends whom we hope before long, to meet again in California.

SEPTEMBER 20, 1864 As I anticipated, we passed a most uncomfortable night crowded together in the stage. Our road all day has been along a most miserable route. We have moved slowly through clouds of alkali dust. Frequently I have been compelled to get out & walk for relief. My seat is the most uncomfortable one in the whole party. We passed three stations or ranches, known as East Gate,[12] Middle Gate[13] & West Gate. The road has been full of holes & the team has moved very slowly. At night, about 9 O,clock, we reach Sand Springs,[14] where we overtook my ambulance & Mr. Ramage & family. Another night of agony is before us.

[12]See ch. 16, n38.
[13]See ch. 3, n42.
[14]See ch. 3, n43.

SEPTEMBER 21, 1864 I know not that I have ever passed a more unhappy night. My rheumatism has given me a great deal of trouble. It has been impossible for any of the party to sleep, cramped & crowded as we are. During the night we passed the sink of the Carson.[15] In the morning about 10 O,clock, we reached Ragtown, when we got a good breakfast. Traveled all day, over a bleak & desolate region, passing a good many stations & trading posts by the way. It seems to me that life would be a burden in such a country. Night overtook us about 30 miles from Virginia City, where we shall be compelled to stop & rest & procure another conveyance.

SEPTEMBER 22, 1864 Arrived in Virginia City this morning about day light & stopped at the International Hotel. Last night I walked almost the entire distance from the foot of the mountain up to the City, a distance of not less than six miles.[16]

---

[15]The usual stage route was through Simpson Pass and along the southern and western shores of the lake. Whether Fackler's stage took this route is unknown. See ch. 3, n44. (See map 8.)

[16]Although it is not entirely certain, it appears that Fackler's coach left the Central Overland Trail a few miles northeast of Dayton and reached Virginia City by traveling up Six Mile Canyon. (See map 9.)

CHAPTER 19

Wilson Fryberger

1864

WILSON FRYBERGER made the journey with his wife, Ellen, and a traveling companion identified as Ab Coriell. A son, whom the couple named Andrew, was born shortly after they left Salt Lake City. Fryberger's grammar leaves much to be desired, and his spelling was highly imaginative, but his diary is interesting and contains significant information about the trail. The Frybergers left Muscatine, Iowa, on March 25 and arrived in Salt Lake City on July 7.

Jim Hall obtained a copy of the first part of the handwritten diary from the State Historical Society of Iowa, and the editor transcribed these pages. Later, the editor obtained a copy of a version of the diary that had been transcribed by Jesse Fishburn. Permission to publish was granted by the State Historical Society of Iowa (Wilson Fryberger Collection, BL 61 f. 1&2).

JULY 7, 1864 Travild 25 good miles camped in the sity had hay enough to do till noon the next day but no wood

JULY 8, 1864 staid all day in the sity pretty warm put my horses in to a large yard and they charge 1.00 a hed for 24 hours I was offered 160 dollars for my wagon I received 2 letters from pap and one from John good news

JULY 9, 1864 travild 17 miles[1] camped next to a mans house by the name of smith poor grass Ellen was taking sick and grunts prety hard prety warm we are 17 miles south of the sitty poor grass

JULY 10. 1864 at 2 (morning) o,clock we received a fine son prety cold at night and hot in the day time lade in or around the tent all day I thought it was Saturday

JULY 11, 1864 still in the same place tried to get in

JULY 12, 1864 " " " " " very hot days

JULY 13, 1864 still in the same place very warm Ellen is prety smart

JULY 14, 1864 I [stayed] around the tent prince in pasture Ab went to the sity to work

JULY 15, 1864 around the tent

JULY 16, 1864 " " "

JULY 17, 1864 " " "

JULY 18, 1864 had som rain

JULY 19, 1864 around the tent very warm

JULY 20, 1864 went to salt lake sity and baught over halls and over shirt 4.75 2 llbs sugar and som other things prety warm

JULY21, 1864 around the tent Ellen got up Andrew[2] is a little sick

JULY 22, 1864 around home prety warm

JULY 23, 1864 went in swiming with stewart son and after noon helped him kill a beef and got 10 pounds at 15 cents pr pound

JULY 24, 1864 ab came from the sity and I went to Jordan and went In swiming with mat stewart nice and warm This is the greatest country I ever seen it is as dry as it can be every thing is dride up and it rains every day in the morning

JULY 25, 1864 around the tent prety warm

---

[1]When the Frybergers left Salt Lake City, they headed south, following the stage road toward Camp Floyd. After traveling seventeen miles, they would have been in the area of present-day Draper, on the east bank of the Jordan River. (See map 2.)

[2]The name of the new baby.

July 26, 1864 " " "

July 27, 1864 it raind som

July 28, 1864 cradling for Isic Stewart and binding prety warm to pay for what time I was in his paster

July 29, 1864 around the tent very warm Ab quit work to he worked 2 dayes for banksheds and got 2 bushel wheat and I traded it to stewart for 40 pounds flour and 60 pounds barley for feed and traded my gun for 3 bushel of barley and 4 dollars in blacksmithing

July 30, 1864 Went to the sity and baught som copperas and salaratus and sale my spurs for 3 dollars and a hors to ride to town

July 31, 1864 around home prety warm I fix it up to start on Monday [the following day] got all redy I have travild only about 100 miles this month

August 1, 1864 Started on and travild 8 miles and crost Jordon[3] and then had to go 18 miles with out water to camp floyd[4] found no grass but good water

August 2, 1864 25 miles to water to a crick travild 1 mile up the crick to a stage station[5] and camped good water som grass no wood

August 3, 1864 Travild 28 miles to government spring or to the spring run[6] we had no water only what we cared [carried] plenty grass som 2 or 3 big hills the rode is prety good dusty

August 4, 1864 Traveled 5 miles to mountain springs[7] and camped for noon very bad rode after noon traveld 3 miles to Indian springs very bad rode and camped at government springs[8] and took our horses about 1 mile out to mountain grass

August 5, 1864 staid at government springs till 4 o,clock then started acrost the or what they call the desert 45 miles We got

---

[3]This crossing was about four miles north of Lehi. See ch. 2, n5.

[4]See ch. 2, n6.

[5]The stream was Faust Creek and the station, Faust station. The distance traveled was eighteen miles, not the twenty-five Fryberger indicated. See ch. 8, n2. (See map 3.)

[6]Fryberger was almost certainly at Government Spring. By using the term "spring run," he seems to indicate that the spring was the source of a flowing stream. See ch. 12, n5.

[7]These springs were probably the headwaters of Lee Creek, which flows down the eastern slope of the Simpson Mountains.

[8]Although he had just indicated that he was at Indian Spring, Fryberger mistakenly refers to his campsite as Government Springs. See ch. 8, n30.

there about 10 on saturday about 55 miles we traveld 10 miles up the valey after we first struck the springs a awful hill to go over[9]

August 6, 1864 staid the rest of the day and all night poor water and poor grass hall your water from indian spring to drink it will do for horses but not for man these springs is called fish springs[10] this is all desert . . . som little sand but more rocks and dust.

August 7, 1864 Travild 28 miles to willow springs[11] no grass nor water prety good rodes and poor grass and water when you git there[12]

August 8, 1864 Traveled 28 to deep crik[13] som grass no water till you git there and not good grass there the water is a little better here

August 9, 1864 Travild 22 miles to antelope springs[14] good water no grass we fild our cags and traveled about 6 miles found good mountain grass west of the rode a mile no water staid all night plenty wood[15]

August 10, 1864 Travild 10 miles to spring valey station poor water and poor grass so we went on 8 miles further past several springs in the canon and camped pretty clost the top of the hill The best kind grass and water and wood staid the rest of the day the horses is prety week[16]

August 9, 1864 is a mistake we traveld only 8 miles and staid all night and travild the other on wendsdy [August 10]

August 11, 1864 is the what we traveld Wenesdy

---

[9]A very confusing entry. What Fryberger was probably saying was that he traveled fifty-five miles and came to Fish Springs. Then, after passing by the first spring in the Fish Springs area, he continued on another ten miles before stopping for the night. If this is what he meant, his ten-mile figure was somewhat high; it could not have been any more than six miles. Then he parenthetically adds that during the day's journey he had to cross "a awful hill," which would have been Dugway Pass.

[10]See ch. 6, n4.

[11]See ch. 7, n9.

[12]This statement makes sense if it is interpreted to mean that there was no water or grass along the trail, and that at Willow Springs, what could be found was poor. (See map 4.)

[13]See ch. 7, n11.

[14]See ch. 7, n13.

[15]The fact that Fryberger traveled six miles and failed to find any water indicates that he was following the stage road rather than going over the mountain, where he would have found water at Rock Springs. See ch. 8, n10.

[16]Fryberger had passed the Spring Valley station (which modern maps show as Stonehouse), and then continued along the stage road, turning up Stage Canyon and making camp at Schellbourne Spring.

August 12, 1864 laying over at the springs fine grass and water and wood

August 13, 1864 travild 18 to some canion where they was mining som water poor grass[17]

August 14, 1864 traveld 18 miles good water and grass prety hard hill up to the springs[18]

August 15, 1864 traveld 14 miles to ruby springs[19] water som grass after noon traveld 10 miles to ruby valey[20] water and good grass

August 16, 1864 Travild 7 miles and nooned good grass bad hill[21] here is the best grass no water travild 14 miles to a spring[22] not much water or grass got super and traveld 6 miles after dark over awfull hill found good water and grass

August 17, 1864 Travild 16 miles to som springs staid all night poor water and grass[23]

August 18, 1864 travild 16 miles som water no grass mountain grass 3 miles up roberts crik After noon traveld 17 miles to grubs well som water not much grass there has not been any grass along the rode for 40 miles fit for a hors[24]

August 19, 1864 travild 20 miles to dry crick good water and grass the best kind no water or grass for noon prety good rodes[25]

August 20, 1864 traveld 10 miles to simpson park[26] water poor grass after noon travild 5 miles in 2 miles of ostin [Austin] som water and poor grass[27] staid all night and let the horses rest coby and dot give out

---

17Egan Canyon. (See map 5.)

18Pony Springs. See ch. 8, n12.

19Fryberger was confused about the name of the springs. About fourteen miles from Pony Spring, he was at Mountain Spring, but he got ahead of himself and called it "ruby springs," which was still several miles away.

20See ch. 6, n8.

21Fryberger's "bad hill" was the Overland Pass in the Diamond Mountains. See ch. 8, n14.

22The spring was Diamond Springs at the western base of the Diamond Mountains.

23Sulphur Spring. See ch. 10, n23.

24During this day's travel, Fryberger crossed Roberts Creek and camped near the Grubb's Wells stage station.

25Dry Creek. (See map 6.)

26The ten-mile figure indicates that Fryberger took the shorter Eagle Butte route from Dry Creek to Simpson Park. See ch. 8, n15.

27Five miles beyond Simpson Park would have put him near Emigrant Pass, where he would have still been about four miles from Austin.

August 21, 1864 Went over to ostin on charley to see the sits [sights][28] found george maylone and talked a little he says it is hard times there or here I got 10 cents worth of tobaco I have 50 cents left and I am straped and only a sack of flour to last this week and out of meet prety shortly

August 22, 1864 got up the horses after noon pulled over to ostin and camped at the first house and took the horses in the mountains about 2 miles to good grass and baught 2 pounds stake

August 23, 1864 went over to the horses and found bets Dead I think she had the colic we left the rest thare I am sick with the diree

August 24, 1864 still camped at the first in the hed of the canion got some stake the wether is cold Ellen andrew and I are sick

August 25, 1864 Ab corell went to see the horses and prince had fell in a prospect hole and broke his nec so he is dead I got som stakes prety bad luc for a new biginer

August 26, 1864 Went to george maylones and he got me 100 wate flowur and 13 pounds stake and we hitched up and pulled 15 miles Down reec [Reese] river[29] to J T midtlons Rance and calculate to hall in som hay for him we are still sick got thare after dark good water and grass

August 27, 1864 went fishing caut nothing ab is helping make som hay racks prety warm day We are still grunting som better

August 28, 1864 helped midlton lode a lode of hay and he took charley and borrowed another hors and started to ostin

August 29, 1864 laying around midleton came home at night and brought som beef

August 31, 1864 halling in hay till noon after noon . . . begun bilding fence around hay stack in yard

September 1, 1864 helping hall in hay till noon with team after noon bilding fence and splitting posts

September 14, 1864 Ab and I damed reece river in 2 places and turned som dobies and mixed som mud

[28]Fryberger rode his horse Charley to the mining town of Austin. See ch. 12, n21.

[29]See ch. 3, n38.

SEPTEMBER 15, 1864 making dobies we made 549 plesant day it frose last night

SEPTEMBER 16, 1864 making dobies we made 524 and it started the first rain I have seen to wet threw the shirt since I left salt lake I helped or went to help brooks lode a lode of hay and ab and midleton loded a lode for ostin

SEPTEMBER 17, 1864 midleton went to ostin with hay and I went and helped brookes of Ab and I done nothing but grub a little Ellen and I went and helped milked brookes cow about supper

SEPTEMBER 18, 1864 around home doing nothing midleton came home from ostin at night

SEPTEMBER 19, 1864 loded a lode of hay for midleton and he started to ostin at noon ab and I grubed a little brook came here

SEPTEMBER 20, 1864 I went and helped brook lode a lode of hay and milked his cow

SEPTEMBER 21, 1864 around home midleton came home

SEPTEMBER 22, 1864 " " calculate to start

SEPTEMBER 23, 1864 Went to ostin and camped in store clost where maylane lives

SEPTEMBER 24, 1864 sale my things all to our cloes and beding and only had 162.25 in all and hired a man to take us to virginia sity for 19 dollars

SEPTEMBER 25, 1864 started we traveld 35 miles bad rode I pade him our fare

SEPTEMBER 26, 1864 Travild 30 miles bad rods

SEPTEMBER 27, 1864 " " 28 " " "

SEPTEMBER 28, 1864 seen smith traveld 35 miles

SEPTEMBER 29, 1864 traveld 30 bad rods the team is about give out

SEPTEMBER 30, 1864 travild 28 miles got in 12 miles of virginey sity

OCTOBER 1, 1864 travild 12 miles got in Virginey about noon and staid all night and baught Ellen a hat and andrew a hat[30]

---

[30]Fryberger probably left the Central Overland Trail about six miles northeast of Dayton and took the road up Six-Mile Canyon to Virginia City. (See map 9.)

CHAPTER 20

George Edwin Bushnell

1864

In May 1864, George Edwin Bushnell left Kirksville, Missouri, and began a journey to California. Bushnell's trip was unusual in that when he left Austin, he also left the Central Overland Trail and took a route roughly parallel to it but about twenty-five miles to the south. After reaching the Walker River, he turned north and returned to the Central Overland Trail at Fort Churchill. Bushnell began his journey west on May 5 and arrived in Salt Lake City on August 2.

A copy of the Bushnell diary was obtained from the Merrill J. Mattes Research Library, National Frontier Trails Museum (Independence, Missouri), which granted permission to publish it.

August 2, 1864 Went up to the top of the mountain. Got into Emigrant Mountain, and got to the City, stayed long enough to go in the P.O. and get my letters, and drove on 15 mi. We crossed the river Jordan,[1] about 2 mi. from the City. Tonight we are camped by a Salt Spring, at the point of the mountain.[2]

[1]Bushnell crossed the river on the old North Temple bridge. See ch. 9, n2. (See map 2.)

[2]The salt spring campsite was near the northern tip of the Oquirrh Mountains, in an area now covered by an immense mine waste dump.

AUGUST 3, 1864 Layed by and went back to the City, and paid $8.00 for shoeing a mare and 24¢ for flour, and $1.00 a pound for sugar, and saw the foundation of the Temple. It is 190 ft. by 127 walled in with a wall 14 ft. high.

AUGUST 4, 1864 Drove 28 mi. to Stockton.[3] The new silver mines they are building, 2 furnaces, and putting up a quartz mill. About 50 men at work there, we had plenty of wood, and water and the finest grass on the trip.

AUGUST 5, 1864 Three months today, since we left home, went up to the Silver Mines this morning and got a specimen of the ore, and traveled 20 mi. up Rush Valley.[4]

AUGUST 6, 1864 Drove to Government Springs 28 m.[5]

AUGUST 7, 1864 Drove to a spring in the mountains 2 m. of the desert.[6]

AUGUST 8, 1864 Are laying by, or over today plenty of wood, water, and grass of the best quality. It is 1 1/2 mi. to the Indian Springs.

AUGUST 9, 1864 Drove over the mountain to the springs,[7] and stopped there a while, and then started across the desert. It looks from the mountain like a lake frozen over.[8]

AUGUST 10, 1864 Got across the desert this morning about 8 o'clock[9] traveled in about 20 hours, 50 mi. without water or grass, except what we took with us. Stayed till 3 o'clock, and drove up to the spring 4 mi. and camped.

---

[3]When they left the salt spring, the Bushnell party continued west, traveled along the southeastern shore of the Great Salt Lake, and then turned south into Tooele Valley. The town of Stockton is about six miles south of Tooele City. See ch. 9, n6.

[4]This would have put them near Faust Station, where they would have gotten onto the old stage road that came from Camp Floyd. See ch. 8, n2. (See map 3.)

[5]Although the exact location of Government Spring is uncertain, Bushnell's twenty-eight-mile figure is too high. The actual distance would have been closer to eighteen miles. See ch. 12, n5.

[6]It appears that Bushnell meant that the spring was two miles up the canyon. Present-day maps do not show a spring at this point, but the campsite could have been on Lee Creek, which is almost always a flowing stream.

[7]Indian Spring. See ch. 8, n30. Martha Logan, whose diary is included in this book, spent the same night at this location; see ch. 21, n9.

[8]The desert to the west of the Simpson Range is very flat, and the soil is very light in color.

[9]There is a line missing from the transcribed copy that probably indicated Bushnell had reached Fish Springs. See ch. 6, n4.

AUGUST 11, 1864 Traveled today 21 mi. to Willow Springs,[10] good water and grass, and holes here said to be 250 ft. deep, and fish in them.

AUGUST 12, 1864 Drove 28 mi. to Deep Creek Station,[11] good water and grass.

AUGUST 13, 1864 Drove up the creek 4 mi. and cut grass to cross the desert and came on 2 mi. and camped, to stay over today, good water, but poor grass.[12]

August 14, 1864 Today, we traveled 28 mi. to Antelope Springs,[13] and found good grass, 3 ½ mi. to the right of the road, and good water. Today, we fell in company with Dr. Coger, and Mr. Baker, cousins of Mrs. Thatcher.

AUGUST 15, 1864 Come on to Spring Valley,[14] 18 mi. and stopped for dinner, plenty of water, and grass, and Indians too. Drove to spring in the mountains, 8 mi. plenty of wood and grass. 26 miles today.

AUGUST 16, 1864 Stayed in camp till evening and drove over the mountain to Shell Creek, 4 mi. and camped. Plenty of wood, water, and grass.[15]

AUGUST 17, 1864 Traveled 18 mi. and camped in Egan Canyon, 2 mi. above Steptoe City, at the silver and gold mines.[16]

AUGUST 18, 1864 Traveled 18 mi. to Pony Springs,[17] good water, wood, and grass, but rough place to camp on the side of a rough, rocky mountain.

AUGUST 19, 1864 Traveled 14 mi. to a mountain spring water, but poor grass.[18]

---

[10]See ch. 7, n9.

[11]See ch. 7, n11.

[12]After passing the site of Ibapah, Bushnell followed the west branch of Deep Creek for about two and a half miles to get to where he cut the grass. After traveling another two miles, he would have been just beyond the Utah-Nevada border. (See map 4.)

[13]See ch. 7, n13.

[14]Bushnell did not describe the route he took between Antelope Spring and Spring Valley, and his mileage figures are too inaccurate to indicate which route he followed.

[15]This camp was on Schell Creek, near the site of old Fort Schellbourne and present-day Schellbourne Ranch.

[16]See ch. 16, n22.

[17]See ch. 8, n12.

[18]This camp was at Mountain Spring in the Maverick Springs Range.

August 20, 1864 Traveled 12 mi. today, to Ruby Valley[19] got a piece of bacon and paid $1.36 a pound.

August 21, 1864 Drove 19 mi. to a spring to the right of the road about 3 mi. and found plenty of water and grass.[20]

August 22, 1864 Drove 12 mi. over Diamond Mountain to Diamond Springs.[21]

August 23, 1864 Drove 14 mi. to Sulpher Springs,[22] plenty water and grass.

August 24, 1864 Drove 16 mi. to Roberts Creek, a small spring branch but plenty of water and grass 2 mi. to the right on the mountain.

August 25, 1864 Drove 16 mi. to Grubbs Wells, good water but not very good grass.

August 26, 1864 Drove to Dry Creek, 20 mi. plenty of water but poor grass.

August 27, 1864 Drove to Simpson's Park and left old Puss, and drove up to the valley, 4 mi. good water and grass, a good place to lay over awhile. 20 miles today.[23]

August 28, 1864 Went to Austin[24] and found Edwin there.

August 29, 1864 We left Austin late in the afternoon and found our road leading through sage brush plains and flats for almost indefinite number of miles.[25] We have found plenty of grass along the road and passed one attempt at civilization in the shape of a grocery, where we found a man who owned a ranch, and knew there was no grass anywhere but at his ranch. But as we had travelers, we concluded to "Trust to luck and stand fate in the face" and so we did, and finally

[19]See ch. 6, n8.

[20]This camp was in Huntington Valley, somewhere near Jacob's Well. Cottonwood Spring, Alba Spring, and Meadow Springs are all possible locations.

[21]Bushnell makes this sound like just another day on the trail. In actuality, he had crossed Overland Pass, the steepest section of the entire Central Overland Trail. See ch. 8, n14.

[22]See ch. 10, n23.

[23]Based on Bushnell's mileage figures, it appears that he probably took the Eagle Butte route. See ch. 8, n15. The camp could have been on Willow Creek or perhaps a little farther west near Thorpe Spring. (See map 6.)

[24]See ch. 12, n21.

[25]When Bushnell and his party departed from Austin, they left the Central Overland Trail and took a route that went south for several miles and then turned west. They did not get back on the stage route until twelve days later, when they had worked their way to Fort Churchill.

realize, that even luck is more worthy of trust than any man who owns a ranch on the Emigrant Trail. We are now in camp near Big Creek.[26] We found plenty of fine water and possible feed. Nearby is a stream sawmill manufacturing a vast amount of lumber, getting the logs franchiseally from Smoky Valley; and in another direction nearby we find a beautiful garden having flume and power pump with which to irrigate. It was quite late when we got here.

August 30, 1864 We encamped this evening in a beautiful flat or valley through [which] the beautiful Reese River runs.[27] The events of the day's journey were not peculiarly striking. We left our camp at Big Creek at about a half hour after 7 o'clock. After traveling 1 mile we found ourselves travelling the main street which, by the way, is the principal street of Lander City, noted for its want of supplies of any description, not having a full box of matches. A short distance above this, however, is an extensive flume and overshot wheel by the bow of which receiving the entire stream, a large number of entrances under which are furnaces for heating the rock, at the same time it is being crushed. One mi. from Lander City we passed through a small portion of Canyon City, a small but flourishing mining town having one or two quartz mills in operation and others are now being built. There seems to be considerable activity here. Turning to the right from this place we passed over rough sage brush hills and travelled over plains of pretty much the same composition until we were convinced we were on the wrong road, when we turned immediately west and travelled 5 mi., without a road and found ourselves at Reese River again. After travelling 15 mi. without water or grass. We experienced but very little difficulty in crossing the above mentioned noted stream. A stream from which the richest silver mines known in the world derive their misappropriate names. After a brisk drive of 5 mi. we reached the camp mentioned at first of the date. Saw about 30 Indians. Travelled nearly to Washington and made in actual travel towards our destination, 25 mi.[28]

---

[26]The town of Big Creek was about twelve miles south of Austin, on a stream with the same name.

[27]They had reached the Reese River, but they were about twenty-five miles upstream (the river flows from south to north) from the point where most emigrants crossed it near the site of Jacobsville. See ch. 3, n38.

[28]Washington was about twenty-five miles south of Austin and six miles east of the Reese River.

August 31, 1864 Camped near Ione. Our road has continued all day along the river sometimes through open fields and sage brush finding much of the country populated by stake and brush fences, and occasionally a house. Late in the evening left the Reese River Valley and entered a canyon which brought us to our present camp.[29] We find plenty of good bunch grass 1 ½ mi. from camp through a deep mountain pass, The water is not abundant in quantity but excellent in quality. Plenty of wood and abundant need for fire.

September 1, 1864 We are camped this evening near the road among rocks and sage brush. A dreary waste is spread out above, beneath and all around us. We left our encampment this morning as early as circumstances would allow. Our camp might justly be styled a Grand encampment for the rocks, the hills, a large rock cave into which we could not gain admittance, and indeed everything, except the little spring and the unfinished walls of wooded buildings was grand. The former were beautiful and the latter wonderous. We left our camp this morning and passed through Ione,[30] the capitol of Nye County, this, I mean, the town is a small cluster of houses situated in a canyon or mountain gorge, like most of the mining towns. And would be a great place if it were not for a few wants under which the builders struggle. 1st. they want a better country upon which to build a town, 2nd something out of which to build and 3rd object in building. After leaving this place we travelled in a some-what of a western direction, first over a rocky country of sage brush and then through a beautiful plat in which was superb grass, and near this an effort to dig a well which effort has been abandoned. After this we passed through a deep mountain pass, or a Westor, and then through a deeper one which was grand. At Westor we found good water though scarce. At the next springs we had good water and more abundant. Ranch man tried to collect toll but failed. We have travelled 20 mi. today and are with out water but having good grass as before stated.[31]

---

[29]From the previous camp, Bushnell would have traveled southward along the Reese River for about fourteen miles and then turned west to go through Ione Canyon. The campsite may have been at Ione Spring, about two and a half miles east of the now-abandoned town.

[30]The abandoned mining town of Ione is located about forty-five miles southwest of Austin.

[31]Bushnell's description of the route is becoming increasingly difficult to follow, but it appears that this camp was about twenty-eight miles south of Middlegate in Gabbs Valley, and near present-day State Route 361.

September 2, 1864 . . . of a grade 80 ft. deep and but little water. Found good grass in valley. Travelled over and near the ocean bed variegated pebles scattered in profusion over the earth, vegetation scarce and scattering. Country undulating and sands just to the right, and left to immense chains of mountains composed of black apparently volocanic rock. The one to the right up to an immense hight, and the two converge near the immense alkili flat that lies in front only seen through the low gap and pass way that lies between their points. The road leads the traveller over the loose rock through this gap, and we find ourselves in a rocky flat just scenting the alkali desert eluded to above. The prospect is dreary and cheerless. Abundance of alkali water in well. Emegrants encamped. Hot springs to the south 3 mi., salty grass. No feed nearer that 3 1/2 mi. over drifts of sand. Boys gone with stock.

September 3, 1864 Boys travelled until midnight lost 3 head of stock but found no feed they returned and slept near us. Rancher kindly offers to show us grass, offer accepted. Lost stock recovered, and plenty of feed found. Doleful day around the desert sands. The same picture as presented yesterday. Not traveling. Stock doing well. Sleepless nights among greesewood and sand hills.[32]

September 4, 1864 Started early over alkali flat singular appearance. 15 mi. to an excellent well of water. Met movers suffering. Passed by the . . . and stopped for supper and feed. Sand hills 5 mi. west. No water but plenty of fine feed. We remained about 2 hours and commenced our toilsome march across a wilderness of sand. Our general direction is west and south of west. The country for 6 or 8 mi. gently ascending and then gradually sloping off over drifting sand to Walker Lake and river. We reached Walker River bridge about 4 A.M. having travelled . . . without serious inconvenience and are now encamped west side of Walker River having travelled 15 mi. in 24 hours. We are now encamped near Walker River bridge in the Pierce Indian Reservation.[33]

---

[32]Bushnell's eloquent description of the country through which they were traveling provides little information that can be used to determine the route. It may be safe to assume that after passing through Ione Canyon, he traveled west in a fairly straight line. If so, the camp would have been about eight or ten miles southeast of the ghost town of Rawhide.

[33]The location of this camp and the Walker River bridge remains uncertain, but it may have been near the present-day community of Shurz. Bushnell makes it clear that he and his party crossed to the west bank of the river at this point.

SEPTEMBER 5, 1864 Arrived here about 4 o'clock. This morning Indians in great numbers gathered around us, many of them having fish to sell, and all of them asking for biscuits, crackers, tobacco, etc. They ask us enormous, exorbant prices for everything they offer to sell, and even willing to pay a fair price for what they want when they have the money. They asked us 25¢ per head for grazing stock. We find bunches grass 3 mi. from the bridge north side of road among sand hills. The day has been spent in sleeping, eating, etc. Women folks very much alarmed for fear of Indians. Moved up the river about 5 mi. and encamped on the bluff and found fine feed near the mountains.[34] Cooked up the last flour we had at noon today, and must fast now until we get to settlements. As we advance up the river we find the most delightful valley stretching out for several hundred yards on each side of the river covered with luxuriant grass and underbrush offering a magnificent place to camp, but then that wretched Reservation prevents, and the boys have gone to the mountains and I must go awhile to dreamland and explore the lights of vision, somewhere in its hidden caves.

SEPTEMBER 6, 1864 At a very early date this morning the mules returned to the river and by a little white lie, we managed to gain them greater grazing on good green grass, for about 2 hrs. and at an early hr. we were on the move. We traveled at some distance from the river for a considerable time over deep sand with but a dim road but an abundance of excellent bunch grass, to the right of the road. After passing this slope were suddenly discovered by Indians, travelling along the beautiful valley to which allusion has been made. Oh, what meadows of untouched grass waves in the gentle breezes that stir also the rich green foliage of the cottonwood, and willos trees that skirt the Alkali stream. About 2 o'clock we reached the "Reserve House," whose keeper, as subsequent information proved to be a cousin of my mother, and hence a second cousin of my brothers and sisters, and myself. He has proved himself worthy of the name he bears, (Bligh). From him we have procured 4 lb. of flour, nearly 1/4 of all he had, 4 lbs. beans,

[34]In the area five miles upstream from Shurz, the Walker River flows through a narrow and shallow canyon with steep bluffs on both sides. The campsite may have been on the bluffs above this canyon.

1/2 of all he had, and through his generosity, we were presented this evening with a fine veal quarter, and a nice bucket of milk. We are now encamped just above his place at a ford of the river.[35] We pay him, in behalf of the government, $10.00 for pasturing the stock tonight for the present we have everything that emegrants need except money.

SEPTEMBER 8, 1864[36] Accompanied by our friends (D. R. H. Bligh) we left camp this morning and have slowly moved along the serpentine way that leads the weary traveler who follow it to the Carson River. The country over which we have passed today is not entirely without its due amount of interest, but never-the-less, is some-what mountainous and is really more noted for this than anything else. For a distance of 10 mi. we traveled near the river, with sage brush and sand plains to the right as we circle to the westward around meandering stream. Feed seems to be entirely out of the question. After the above drive we move in a north-western direction for 5 mi. over Alkali flat with low volcanic hills to the right and front. 5 mi. from the river we halted near a spring water hot enough to scald the fingers. In this vicinity we found a great deal of salt and Alkali, no grass. Seeing this untilable spot we moved on north and northwest with but little change, in the country until we reached the Mason Road, we turned our course northward and moved directly down an incline canyon road toward Fort Churchill.[37] The hills on either side are decidedly volcanic in their appearance. Immense sage brush forming a minature forest. We found no prospect of feed along the road until late this evening we traveled through little flats that are covered with alkali grass and near by the road are plenty of sloughs filled with Alkali water. Near the hour of sunset we found a very delightful spring issuing from a mountain side.[38] Plenty of wood and water, but no grass that is worthy

---

[35]Bushnell indicates that he was camped near a ford, but does not say if they crossed the river.

[36]There may be a problem with the date here. The previous entry was dated the 6th. Bushnell either got his dates mixed up, or they stayed in camp on the 7th, and he failed to make an entry in his diary.

[37]They were now in Adrian Valley, following Simpson's outbound trail to the Carson River, where they would get back onto the Central Overland Trail.

[38]The "delightful" spring was probably Churchill Station Spring. On June 9, 1859, James Simpson reported that his expedition passed this spring: "In this cañon, on left side, fourteen miles from last camp, embowered among wild roses and willows, is a small spring of good, cool water" Simpson, *Report of Explorations*, 88).

of the name, but we are now encamped near the springs having traveled 27 mi. since morning. To the right of the canyon is an immense pile of rock forming a mountain of considerable altitude and magnitude

SEPTEMBER 9, 1864 We are now encamped on the farm of T. Terford Esq. 9 mi. below Dayton. Our jog today is almost without interest. 3 mi. drive brought us to the crossing of Carson River,[39] near which is situated the neat little garrison Fort Church-hill. Near the Fort, we had the privilege of looking at some specimans of the game tribe, in the shape of dromadaries.[40] I paused at the Fort with some friends, and accepted from them an invitation to dine after having witnessed a grand review of the troops. The train continued traveling up Carson River. We had a heavy wind during the entire day and the dust has been almost intolerable. There are a number of settlements along the river but little feed. Traveled 20 mi.

SEPTEMBER 10, 1864 We are encamped tonight at Penrods farm on Clear Creek 3 mi. from Carson City, Capitol of Territory, having traveled 23 mi. over rough roads. Passed through Dayton's thriving town. Capitol of Lyon Co. Quartz mills etc. and etc. From Dayton to Carson City 12 mi. mostly rough. Carson City a beautiful little city. Territorial prison opposite side of valley. We have good feed tonight, barley stubble, (costing $10.00) Lost a mule at Dayton.

SEPTEMBER 11, 1864 Train remained in camp until Monday. I went back for mule. Road enters the edge of Carson Valley and follows it for a number of miles. 10 mi. to Genoa. Over-took train 2 1/2 mi. above Genoa traveled 45 mi. arrived at 9 o'clock.[41]

[39]The Bushnells must have forded the Carson River at Fort Churchill and gotten back onto the Central Overland Trail. There was a bridge across the river at this time, but it was about two miles to the east at Bucklands. (See map 9.)

[40]The "dromadaries" could have been a part of the U.S. Army's experiments with a camel corps during the 1860s, or some that were being used to transport salt from Salt Wells Basin to Virginia City. Five others mentioned seeing camels on the Central Overland Trail. See ch. 14, n21.

[41]When they reached Genoa, Bushnell's party had reached the western end of the Central Overland Trail. If he and his party had not deviated from the usual route between Austin and Fort Churchill, they would have traveled the entire trail from Salt Lake City to Genoa.

CHAPTER 21

Martha Logan

1864

MARTHA LOGAN traveled from St. Joseph, Missouri, to Sacramento, California, in 1864. She was traveling with relatives, but not members of her immediate family. Her age at the time is uncertain, but from comments in the diary, it would appear that she was probably in her late teens or early twenties. Her diary provides a good description of life on the trail, with something of a flair for the dramatic. Logan's group of emigrants gathered in St. Joseph, Missouri, began their trek west on April 27, and arrived in Salt Lake City on July 28.

A copy of a transcribed version of the Logan diary was obtained from the University of Missouri at Columbia, which granted permission to publish it (Logan Family Papers, 1836–1866, Western Historical Manuscript Collection–Columbia, University of Missouri).

JULY 28, 1864 Salt Lake City We arrived here about noon today. I have not seen much of the city yet, though from all appearances I do not think it as grand a place as I had expected. I think it a fine place to get good eatables, as there has been Mormon women every moment since our arrival, with vegetables and fruits for sale. We had plenty of onions and beef steak for supper. I had one letter from home—greater troubles in Missouri. I wonder what will be her fate—poor downtrodden state. The weather is very warm now—I have suffered very much with heat in the last day or two. This place has a great many shade trees.

JULY 29, 1864 Another day in Salt Lake City. I walked around today to see "Brigham's" residence, also the foundation of the "Temple" which was very grand, though I think it will not be finished in our day. B. and John went with us to the Ice Cream saloon. Altogether I think this is a very nice city.

JULY 30, 1864 A dull day this has been and O! so warm. I nearly suffocated up on that dirty Emigrant Square,[1] but thank goodness we are now in a nice green spot about half mile out of the city. We had plenty of callers today. The Theatre comes tonight, but aunt will not permit me to attend.

JULY 31, 1864 What a dreadful Sabbath I have spent. I have never felt more miserable and lonely in all my life before. I went up to see Kate Wise before she left town, and this evening I went to hear "Brigham Young," the president of Utah, preach. He speaks well, and is a very fine looking man. They had good singing by the Choir and there were some good looking ladies there. I walked more than two miles to church. We have some visitors today—Mr. W., and Mr. Tom were here.

AUGUST 1, 1864 Another warm day. Mrs. Persinger went up in the city this evening to the office. Aunt S. and the others went out to camp Douglas. I stayed and kept house.

AUGUST 2, 1864 Still in Salt Lake waiting to start. I have got the blues so badly. O! Lord, dispel the gloom that is gathering over me, or I cannot bear up any longer with the burdens I have to bear. There was company and as usual I went to the Office and sent a letter to Aunt G. O! when will I see her, my dear, dear Aunt. I am so anxious to be getting on to Cal.

AUGUST 3, 1864 Our last day in Salt Lake I think as we are expecting to start out tomorrow, and go a few miles to grass. The weather

[1]See ch. 14, n1.

is still warm and sultry. I have been sewing all day on a bonnet for Aunt. I am weary. O! God watch over me and protect me from the snares of this sinful world.

AUGUST 4, 1864 Left the Great Salt Lake City this morning about ten o'clock. I never expect to behold it again in this life. I left some good friends behind me. We are now camped in full view of the Salt Lake, and right under a high mountain, near a Mormon house.[2]

AUGUST 5, 1864 We passed the Salt Lake today—it was a grand sight—so clear and beautiful. We are camping in a very pretty place in a Canyon[3] and such good water I never saw.

AUGUST 6, 1864 Travelled thirty miles over very good roads. Camped on a little clear stream near a Ranche.[4]

AUGUST 7, 1864 We travelled four miles this morning and stopped here at stage station.[5] Met with Mr. Duncan's train again. One of their number, Hugh Todd, is lost tonight in the mountains. They are still hunting him, his mother looks so distressed—it was only last winter her husband and son were lost in the mountains in a snowstorm. How sad is her fate-yet thou God knowest what is for the best. O! continue to watch over and protect us all.

AUGUST 8, 1864 We are at Government Springs tonight[6]—traveled late through dust and heat, good many campers here—had a terrible hill to walk up after leaving camp.[7] No tidings yet from lost Hugh.

AUGUST 9, 1864 Travelled today through a "Canyon"[8]—had one of the awfullest hills to come down I ever saw. I walked eight miles. Are now camped at Indian Springs[9]—the coldest, best water I ever drank—there are a good many here getting rested, ready for the "desert." I hope we get through it safely.

---

[2]This camp was somewhere along the northern base of the Oquirrh Mountains. (See map 2.)

[3]After passing by the southeast shore of the lake, Logan's party continued south through Tooele Valley. The canyon would have been somewhere along the western slope of the Oquirrh Mountains.

[4]The stream was Faust Creek, and the following entry indicates that they made camp about four miles north of Faust Station.

[5]This camp was near the Faust stage station. See ch. 8, n2.

[6]See ch. 12, n5.

[7]The "terrible hill" was the eastern approach to Lookout Pass. (See map 3.)

[8]The canyon was Lee Canyon, on the eastern slope of the Simpson Mountains.

[9]On this very same day, George Bushnell was also at Indian Spring; see ch. 20, n7 and ch. 8, n30.

August 10, 1864 What a hot dusty day this is. Still in Indian Springs. Will not cross the desert till tomorrow night. We washed today and have been very busy getting ready to go on. Mr. Duncan came up today but no tidings from the lost boy in the mountains, How sad is his fate. God preserve him, is my prayer.

August 11, 1864 Desert. Started at three o'clock and traveled through the desert a distance of fifty miles. The road was much better than I had anticipated. We had a nice walk by moonlight over one of the steepest mountains imaginable.[10] Got through the desert by noon and camped near a telegraph office[11]—found it a very nice clean place, no one there, but men to do the work.

August 12, 1864 Fish Springs Here in camp. Are going to travel tonight again. One of the mules has been sick. I am sorry for we may have to stop a long time on account of it—the weather is extremely warm now.

August 13, 1864 In camp here at the stage station,[12] travelled last night till midnight. I drove as the night was light and beautiful. We have come twenty-five miles, got here in time for breakfast—there are a good many campers here—the water is very good though the swamp is dangerous. There are such deep holes of water—one mule got into one today and came near getting killed. Tomorrow will be Sunday.

August 14, 1864 At Willow Springs—a very pretty place—plenty of company here—are going to travel again tonight—not through the desert yet.

August 15, 1864 Deep Creek[13] Got here by breakfast—stayed all day—had very nice camping ground—a great many here. J. B. came up to-day, will leave soon. I have felt very lonely for the last day or two.

August 16, 1864 Camped again on Deep Creek[14]—It is such a deep beautiful stream—so many here to-night. We will remain till

---

[10]The steep mountain was Dugway Pass, in the Dugway Mountains.

[11]The telegraph office was at Fish Springs. The telegraph line through this area had been installed in late 1861. See ch. 6, n4.

[12]They were at Willow Springs. See ch. 7, n9. (See map 4.)

[13]See ch. 7, n11.

[14]It is not clear if they remained at the same campsite or moved upstream to another place. They could have gone as much as eight miles before leaving the west branch of Deep Creek. This would have put them at Eight-Mile station, where Logan could have mailed her letter.

to-morrow evening and then travel again at night. We had such a good shower this evening, which is a rare occurance in this part of the country. The weather continues warm. We have been troubled so much with the Indians, and the hatefulest ones I have seen. I sent a letter home to-day to sister A. I wish I could hear from her.

August, 17, 1864 Just three months exactly since I left St. Joe. A long sad journey I sometimes think and not very near California yet—been travelling to-night by moonlight—passed through Prairie Gate,[15] a very pretty place in the mountains. Camped at Antelope Springs[16] till day light—had such good water —had a nice walk by moonlight—Aunt was quite sick.

August 18, 1864 Came on to Spring Valley this morning, it is a very good camping place, only there are too many soldiers and Indians here.[17]

August 19, 1864 Only came eight miles to-day—here in a canyon,[18] such a pretty place. The mountains so high—there are a great many campers here.

August 20, 1864 Still in the canyon, I don't know any name for it, northing of importance occurring,

August 21, 1864 What a lonely Sabbath here in the same old canyon. L. and I climbed up a high mountain to try and while away some of the weary hours. Barnett called twice—cousin J. left this morning. I may not see him again.

August 22, 1864 Gold Canyon Arrived here about two o'clock—had a pleasant cool day to travel—there a good many here in this canyon trying the new mine—it is quite a pretty place—good many little houses put up, stores and so forth. We passed an office, but I got no letter.[19] O! for one more in this dreary world.

August 23, 1864 This has been a dreadful rainy day. One of our mules broke down today and we had to walk in the rain several miles.

---

[15]Prairie Gate was a shallow but very narrow canyon about three miles southwest of Eight-Mile station, which was sometimes called Prairie Gate Station.

[16]See ch. 7, n13.

[17]Logan includes no information about which route they followed to Spring Valley, but because they saw a number of soldiers, it seems likely that they took the route around the south end of the Antelope Mountains and stopped at the Spring Valley stage station. See ch. 8, n10.

[18]This camp was probably at Schellbourne Spring, about a mile east of Schellbourne Pass.

[19]Logan's "Gold Canyon" was Egan Canyon. See ch. 7, n14. (See map 5.)

At last, we had to stop. Lizzy and I waited all alone till they could send back other mules for the wagon, it was lonely in the desert. Camped in a Canyon[20] where there are a good many others.

AUGUST 24, 1864 Ruby Valley, N.T.[21] Here at last; the long talked of spot—there are so many Indians and Soldiers—they have a Fort—there is also a store and several dwellings. A great many in camp at this place—they had a dance somewhere here, but we did not attend.

AUGUST 25, 1864 Jacob's Wells[22] This has been a long weary day. I thought we would never get to our camping ground—and such a time as some of the folks had quarelling soon after we got here—it will make a lasting impression on me—we have travelled eighteen miles to-day.

AUGUST 26, 1864 Diamond Springs Got here tolerably early, the water is warm though very clear and good; we came over such a steep mountain to-day.[23] Had to walk. Only travelled twelve miles!

AUGUST 27, 1864 We travelled about thirty miles, to Robert's Creek, what a weary day this has been. We are getting close to Austin—I hope we may meet some friends there.

AUGUST 28, Sun, 1864 This is a dreadful lonely Sabbath here in the dust, and no one but Shoshone Indians for company. I broke the Sabbath by washing, such a thing I never did before. I hope I will get forgiveness for it, and all my sins, too.

AUGUST 29, 1864 What a dreadful days' travel this has been, camped just this side of Dry Creek on the Mountain side.[24] Got here after dark and had quite a time of it in the night getting supper. An old acquaintance of the family met us this evening. We had quite a shower this afternoon. One lady here in camp had a pair of twins of to-day.

AUGUST 30, 1864 Another hard day's travel, so many high mountains and rocks[25]—got to Simpson's Park to-night—it is a very pretty

[20]This camp was probably at Pony Springs. See ch. 8, n12.

[21]See ch. 6, n8.

[22]Jacob's Well was a stage station on the west bank of Connors Creek in Huntington Valley.

[23]Logan is referring to the steep road across Overland Pass in the Diamond Mountains. See ch. 8, n14.

[24]They were in the mouth of Dry Creek Canyon. (See map 6.)

[25]Based on Logan's comment about the high mountains, it can be assumed that her party followed the Pony Express route past Eagle Butte. See ch. 8, n15.

place and a nice ranch here. We are in six miles of the Great City of Austin. I do hope I will hear from home and get to see some of my old acquanitances while there.

August 31, 1864 Came into town to-day. I like the place very well. Austin is a considerable place situated in a canyon of the mountains. We have had plenty of nice pears and grapes. I met with two acquaintances, Will Grant, and L. Farthing, and heard of the death of some others. G. Allcorns died here a few days since—how sad I was to hear of it.

September 1, 1864 Austin[26] How far I am from the spot I was this time last September—how swiftly time flies by! I have been walking around Austin some to-day—think it quite a nice little place—it seems strange that a town can be here in this gully between the mountains. We have had such nice fruit of every description here.

September 2, 1864 This has been a dreary day to me. I have shed most an ocean of tears. I have been so sad I could hardly live. Lizzie sent me a note by her friend Mr. Shobe that she would send for me to-morrow. If she does not I will be dreadfully disappointed. O! Lord watch over me.

September 3, 1864 This has been a bright day and very pleasant. Cousin J. came in for me to go out to Mr. Tucker's. We had a very pleasant ride, Mr. Shobe and Mr. Fike also accompanied us. I found Lizzie and Lucie and Zack quite sick, though all seem to be very well pleased with this country. Dr M. and Mr. De– called this evening. I like them very well.

September 4, 1864 This day has passed off very pleasantly. Diana and I rode down to Canyon City with the Doctor and Mr. De–. Also attended church to-night down there. Lander City and these other little towns, I think are quite nice—and there are so many good vegetables here, that I am afraid I will founder.

September 5, 1864 I had quite a nice buggy ride to-day back to Austin, found Aunt S. Had gone on in the stage to Cal. Lizzie and I went down to the Ice Cream Salon, had a very pleasant time, we will leave here Wednesday and I will not be sorry.

[26]See ch. 12, n21.

SEPTEMBER 6, 1864 Still in Austin, though now fixing to leave in the morning. I saw Mr. and Mrs. Overton to-night. I am so glad this is our last night here.

SEPTEMBER 7, 1864 This day one year ago, I was in Clay College—had commenced school. I wonder if any one there ever thinks of me! Now, I am on my road to California. Left Austin this morning—came 25 miles to Mount Airy.[27]

SEPTEMBER 8, 1864 We made a good day's travel—came about thirty miles, camped again at [a] Station.[28] We find it quite lonely without any other wagons along. I saw ten camels yesterday in the road, going toward Austin.[29] I am Cook now, but do not mind it at all, we haven't got a great deal to do.

SEPTEMBER 9, 1864 We are camped at West Gate tonight, not a very pleasant place, too much dust to suit me—the Alkali is very bad on this part of the route, though the roads are smooth so far. I wrote a note back to Lizzie T, to-day from Cold Springs which we passed this morning. Heaven only knows when I will hear from home, we are not going by Virginia as we intended, but by Carson City. There was Ice this morning on the Bucket of water.

SEPTEMBER 10, 1864 We have made a good day's travel, came forty miles to-day. Are now camped on Carson Lake, it is very pretty here[30]—the lake is fifteen miles wide. What a dreadful sand hill[31] we had to walk over on the Desert. I never was so tired in all my life. We were late getting here—this is Saturday night and to-morrow will be Sunday.

SEPTEMBER 11, 1864 We travelled this morning for five miles on the bank of the Lake,[32] it was beautiful, but as soon as we left the shore,

---

[27]Logan was one of only two of our diarists to take the Mount Airy route, which had recently been opened as a replacement for the Smith Creek-Edwards Creek route (Townley, *The Overland Stage*, 253). The other one was William Pennebaker. See ch. 26, n26.

[28]This camp was near a stage station that had been established in 1862 on Edwards Creek near the point where Edwards Creek crosses present-day U.S. 50. Prior to the opening of the Mount Airy route, the Edwards Creek station was in the canyon, about five miles south of U.S. 50.

[29]Five other diaries in this collection mention seeing camels. See ch. 14, n21.

[30]We cannot be certain about where on the shore of the lake they were camped, but wherever it was, they had probably gotten there by traveling through Simpson Pass. (See map 8.)

[31]The "dreadful sand hill" must have been the slope leading to Simpson Pass. See ch. 3, n44.

[32]This comment suggests that they had camped somewhere near the southeast corner of the lake and that after leaving the camp, they had traveled along its southern shore.

the road was heavy & sandy, so, of course, we had to do a good deal of walking. Were till late getting to camp at the Deep Wells.[33] What a lonely Sabbath it has been! I wonder what they are doing back home!

SEPTEMBER 12, 1864 Carson River Came twelve miles, are now in camp on the bank of the River, this Valley is very pretty and there are a good many houses here, and some very good timber. This is the loneliest evening I ever spent. Uncle W. has gone off somewhere, to a ranch I reckon, and the Niggers have gone off somewhere fishing,[34] no one here, but Lizzie and I. The leaves are falling, and the winds are sighing like the fall of the year. I felt that "the meloncholy days are come, the saddest of the year." We are three miles from Fort Churchill. Will get to Carson City by Wednesday, if no accidents prevent us from traveling.

SEPTEMBER 13, 1864 Carson River Passed Fort Churchill this morning, saw quite a number of soldiers. It has been so warm to-day. Camped here at a ranch on the river—in sight of Virginia City, it is a romantic looking place, situated on the side of a mountain.[35] We have had a very pleasant time to-night swinging in the "Cottonwood Grove." Some gentlemen here at the ranch went with us, though we did not hear their names.

SEPTEMBER 14, 1864 Carson City This is quite a pretty place, in a Valley, and much larger than I expected. It was so cold this morning, but has been very warm & dusty. I have a school mate here, but cannot find her. We are camped out on a beautiful spot about half miles from town.

---

[33]Logan's "Deep Wells" was probably Desert Wells, at the western base of the Dead Camel Mountains. If so, her party followed Simpson's return trail across these mountains. See ch. 3, n46.

[34]Logan is the only one of our diarists to mention the presence of African Americans on the Central Overland Trail. It appears that Logan was referring to either slaves or servants, and knowing that her relatives were affluent enough to own slaves or to hire servants might explain some of Martha's rather dramatic and self-absorbed comments about her loneliness and the discomforts of the journey.

[35]Logan's comment about being able to see Virginia City from the banks of the Carson River indicates that they had emerged from the narrow canyon through which the river flows after bending to the east. This would have put them at a place that James Simpson called Pleasant Grove. It was also the site of a mail station that was called variously "Miller's," "Reed's," "Ten-Mile," and "Clugagis Station." (See map 9.)

SEPTEMBER 15, 1864 Carson City We have spent a very pleasant day at Mr. Redford's. Also walked around the town a little to see the place. I have got no letters here. We heard from Aunt S. She has got to Sacramento. I wrote to Sister Annie from here. Mrs. Ringo called to see us, and we went home, and stayed all night with her, found them very nicely fixed, and so pleasant.

SEPTEMBER 16, 1864 Carson City Still in the city—will not leave till tomorrow. I have at last found Mollie Bright, my friend and old schoolmate, living here in town. I was really glad to meet anyone from Mo. Especially one that I had gone with at the Old Seminary. Well, now only six more days to travel and then at our place of destination. God! be with me when I get there!

SEPTEMBER 17, 1864 Spooner Station Left Carson this morning, travelled over the Sierra Nevadas for the first time—they are beautiful. I never saw such grand pines in all my life and so many of them. Camped here in such a pretty place near the station on top of the mountain.[36]

---

[36]Spooner's Station was probably established in 1863 near the junction of present-day U.S. Highway 50 and State Route 23. This entry suggests that Logan's party left the Central Overland Trail at Carson City and took the Kings Canyon road going west into the Sierra Nevada.

CHAPTER 22

Mary Ringo

1864

Mary Ringo, with her husband, Martin, and their five children, left their home in Liberty, Missouri, in 1864 and began a trip to California. Mary was thirty-eight years old. The children ranged in age from two to fourteen. On July 30, when they were a few days west of Fort Laramie, Martin Ringo was killed by an accidental gunshot from his own rifle. He was buried by the trail, and Mary and the children finished the journey without him. The Ringo family began their trip to the west on May 18 and arrived in Salt Lake City on September 6.

In 1956, Ringo's descendents transcribed and privately published her diary under the title The Journal of Mrs. Mary Ringo. *The editor obtained a copy from the website of the Library of Congress (http://memory.loc.gov). In 1983, the Arthur H. Clark Company published the diary in* Covered Wagon Women: Diaries and Letters from the Western Trails, 1840–1890, *compiled and edited by Kenneth L. Holmes. In 1989,* Covered Wagon Women *was reprinted by the University of Nebraska Press; in 1999, that press published it again in a Bison Books edition.*

SEPTEMBER 6, 1864 We start early and have reached the great Salt Lake City. I have not been up in the City are camping on the Emigrants Square.[1] Expect I will go up in the morning. I received two letters one from sister Mattie and one from Mr. Halliday and no tongue can tell how sad I feel for each letter was written to my dear husband for they know not that he is dead.

SEPTEMBER 7, 1864 I wait for Major Barron to come down and as he does not I go up to see him and present my letter of introduction, he receives me very politely and promised to assist me in selling out my outfit and procuring me a passage in the coach for California but took good care not to come down. I am at a loss what to do. Mrs. Belt called down awhile this evening to see Mrs. Davise. This City is handsomely laid out, every house has an acre of ground ornamented with trees and flowers but I would not live here if the whole city belonged to me among such a class of community. I haven't seen a handsomely dressed lady since I have been here. Morman communities are poor excuses to me and there are more dirty little children running around begging than a few, we buy some nice peaches but they are 25cts. a dozen. I tell you, you have to pay high for everything you get here.

SEPTEMBER 8, 1864 I sent up for Major Barrow to come down as I did not know what to do, he came down looked at my wagons, oxen and mules and seemed to think they were worth so little that I thought I had better not try to sell them and have hired a Mr. John Donly to drive my oxen and am going to try to go through in my wagons. We leave Salt Lake City about noon and travel some 15 miles and camp near a ranch where they have a large spring but the water is salty and makes us all sick.[2]

SEPTEMBER 9, 1864 We lay over all day.

SEPTEMBER 10, 1864 We hitch up and travel some 12 miles and camp at a village called E.T.[3] here the water is very salty as well as the grass, our mules come very near dying from the effects of it.

---

[1]See ch. 14, n1.

[2]Leaving Salt Lake City, Ringo's party headed west toward the Great Salt Lake. The camp that night was somewhere along the northern base of the Oquirrh Mountains. There were a number of springs in this area, but they are now covered by an immense pile of mine waste. (See map 2.)

[3]See ch. 9, n4.

SEPTEMBER 11, 1864 We leave Mr. Davises family and travel on to a small town, I do not know the name of it[4] and here we get some hay for the stock and buy some nice peaches. We drive out about a mile from town and Mr. Davises family comes on and correll with us.

SEPTEMBER 12, 1864 We drive some 10 miles and camp by some fine springs and our stock has fine grass, we stay here for the rest of the day.[5]

SEPTEMBER 13, 1864 We hitch up and go through a settlement[6] where we buy some excellent Irish potatoes. We drive some 21 miles and my mules give out,[7] we have poor grass and I buy hay and oats for the mules for which I pay $6.00

SEPTEMBER 14, 1864 We travel some 5 miles and camp near a mail station[8] and we have to drive our stock 6 miles to grass, we stay here the rest of the day and I buy some most excellent mutton. Mr. Davises overtake us again.

SEPTEMBER 15, 1864 We go some 10 miles to a station called Look-out, stay here all night.[9]

SEPTEMBER 16, 1864 We travel 12 miles and camp at Government Springs[10] and have excellent grass for our stock.

SEPTEMBER 17, 1864 We lay over here and I wash our dirty clothes, they cut some excellent grass for the stock as we will soon cross the great desert and will need all the feed we can haul for them.

SEPTEMBER 18, 1864 We lay over here as our stock is improving so much.

SEPTEMBER 19, 1864 We leave this place and travel some 10 miles to Indian Springs,[11] here we again lay over for the rest of the day so the stock may all fill up.

---

[4]The city of Tooele. See ch. 9, n6.

[5]This camp was about two or three miles south of the town of Stockton, near some springs on the eastern shore of Rush Lake.

[6]This was probably the town of Saint John, which was about three miles off the main road.

[7]According to the following entry, they were about five miles from the Faust stage station.

[8]This camp was somewhere near the Faust stage station, now the site of a sod farm. See ch. 8, n2. (See map 3.)

[9]The Point Lookout stage station. See ch. 3, n8.

[10]See ch. 12, n5.

[11]See ch. 8, n31.

September 20, 1864 We remain here unto one o'clock and then start for the desert. We travel all this evening and all night and have come some 36 miles and are now resting in the desert.[12]

September 21, 1864 We travel some 10 miles and noon at Fish Springs Station,[13] our Bet mule is a little sick and we fasten our wagon under the ox wagon and go to the next station from here we move up some 2 miles to a fine spring and camp for the night. The grass and water here are quite salty.

September 22, 1864 We hitch up and start again, the stock seem rested and we have traveled some 10 miles and are now nooning[14] but there is not a sprig of grass for our teams. We travel some 24 miles and camp at Willow Springs[15]—good water and grass.

September 23, 1864 We start before day and travel some 30 miles and camp at Deep Creek,[16] this is a narrow stream but very deep, grass good.

September 24, 1864 We remain here until noon and then travel some 6 miles and camp as this is the last good grass we will have for some miles.[17]

September 25, 1864 We start early this morning and travel 28 miles and camp but find very little grass, our mules are very tired as well as the oxen and we camp for the night, it rains very hard and is very windy.[18]

September 26, 1864 We start early and travel 16 miles, we find some good bunch grass and stop and let the stock graze.[19]

September 27, 1864 We travel 16 miles and camp near a station and have good grass, the water here is quite warm.[20]

---

[12]They were near the Black Rock stage station at the northwestern base of the Black Rock Hills.

[13]Upon reaching the Fish Springs area, they stopped for a while near the stage station, then moved north and camped near North Spring or possibly Wilson Spring. See ch. 6, n4.

[14]They were stopped somewhere near Boyd's stage station. (See map 4.)

[15]The Ringos were camped somewhere near present-day Willow Springs ranch. See ch. 7, n9.

[16]See ch. 7, n11.

[17]This camp was about two miles east of the Eight-Mile stage station. See ch. 10, n13.

[18]Although Ringo does not say anything about water in this entry, they were probably camped at Antelope Spring. See ch. 7, n13.

[19]They were now in Spring Valley. Ringo's distance of sixteen miles indicates that they probably followed the stage route around the southern end of the Antelope Mountains. See ch. 8, n10.

[20]They were now at the Schell Creek stage station, which later became the site of Fort Schellbourne and is now occupied by the Schellbourne Ranch.

SEPTEMBER 28, 1864 We travel 25 miles and pass through Egan Canyon, here we saw a good many emigrants stopping here for the winter to try their luck in the mining process, tis thought that these are rich mines. At night when we camp[21] we have a fine camp fire, near us is camped a woman who is confined and gives birth to a son, her name is Richerson.

SEPTEMBER 29, 1864 We travel 27 miles and have a very tiresome drive our mules and cattle both give out and we do not get into camp till almost midnight.[22] I am very tired.

SEPTEMBER 30, 1864 We start as early as we can and go some 10 miles to Ruby Valley,[23] we stop here and rest our stock, we find everything very dear, I buy some coffee at one dollar a pound and give my tin can to pay for it.

OCTOBER 1, 1864 We start early, travel 24 miles and camp at the foot of Diamond Mountain,[24] this is a very high peak, the highest I have seen yet—our mules give out again and we haul our wagon with the oxen, it is a very cold night.

OCTOBER 2, 1864 We hitch up and climb the high hill,[25] we get up safely and then descend to a beautiful valley and remain there the rest of the day and night and have a very windy evening and night.

OCTOBER 3, 1864 We get an early start and have traveled very well but our mules are tired and I am getting so tired traveling. This evening we have a great time climbing to the top of a high hill[26] and are very glad to get to the top, we then camp near a ranch and buy some hay for our oxen—we traveled 24 miles today.

OCTOBER 4, 1864 We traveled 20 miles have no grass and poor water.[27]

---

[21]The camp was a short distance west of the western end of Egan Canyon.

[22]This camp was at Mountain Spring in the Maverick Springs Mountains.

[23]See ch. 6, n8.

[24]They were in Huntington Valley, at the eastern base of the Diamond Mountains.

[25]The "high hill" was Overland Pass in the Diamond Mountains. See ch. 8, n14.

[26]They were at Roberts Creek. Perhaps they climbed the same hill that Simpson did when his expedition camped here on May 22, 1859. Simpson wrote; "This evening, before sundown, I ascended, with Messrs. Jagiello and McCarthy, the high peak to the northeast of our camp, for the purpose of viewing the surrounding country" (Simpson, *Report of Explorations*, 73).

[27]This would have put Ringo's party at the Grubb's Well stage station.

October 5, 1864 We travel 22 miles and have good grass and water—camp in a canyon.[28]

October 6, 1864 We travel 20 miles over a very bad road, had a very bad hill to climb and a worse one to descend.[29] I walk down which brings on a spell of sickness for tonight I am very poorly. We camp in Simpson's Park.

October 7, 1864 We travel 10 miles and reach Austin, Nevada,[30] where I have the pleasure of seeing cousin Charley Peters and my old acquaintance Mr. Ford from Liberty, Mo. They are very kind to me and assist me to dispose of my oxen and wagon.

Thus ends Mary Ringo's diary. After spending a short time in Austin, Mary made arrangements to obtain transportation to California. Most likely, she and her children found passage on the Overland Mail stage.

At the end of the published version of Ringo's diary is a note added by her daughter Mattie. This note tells us that while she was at Austin, Mary gave birth to a stillborn baby. Although Mary had mentioned a few times that she was not feeling well, nothing that she wrote in her diary even hinted that she had been pregnant during her arduous journey.

And while it has nothing to do with the Central Overland Trail, an interesting sidenote is that within a few years, Mary's son Johnny had become a notorious cattle rustler, spending much of his time in Tombstone, Arizona, where in 1882 he died by his own hand.

[28]Dry Creek Canyon. (See map 6.)

[29]Ringo followed the old Pony Express route past Eagle Butte. See ch. 8, n15.

[30]See ch. 12, n21.

CHAPTER 23

H. D. Barton

1865

H. D. Barton left Wright County, Iowa, in April 1865. His diary entries are quite brief, including little more than the weather conditions and where they made camp. Like George Bushnell, Barton left the Central Overland Trail just west of Austin. Unlike Bushnell, Barton never did return to the central trail, staying well to the south and entering California by way of Ebbetts Pass and the Big Tree Road. Barton began his journey on April 30 and reached Salt Lake City on July 20.

A copy of a transcribed version of the Barton diary was obtained from the California State Library, which also granted permission to publish it. A note on the first page indicates that the transcription was copied from the original in 1961. (Courtesy California History Room, California State Library, Sacramento.)

July 20, 1865 Started and traveled into Salt Lake City 12 miles and layed over the rest of the day.

July 21, 1865 Left the city early in the morning traveled all day and camped in sight of the city hot weather stoped by a hot water spring.[1]

[1]This entry indicates that Barton headed south when he left Salt Lake City. The camping spot was probably near the hot springs that are just south of the state prison. (See map 2.)

July 22, 1865 Fine morning traveled along near utah lake crossed the Jordan river traveled 15 miles without water and camped at camp Floyd[2] poor grass 5 miles over

July 23, 1865 Hot morning got a late start on account of having to go so far after our horses among the mountains where we had driven them the night before traveled about 20 miles and camped by a creek[3] good feed for horses had a morman take supper with us I stood guard.

July 24, 1865 Fine morning started in good season traveled 21 miles had verry little water considerable of wind in the afternoon and a little rain camped at government springs[4]

July 25, 1865 Layed by all day to recruit our stock

July 26, 1865 Moved about 12 miles and camped at a spring in the mountains by the side of a desert 45 miles across fine shade tree[5]

July 27, 1865 Layed by and cut grass and made preparations to start across the desert at 3 oclock in the afternoon calculating to cross in the night so we shoved out and traveled all night the road was good the desert is composed of clay and salt when it rains the salt rises to the surface and crystallizes thus in the day when the sun shines it creates an intense heat.

July 28, 1865 We were moving when morning came at 9 oclock we came to fish spring[6] the water here was so salt that we started again at 4 oclock to cross another desert 25 miles across we reached willow springs[7] at one oclock in the night

July 29, 1865 Hot morning we layed by all day got three

[1]This entry indicates that Barton headed south when he left Salt Lake City. The camping spot was probably near the hot springs that are just south of the state prison. (See map 2.)

[2]Barton was the last of our diarists to take the old route through Camp Floyd. The camp had now been closed for four years, and most emigrants were taking the Tooele Valley route. The Overland Stage would still use the Camp Floyd route for another year; then it too would go through Tooele. See ch. 2, n6.

[3]This campsite was in Rush Valley on Faust Creek, not far from the Faust stage station. See ch. 8, n2.

[4]See ch. 12, n5.

[5]Although the actual distance is only seven and a half miles from what the editor believes to be the site of Government Spring, Barton was now at Indian Spring. See ch. 8, n31.

[6]See ch. 6, n4.

[7]See ch. 7, n9.

horses in the evening I wrote four letters other emigrants came up this after noon

JULY 30, 1865 Started early traveled 25 miles got into the state of Nevada camped at deep end[8] our horses stoped behind in the mountains hot day

JULY 31, 1865 Layed by all day to recruit teams good morning Indians around beging

AUGUST 1, 1865 Traveled 8 miles and layed by the rest of the day and cut grass to and prepare to cross a desert and mountain[9]

AUGUST 2, 1865 Started at 10 oclock traveled 25 miles and came to antelope springs[10] hot weather road dusty no grass except what we brought along the previous night was so cold that ice was formed over ¼ inch thick

AUGUST 3, 1865 Traveled 16 miles over mountains road rough weather cloudy we come to spring valley good grass and water some more holes that were swampy so we pulled up and moved ahead 6 miles farther to some springs in the mountains poor grass[11]

AUGUST 4, 1865 Had some trouble finding horses rough road forenoon afternoon crossed a little desert road verry dusty traveled about 27 miles came to Egans Kanyon fine water poor grass here some silver mines have been discovered two quartz mills are being erected and one that is running it is said to produce $1000 a day went to see an Indian pow wow at night

AUGUST 5, 1865 Started about 8 oclock traveled 17 miles came to a spring[12] in the mts took our horses 2 miles to grass found canteen

AUGUST 6, 1865 Layed by I wrote some letters fine day rather windy folks traveling with us went on we started at 5 oclock PM traveled 15 miles stoped at 11 oclock at night left the old horse in the night

---

[8]This was Deep Creek, not "deep end," and Barton was mistaken about being in Nevada. See ch. 7, n11. (See map 4.)

[9]Barton was probably near the Eight-Mile stage station. See ch. 10, n13.

[10]The actual distance from Eight-Mile Station to Antelope Spring is closer to twenty miles. See ch. 7, n13.

[11]Because he mentioned traveling over the mountains, it appears that Barton took the Rock Springs Pass route. The camp was probably near Schellbourne Spring. See ch. 8, n10.

[12]Pony Spring. See ch. 8, n12.

August 7, 1865 I got up my team and started the other teams staid to hunt the old horse I moved along 10 miles to some springs[13] where the other emigrants were camped and stoped to wait till the other teams came up they came up late I took dinner with Harberts rhuby valley[14]

August 8, 1865 The rest of the train moved on but we remained more emigrants came in the old horse was brought up Hallegan came up

August 9, 1865 Just changed camp ground and remained all day hot weather

August 10, 1865 Hallegans horses were so sick that he could not move so we had to leave him we traveled 22 miles and camped at diamond springs[15] here we fell in with the emigrants I spoke of as traveling with before we came to Ft Kearney

August 11, 1865 Started earley crossed diamond mountain[16] came to some springs of warm water[17] here we stoped for noon having made about 7 miles we then started and came to mountain well making about 25 miles more road rough weather hot

August 12, 1865 Traveled about 18 miles and came to Grubs wells in a small desert road level and verry dusty weather hot crossed Roberts creek[18] took dinner at a pond spring 4 mile east of here the water is quite bad

August 13, 1865 Traveled about 20 miles weather hot no water along the road I was quite sick awhile from the effects of the water we camped at dry creek good water and grass took a passenger for Austin.[19]

---

[13]This was Mountain Spring in the Maverick Springs Mountains.

[14]See ch. 6, n8.

[15]The actual distance from Station Spring to Diamond Springs is closer to 24 miles. The road would have taken Barton across the Overland Pass that is located at the southern tip of the Ruby Mountains and then across the Overland Pass that is found on the ridge of the Diamond Mountains. See ch. 8, n14.

[16]The word "mountain" was probably a transcription error. Barton had already crossed the Diamond Mountains and would now be crossing Diamond Valley.

[17]This was Sulphur Spring. See ch. 10, n23.

[18]Barton was a little confused about the sequence of events. He had crossed Roberts Creek before coming to Grubb's Well.

[19]This camp would have been near the Dry Creek stage station. (See map 6.)

August 14, 1865 Here we left the stage road and took a cut off had some hard hills to descend rough road all day[20] water plenty weather hot traveled about 18 miles and camped at a spring just west of Simpsons Park poor grass

August 15, 1865 Started quite early traveled 5 miles came to the town of Austin[21] this is a place where some silver mines have been discovered and some mills have been built there is about a dozen mills here was the first Chinees I ever saw James stoped here to get work after buying a few things we Started and traveled about 12 miles farther and camped on Rees river[22] got grass of some ranchers

August 16, 1865 This morning we sold the old black horse for five dollar weather rather cloudy and some rain Traveled up the river about 18 miles this river heads in the mountains and sinks in a desert camped at five oclock good grass[23]

From here, Barton and his party turned to the west, made their way to Walker Lake, and then over the Sierra Nevada by way of the Big Tree Road and Ebbetts Pass, reaching the town of Columbia, California, on September 6, 1865.

[20]Barton followed the Pony Express route past Eagle Butte. See ch. 8, n15.

[21]See ch. 12, n21.

[22]See ch. 3, n38.

[23]Sometime during this day's travel, Barton left the Central Overland Trail for good. Making his way to Walker Lake, he turned to the south and crossed the Sierra Nevada by way of Ebbetts Pass.

CHAPTER 24

Dennis and James Colwell

1865

In May 1865, Dennis Hand Colwell and James McNabb Colwell left Harrison County, Missouri, and began a journey to California. These two brothers left two different records of their journey. Throughout the trip, James maintained a detailed diary, never missing a day. Although the heading on the second document indicates that it is the diary of both Dennis and James, a number of entries seem to indicate that it was written by a single individual; since the other diary was written by James, the logical conclusion is that this one must have been written by Dennis. Since James's diary is somewhat more complete, the editor has included the entire portion written while he traveled between Salt Lake City and Carson City. Rather than include all of Dennis's diary, the editor has inserted selected entries that seemed interesting and appropriate. These entries are preceded by the name "Dennis" and follow James's entry for the day. The Colwells began their journey on May 15 and reached Salt Lake City on August 25.

James Colwell's day-by-day diary has been transcribed and copied but, as far as can be determined, has never been published. The editor obtained a copy of James's diary from Alene M. Thille. Dennis Colwell's diary was published in the newsletter of the Columbia Gorge Genealogical Society in two installments in 2005. Alene Thille, who is a direct descendant of James Colwell, granted permission to publish both documents.

AUGUST 25, 1865 It is twelve miles from Mountain Dale to the Great Salt Lake City. We came by way of camp Douglas. Got to the camp at eleven o' clock. Laid by till evening. Went to the . . . and drew rations. Camped here tonight. Ten miles today.

DENNIS: We only halt long enough to see the head and neck of this wonderful city, but we drive out of the city this afternoon and camp close to the Lake, the odor of which (to us) is very disagreeable, as it smells like all the old meat barrels in America had been brought to camp and turned over.

AUGUST 26, 1865 Three miles from Camp Douglas to the city, two miles through the City and fifteen miles to the mountain west. We came to the City this morning and were detained till after noon. We then drove out to the point of the mountain. Twenty miles today.

AUGUST 27, 1865 It is twenty miles from the mountain point to Twilla City,[1] three from this city to the beaches. We visited the Salt Works this morning and traded a horse for a mare then drove to the beaches and stopped. Twenty three miles today.

DENNIS: As we came near Twilla City (a Morman town 35 miles from Salt Lake) we meet Mr. Brigham Young in company of about 20 carriages. Brigham has his escort of soldiers and we think it becomes a White man to give the road to so great a man. Brigham's fine Chariot comes along and we feel almost like springing to save the poor man's life as he bows so politely and so low to us that we think he certainly will fall from his Chariot but he recovers and we meet his followers who are all trained to be polite to Gentiles as they meet them, but a few minutes and the sight of Brigham and his followers is gone.

AUGUST, 28, 1865 [9] miles from Twilla to Stockton. We drove to Stockton before breakfast, and traded our wagon for a lighter one. Left Stockton at one o'clock and drove out fifteen miles and camped. Good grass and water. Twenty one miles today.

[1]See ch. 9, n6.

AUGUST 29, 1865 It is twenty miles from Stockton to Forter's [Faust] Station, eleven from Forter's to Point Lookout. Point Lookout is at the head of Rush Valley.[2] Good Grass here. Sixteen miles today.

AUGUST 30, 1865 From Point Lookout to Government Springs is fifteen miles and from the spring to Indian Springs is ten miles. We drove six miles and left the Telegraph Road. Took the left hand drove to Government Springs to dinner, concluded to camp here. Good grass and water. Fifteen miles today.

AUGUST 31, 1865 We only drove about three miles this morning and found excellent grass, water and wood. Turned out and prepared . . . to cross the desert. Three miles today.

SEPTEMBER 1, 1865 It is seven miles from Government Springs to Indian Springs[3] and ten miles from Indian Springs to River Bed Station and twelve from that to Dugway Station and eighteen on to Blackrock and eighteen from that to Fish Springs. We started on the Great American Desert at two P.M. and drove to Dugway Station and turned out. Twenty six miles today.

DENNIS: These springs [Indian Spring] are on the edge of the great American desert. We often heard of the hardship and suffering of both men and stock in the crossing of this desert. It is but 75 miles without water or grass. We find good grass in great abundance at these Springs. We turn our animals on grass, go to work and (with a caseknife apiece) cut 7 large bundles of green grass, and then take some short green grass, chop it up and mix it with some shorts and wet it completely. We then fill our vessels with water about 11 gallons. The weather as providence will have it is very cool.

SEPTEMBER 2, 1865 We started on this A.M. and drove to Black Rock station for dinner. Drove to the springs and unhitched two miles from the station.[4] Twenty eight miles today. Grass and water poor.

SEPTEMBER 3, 1865 From Fish Springs Station to (Boyd's station, fifteen) Willow Springs Station it is twenty five miles. We started on this morning. We reached Willow Springs Station after dark.[5] Plenty grass and water here. Twenty seven miles today.

---

[2]See ch. 3, n8.

[3]See ch. 8, n31. (See map 3.)

[4]They were at Fish Springs. See ch. 6, n4.

[5]See ch. 7, n9.

DENNIS: We have crossed the desert known by all who have crossed it [as] the Great American Desert. We rest here a couple days (as it is quite customary with all emigrants and freighters) through we and our little train have fared quite sumptuously to what others have in crossing the same dreaded road.

SEPTEMBER 4, 1865 We layover today resting our horses at Willow Springs.

SEPTEMBER 5, 1865 We still laid over today preparing feeds, shoeing etc.

SEPTEMBER 6, 1865 It is fourteen miles from Willow Springs to Cannion Station and fifteen from that to Deep Creek Station. We drove eleven miles past Cannion and struck Deep Creek and camped.[6] Twenty five miles today.

SEPTEMBER 7, 1865 We drove two miles this morning and turned out. Only two miles today.

SEPTEMBER 8, 1865 We came past Deep Creek to Eight Mile Station and stopped. It snowed nearly all day. Very disagreeable. Grass and water. Eleven miles today.

DENNIS: We drive to 8 mile station today. Today it snowed very hard. am barefooted, common shoes are $5.00 per pair, too much for me. Snow will be off soon.

SEPTEMBER 9, 1865 It is twenty two miles from Eight Mile Station to Antelope. We came to the latter today. No grass, planty water. Twenty two miles today.

SEPTEMBER 10, 1865 From Antelope to Spring Valley it is sixteen miles. We came to the latter today. Good grass and water. Plenty wood. Sixteen miles today.

SEPTEMBER 11, 1865 From Spring Valley to Shell Creek it is fourteen miles. We came to the latter today and shod our horses hind feet and camped. Fourteen miles today. Water and grass.

SEPTEMBER 12, 1865 It is eighteen miles from Shell Creek to Egan Canyon. We came to the latter today and camped. Crossed the Utah and Nevada line today and came into Lander County, Nevada. Plenty water here. Grass in the hills either north or south.

SEPTEMBER 13, 1865 It is thirty miles from Egan to Mountain

[6] See ch. 7, n11.

Spring (via Buttes). We left the stage road but followed the Telegraph eight miles from Egan. We came to the springs in the Mountain eight miles from where the roads fork. Plenty good water. Good grass one half miles west the spring on side mountains. Sixteen miles today.

September 14, 1865 It is ten miles from Mountain Springs to Fort Ruby.[7] We only drove out about two miles this evening. Good grass on side hills. We brought water from the station. Plenty good wood. Sixteen miles today.

Dennis: After leaving Egan we come along by way of Mountain Springs to Fort Ruby having a very rough road. The Military refuse to let us come via Gravey [Gravelly] ford but we must continue on Stage coach [road].[8]

September 15, 1865 From Ruby to Jacob's Well fourteen miles. We came to latter today. Plenty water. Grass in the mountains northwest. Twenty two miles today.

September 16, 1865 From Jacob's Wells to Diamond Spring twelve miles. Grass on bottom. We left the Wells this morning and struck Diamond Mountain five miles from spring. A good spring at foot of mountain. Two miles to top of mountain.[9] The worst hill from Mo. [Missouri] to the Sierra Nevada Mountains. Twelve miles from Diamond Springs to Sulphur Springs. We came six miles past Diamond. Good road. Camped on a little [spring] branch. Short grass. Eighteen miles today.

Dennis: [referring to Overland Pass] a most dangerous Mount to climb . . . water plenty, rest our animals. Our women (with their little ones) get out and walk. We start and without trouble we reach the top of this mountain. We now go back and assist our wifes and children in reaching to Summit and we rest and start down. We have 3 miles steep hill to go down but by locking all the wheels we make it without any particular damage. We reach camp tonight and all feel glad to retire.

---

[7]While most of our diarists made camp near Station Spring, the Colwells continued on until they reached Fort Ruby. See ch. 6, n8.

[8]It appears that the Colwell brothers were planning to leave the Central Overland Trail when they reached Huntington Valley to follow the old Chorpenning mail route to the Humboldt River at Gravelly Ford. The unanswered question is, why did the army refuse to let them do so? It might be safe to assume that it had something to do with Indian troubles.

[9]Overland Pass in the Diamond Mountains. See ch. 8, n14.

September 17, 1865 Twelve miles from Sulphur Springs to Mountain Wells. Rough road. (Mountain Wells Ranch). We drove to the latter and turned out. Grass on hills if not at ranch, one and one half miles north. Good water. Eighteen miles today.

September 18, 1865 Four miles from Mountain Wells to Roberts Creek. We had to layover today because of our horses being gone and we not able to find them.

September 19, 1865 Our horses came up last night. It is fourteen miles from Roberts Creek to Grubb Wells. (No grass at wells Water). Nineteen miles from the Wells to Dry Creek. We came to Dry Creek today. Feed on hills one mile up creek. Thirty nine miles today.

September 20, 1865 It is eleven miles from here to Cape Horn. From Cape Horn to Simpsons Park is ten miles. (Stage Road) No feed, No water. But here is a cut-off across mountain. Sixteen miles across to Simpsons Park. Good grass and water on this road. Very rough road. We took the cut-off this morning, drove two miles for breakfast at springs. We concluded to stop here today to wash and rest our team. Two miles today.

September 21, 1865 We came on this morning and found this cut-off to be very rough and too bad for a team.[10] We got across to Simpsons Park and stopped. No grass, water plenty. Fourteen miles today.

Dennis: We are quite much rejoiced to see those Parks as we are near to Austin and we feel as though we need rest and refreshment. Find the Keeper of these Parks to be very kind and generous we feel ourself at home. They invite us in to enjoy each others society. We cook and eat in their rooms and make a sojourn of 10 days, having a very pleasant time.

September 22, 1865 We layover today.

September 23, 1865 We still lay over today.

September 24, 1865 We are still at Simpsons Park

September 25, 1865 Still we lay at Simpsons Park.

September 26, 1865 We still remain at the park.

September 27, 1865 Still we layover another day.

---

[10]It seems quite clear that the Colwells took the Eagle Butte route. See ch. 8, n15. (See map 6.)

SEPTEMBER 28, 1865 Yet at the Park. Very pleasant weather. Cool nights.

SEPTEMBER 29, 1865 We still remain in camp at Simpsons park

SEPTEMBER 30, 1865 Waiting today yet at the Park.

OCTOBER 1, 1865 It is seven miles from the Park to Austin.[11] We start on this morning. Eight miles from Austin to Jacobsville (Reese River).[12] We drove to the latter today and unhitched. Fifteen miles.

DENNIS: Seeing the advancement of the season we think it good policy to be making some headway to the coast. We bid adieu to our newly made friends and come along, we reach Austin, at 11 o'clock. Here we make a halt of an hour. Austin, we find is quite a flourishing mining town situated on Reese Creek, Nevada.

OCTOBER 2, 1865 We laid over and wasted all day today.

OCTOBER 3, 1865 Had quite a rain last night. Our horses being gone we had to layover today. Grass and water here.

OCTOBER 4, 1865 Horses not found. We got the horses and started at 10 A.M. and drove two miles and crossed Rose River at Railroad Station then twenty to Smith Creek Ranch[13] and stopped. Pasture here and plenty water. Twenty two miles today.

OCTOBER 5, 1865 From Smith Creek Ranch to the Junction House is twenty four miles. We go ahead this morning. Struck Smith Creek about five miles from camp. Followed the same some miles. Good grass water all up creek. Crossed the summit and camped at Lowes Ranch. Seventeen miles today.

OCTOBER 6, 1865 Seven miles from Lowes to the Junction House and eighteen miles from that to East Gate[14] thence to Middle Gate.[15] Eleven from Middle Gate to West Gate. (White Rock) We got to White Rock today. Plenty water. Twenty two miles today.

OCTOBER 7, 1865 We drove to West Gate and turned out on account of the desert ahead. Seven miles today.

OCTOBER 8, 1865 It is twenty two miles across the desert to Sand

---

[11]See ch. 12, n21.

[12]The Reese River is actually five miles from Austin. See ch. 3, n38.

[13]Smith Creek Ranch was near the mouth of Smith Creek Canyon at the eastern base of the Desatoya Mountains. (See map 7.)

[14]See ch. 16, n38.

[15]See ch. 3, n42.

Springs.[16] We start on this morning. Made across the desert through sand and dust. Met a train of camels today.[17] Twenty two miles today.

DENNIS: We stop for dinner turn our wagons from the wind and while eating we look at a time of a little cessation of dust and sand, and behold a train of 20 camels coming. Quite new to us as they come along with their noses pointing upward.

OCTOBER 9, 1865 From Sand Springs to Carson Sink six and one half miles. (To Salt wells twelve miles.) We roll on today. Took dinner at Salt Wells then drove to the sloughs on Sink of Carson River.[18] Eighteen miles today.

OCTOBER10, 1865 From Sink of Carson to Ragtown eighteen miles. We only got to Willow Ranch and stopped.[19]

OCTOBER 11, 1865 We drove to Cottonwood Station today. Only eleven miles today.

OCTOBER 12, 1865 We came to Old Log Cabin[20] and I and Carrie took passage on a freight wagon and drove to Newman Station. Thirty miles today.

OCTOBER 13, 1865 We came to Carson City today via Dayton. Twenty five miles today.

OCTOBER 14, 1865 We are waiting for the train to overtake us. Remain here tonight.

OCTOBER 15, 1865 We are still waiting for the wagon to come.

OCTOBER 16, 1865 And still we wait for the train to come.

OCTOBER 17, 1865 We left Carson City this morning and drove past Mile station to Waggoner Valley Mill and stopped. Washoe County, Nev. Eight miles today.

DENNIS: we leave Carson City this morning and come out to Washoe Valley[21] and stop to rest our team and while the ponies rest we help on Mr. Miller in digging potatoes at $2.00 a day.

---

[16]See ch. 3, n43.

[17]Five other diaries mentioned seeing camels in the desert. See ch. 14, n21.

[18]It appears that the Colwell brothers followed Simpson's outbound trail to the north end of Carson Lake. See ch. 3, n44.

[19]The Colwells were now on the banks of the Carson River, a few miles west of Fallon. See ch. 3, n46. (See map 8.)

[20]The location of Log Cabin is unknown to the editor, but William Pennebaker and Mary Jatta also mentioned it.

[21]The Colwells left the Central Overland Trail and headed north, eventually reaching Susanville, California, where they settled for a time.

CHAPTER 25

Elizabeth Duncan

1867

Elizabeth "Bettie" Duncan; her husband, Wesley; and their children, William, Katie, and Lucetta, left Lawrence, Kansas, in June 1867 and joined a small group of emigrants bound for California. The diary that Elizabeth kept during her journey is not the most eloquent in this collection, but it is certainly the most poignant as she records her thoughts during the sickness and death of her daughter Katie. The Duncans began their trip rather late in the year, not leaving their home until June 24. They arrived in Salt Lake City on September 2.

The editor obtained a copy of a portion of Duncan's handwritten diary from the Kenneth Spencer Research Library at the University of Kansas, which also granted permission to publish it. Her handwriting is very difficult to read, and many of the words and phrases in this transcription are guesswork (Kansas Collection, Spencer Research Library, University of Kansas).

September 2, 1867 We left camp this morning at 6 we came several miles down the mountain in the kanyon and then entered the great City of Salt lake came 7 miles more and then reached the city O how glad when we drove in camp in the emigrants corell[1] Got some nice fruit and vegatables for dinner . . . then once we thought and talked of loved ones at home yes and we got 8 letters from our dear friends I am very tired to night

SEPTEMBER 3, 1867 We had rather late breakfast as we did not have to travel to day but as soon as we got breakfast over the children and our selves dressed Mrs Mcgrew the children and my self went out in town we went as far as we could seen many nice stores and nice fruit stands and very many beautiful residences and so many fruit trees loaded down with fruit how nice this seems we bought some splendid peaches and a nice melon and returned home rested a while and went out again Mrs Berry went with us this time we done some shopping and seen all we could and returned home and found our men had a good dinner or supper which ever it might be called most ready we were very thankful all of us partook of it very heartily I have been trying to write some letters home but find it hard work amongst so much noise and confusion I wold love to be home with my friends to night

SEPTEMBER 4, 1867 I can hardly compose my mind enough to write to night I have seen so many things that I hardly know which to speak of first Well soon after breakfast Mrs Berry Mrs Mcgrew Willie the children and my self all started out to see as much of the wonderful city as we could in the first place we went to the great Tabernacle and temple that is being built This is a beautiful sight all enclosed in a very high cement wall Mrs Mcgrew and my self went upon the very top by assending twelve very long flights of stairs when upon the top we could see all over the city What a pretty city with its pretty houses green trees and running brooks all over the city When we came down we then went to Brigham Youngs residence this is not far from the temple is also enclosed by a high stone wall with plenty of fruit trees and many curious things that us Gentiles could not understand I am very tired to night and can not write much more

SEPTEMBER 5, 1867 This morning we had breakfast early then Mr Duncan took all the things out of our small waggon and Mrs Berry

[1]Emigrant Square. See ch. 14, n1.

Mrs Mcgrew and children my self all went up to the hot springs[2] which is 2 miles from the city this is truly one of the wonders of the world this spring runs out of a crack or crevice in the rock and is boiling hot and is a little salt and considerable sulfer and is the clearest water I ever saw We stayed there some time and then came one mile and a half farther toward town and there is sulfer warm springs here is a house fitted up for bathing purposes here we all stoped went in and got bath rooms for bathing the water is just too warm I think to feel comfortable but all the others like it fine after bathing we came on into town and then got dinner and began to prepare to leave the great city about 2 we drove into town and got some fruit and other . . . and to take along our journey and then left the city drove out 8 miles and are in camp at rather a pretty place where there looked to be good grass but we soon found that it was so salt that the stock wold not eat it one of the little girls went out and diped up a cup full of salt with a spoon surely this is a strange country strange in many ways O how mysterious are the ways of providence as how little we studdy the greatness of his works

SEPTEMBER 6, 1867 As there was no grass for our stock we left camp this morning at day break traveled 8 miles came to a splendid spring good grass where we stoped got breakfast and rested a while then drove on about 11 O clock we came to great Salt Lake here we stoped to look at the lake and went in bathing this lake is said to be the saltiest water on the globe any way it is very salt so much so that a . . . will not sink as it will first float to shore and can not . . . with out great difficulty how strange and beautiful is this great lake how much I have wished to day for some of my loved friends here to enjoy some of this beautiful country but they are . . . we are in camp in a beautiful place 5 miles from a small village called Towillow[3] it lays in . . . and is a pretty looking place we will go through it tomorrow

SEPTEMBER 7, 1867 This morning we were on the move again about the same old time and drove up to Towillow and . . . This is a lovely little place I never seen fruit trees so full of fruit in all my life

[2]See ch. 3, n1.

[3]The town of Tooele. See ch. 9, n6. (See map 2.)

but to our great disappointment none of it was ripe so it done us little good only the sight of it we got some nice potatoes and beef and drove on in 7 miles we came to a little mining town called Stockton this is said to be the only gentile town in the territory it is mostly deserted as the silver mines did not prove to be very good We came 2 miles on and stoped on Stockton lake where there is plenty of good grass and a pretty place and good spring water we are going to remain here over Sabbath I am almost sick to night feel very like nothing or doing any thing else O for grace and faith in every trial.

September 8, 1867 To day has been long and lonely I have thought much of home and friends have written some letters back to dear ones We have been in camp all day trying to keep sabbath the best I could but find it pretty hard where there is no church to go to for sabbath class to meet and so little to clear ones mind out for good O for faith courage and grace and O for a more peaceful heart and more faith in God

September 9, 1867 Again this morning we were on the move at an early hour but on every turn there was so little of interest . . . place that it seems hardly worth noting any thing down we have traveled over a very barren country all day but found a pretty green little place to camp on to night[4] I am sick to night feel very little like writing

September 10, 1867 This morning there was a white frost found it very cold getting breakfast We have traveled 23 miles to day over rough road and had to noon without water only some we had in our keg our mules seem very tired to night we are in camp on the prettyest little brook I most ever seen there is a little stream[5] gurgling past our wagons while I write I hear it murmer I am almost sick to night also the little ones

September 11, 1867 This morning we left camp at 7 traveled 9 miles through the mountains and kanyon then come to a pretty spring[6] where there is plenty of wood and grass We are going to stay here until tomorrow at 4 O clock and then start over the Desert how

[4]The Duncans were probably camped near the Point Lookout stage station. See ch. 3, n8. (See map 3.)

[5]The little stream was Government Creek. See ch. 12, n5.

[6]This was Indian Spring. See ch. 8, n31.

much I do dread it as our darling little Cettie [Lucetta] is sick she has not been well for several days and is much worse this evening O how glad I wold be to have her home where I could have the Dr and me take good care of her I try to trust in god and pray earnestly that he may help in this our hour of need

September 12, 1867 I was busy this forenoon in cooking and preparing for crossing the desert my little Cettie was able to be up some but about noon was taken much worse now it is 3 o clock in one hour we expect to start for going over the desert we will travel all night and noon or after tomorrow O how I hate to start with my little lamb so sick but all say it will not hurt her and I must yield as I always have to do O that the Lord will guard and protect my little one and soon make her well

September 13, 1867 We are again permitted to see the light and darkness of another day and night we are now in camp at Fish springs[7] we got here at 2 this afternoon having traveled 45 miles in 16 hours and got over all safe and well save my darling little Cettie she is very sick has the Flux the worst kind O how I have made every effort possible for to help her and how earnestly I have tried to pray to god for assistence in this my greatest time of need

September 14, 1867 I write to night while I sit by my sick darling O how sad my poor heart is how little I care for any thing save my sick little one she gets no better I have done all in my power now I must leave all in the hands of the lord surely he will hear my prayer and save her We have traveled 25 miles over the most barren country I ever seen and are now in camp at Willow spring[8] we hope to reach settlements tomorrow

September 15, 1867 We have traveled 30 miles and are in camp at deep creek station[9] my dear little Lucetta is not better yet I wold give every thing if I was home where I could have the Dr and take good care of her O how much grace and faith I kneed it is very cold to night and how much I feel the kneed of home and home comforts

---

[7]See ch. 6, n4.
[8]See ch. 7, n9.
[9]See ch. 7, n11.

Sᴇᴘᴛᴇᴍʙᴇʀ 16, 1867 We have been in camp all day trying to get our little girl better but no help comes yet Willie is very sick also it is very cold and has been snowing some to day the mountains were covered white last night with snow and it has been snowing some most all day in the valley I never have felt so homesick since we left home as to night O for a renewal of my patience and O for more grace and wisdom in this my time of kneed

Sᴇᴘᴛᴇᴍʙᴇʀ 17, 1867 We left Deep creek at 2 O clock this afternoon drove out 8 miles and camped near a stage station[10] I know not the name it is very cold at night and I am sitting up with my sick children in the tent Willie Katie and little Cettie are all very sick Mr Thorp is complaining I fear we will all be sick yet O how hard to have all these trials

Sᴇᴘᴛᴇᴍʙᴇʀ 18, 1867 I write with a heart full of anxiety and a body almost worn out with fatigue This morning about 4 O clock Mr Duncan was taken with the pluresy very bad and has been very bad all day Mr Thorp is also sick Katie and the little ones are very bad no one to do any thing but George and my self We have traveled 24 miles to day we camped near a station last night called antelope[11]

Sᴇᴘᴛᴇᴍʙᴇʀ 19, 1867 We have traveled 23 miles to day I hardly know over what kind of country or any thing else my mind has all been taken up with my sick ones Willie is very bad also little Katie Mr Thorp and Mr D are some better my little Cettie we hope is better but is very sick yet I my self am almost worn out

Sᴇᴘᴛᴇᴍʙᴇʀ 20, 1867 We have traveled I think 26 miles and now in camp in Egans Kanyon there is some settlement here and a quartz mill well here it is running and pays pretty well I believe but I take little interest in these things I think to much of my sick children Willie and Katie are very bad little Cettie is some little better we are going to remain here until the children are all better

Sᴇᴘᴛᴇᴍʙᴇʀ 28, 1867 I have not written in my book for 8 days O how full of care anxiety and sorrow has this time been When I wrote last we were in Egans Kanyon we remained there until Monday

[10]Eight-Mile station. See ch. 10, n13. (See map 4.)
[11]Antelope Spring. See ch. 7, n13.

[23rd] morning then we traveled again Willie and Cettie were much better we hoped our dear little Katie was better too but we were mistaken we traveled 30 miles on Monday camped at Mountain springs[12] Tuesday [24th] we traveled 26 miles and camped at a station called Jacobs well[13] Wednesday [25th] morning our darling little Katie was much worse but as our camping place was so poor we descended 12 miles to dimond springs station[14] here we camped at the foot of the mountain put up our tent took our dear little Katie and made her comfortable as possible but her little spirit was not long for this world at 8 O clock in the evening she breathed her last and O the agony of our hearts none can tell so none can ever know how we felt O how desolate we felt when we sat in the tent with our little angel and herd the pattering of rain and the wind told how the storm was raging without but not as it was in our hearts O that god may give us grace to bear this the greatest trial of our lives on Thursday [26th] morning Mr Mcgrew and Berry went up on the mountain side and found a place where there was 2 other little graves and there they dug her little grave Mr Berry and the Frenchman there made a little pine coffin Mrs Mcgrew and Mrs Berry dressed her nice and pretty and at 12 O clock on Thursday we all assembled in and near the tent to listen to Mr Mcgrew read a chapter and offer a prayer O how our hearts bled within us my heart is now to full to write they tell me that it is Gods tender mercy that took my lamb my idol away but I can but feel that it is to hard why did he take her here away from home and loved ones there Friday [27th] morning as Mr Duncan and me went to her little grave and there nelt I think if hearts could ever busted with grief ours surely wold O that god will give us some help in this our time of need O for faith and prayer I now feel that what little hope I had of being contented in our new home is all gone O for grace and faith and prayer

---

[12]Located near the summit of the Maverick Springs Mountains.

[13]The Jacobs Well station was on Connors Creek in Huntington Valley. It is somewhat surprising that Duncan passed through Ruby Valley without mentioning the settlement that had been thriving there for several years.

[14]This day's travel would have taken the Duncans across the Overland Pass in the Diamond Mountains, the steepest and probably the most difficult section of the Central Overland Trail. See ch. 8, n14.

October 1, 1867 Again find my self trying to write O how hard for me to try to write but I will try Yesterday we passed through Austin[15] this is a much larger place than I expected to see there is splendid silver mines ten or 12 quartz mills there some fine business houses we saw some fine California fruit but how little interest I took in any thing all my thoughts are for my darling Katie we are in camp 30 miles west of Austin[16] O how sad my poor heart is

October 2, 1867 Another night finds me trying to write this to me has been a long long day one week ago this evening our darling little Katie . . . how long and sad the week has been to day it has seemed more than ever that it could not be possible that our darling has gone O how can it be that I have no Katie O for grace to sustain me in this my darkest hour we are in camp in a beautiful Kanyon[17] we have not traveled any since noon we are trying to rest and improve our stock some

October 3, 1867 All is quiet in camp and I will try again to write We came about 10 miles this morning then camped near the most splendid kanyon[18] I have yet seen and have not traveled only half the day to day we expect to make a big drive to morrow to Sand springs while in this beautiful place how much I have thought of my loved one we laid in the grave one week ago to day how the dear little angle loved the great rocks and hills so much O for grace and faith and prayer

October 4, 1867 We left camp at 6 this morning passed through middle and west gate this kanyon that these passes or gates are in is the most beautiful one we passed through yet we have not traveled only 15 miles to day are again on the stage road are in camp at a ranch and stage station[19] there are some indians in camp at this place poor miserable degraded looking

---

[15]Although it is not certain, they probably took the stage road through Blackbird Canyon and across Austin Summit. (See map 6.)

[16]Although the new Mount Airy route was being used by some emigrants in 1867, the Duncans followed the older Smith Creek route and were camped near the mouth of Smith Creek Canyon.

[17]They were camped somewhere in Edwards Creek Canyon. See ch. 3, n40.

[18]This camp was in the Cold Springs area or possibly near the mouth of the canyon at Eastgate.

[19]It appears that they camped just west of Westgate, but the nearest station was back at Middlegate, about four miles away. See ch. 3, n42.

October 5, 1867 This morning we left west gate at 7 O clock traveled 12 miles and nooned near Fair view ranch this is the most desolate looking country I have ever passed through this is called the desert and truly it has the right name[20] we after dinner came 10 miles more to Sand springs[21] there is a ranch here and the most barren country I ever seen we are now [with]in 18 miles of the sink of the Carson river but how little interest I have my time and mind is all taken up with thoughts of my dear Katie

October 6, 1867 To day has been a peculiar Sabbath to me this morning about 8 O clock it commenced to rain the rain being very cold the folks at the ranch sent up for us to come down to the house Mrs Berry Mrs Mcgrew little Cettie and my self all went down we found them to be very pleasant people especially the lady a Mrs Philips we stayed for dinner they had a splendid dinner fruits and vegetables all brought from California to day 15 weeks ago is the last meal I have eat at table until to day how long these weeks have been and O how full of trial and labor hardships and sorrow have they been but if my darling could have been spared us I would have been willing to have born any thing that came but O how hard to leave my idol my treasure away in this dreary and lonely land but I know her spirit is in life in heaven freed from all the hardships and sorrow that I have to undergo but still I sigh for my dear Katie O my dear angel Katie only O why did you have to leave your mother This morning Mr Thorp and Charlie Babcock left us they thought from what they could hear that wages were better at Virginia city Nevada than in California so they left for their this morning it being 90 miles to that place we cooked them enough to do them there and they got a good way to go in a large waggon we feel lonely without them how small our family seems now our little Katie O how we miss her.

October 7, 1867 Again this morning we were on the move 15 weeks ago this morning we left home O how long and weary and full of sorrow has some of these weeks been we left Sand springs this morning and have traveled 22 miles over a miserable road over the

[20]They were crossing Fairview Valley. See ch. 9, n35.

[21]See ch. 3, n43.

alkali flats and some sand   the flats were very muddy on account of the heavy rains   we are now in camp at the sink of Carson river[22]   there is quite a large lake here and it is a pretty place   O how cheerful I think I could feel if I had my darling Katie

OCTOBER 8, 1867   We were up in good time this morning   our men soon found that our mules were gone   Mr Duncan and George started for them and after walking 9 or 10 miles found them   this made us late in getting started   we did not leave camp until near 10 O clock   we traveled about 10 miles and made a dry camp where there was some little grass and to night I am O so lonely   2 weeks ago to night I watched all night long with my sick darling Katie   how sad I am without her

OCTOBER 9, 1867   This morning we were traveling some time before sun up   we traveled about 8 miles and came to a ranch where the people were just moving   there was a good well of water   we got breakfast and were soon moving slowly on   we soon came in sight of the Carson [river]   O how fine the green cotton wood trees looked in the distance but to me there was nothing joyful in the sight of them for I had not my Katie with me to admire them   2 weeks ago this evening her little spirit left us and only is the cold form of clay   O how long and weary these 2 weeks have been to me   there has years of my life offered to me much shorter than these 2 weeks   O that I may have more grace given to me in this my time of distress   I can but ask again why was my darling taken O why was she not spared for me but I ought not to murmur   yet I can not help it   O for more of a spirit of submission.

OCTOBER 10, 1867   We left camp at about 8 O clock   I started out before the teams a little and walked 2 or 3 miles to the bridge of the Carson river and as I walked I looked and thought . . . and as I looked at the beautiful cotton wood trees and seen the leaves some of them beginning to turn yellow and fall off how much I thought these trees resembled human nature   here were the large old trees   the middle sized ones   those of only a few years groth   then the tiny ones that

[22]The Duncans followed the stage road across Four Mile Flat, over Simpson Pass, and along the southern shore of Carson Lake. Along this route, it is just twenty-two miles to the site of the Carson Sink station. See ch. 3, n44 and 45. (See map 8.)

only sprang up a few month ago all fading and dieing how much like nature this is yes the old the youths the children the infants all fade and age like those trees how great a change a few days or even a few hours make in us as well as the trees but in the spring these trees will again put forth there beautiful foliage in all its splendor and so after our poor boddies have laid in the silent tomb we if having been good and faithful we to will arise and put on the beautiful robe of righteousness and enter heaven not fade then we will not have to bid adieu to loved ones or grieve after dear ones and see them left in the cold silent grave so bless god there will be no sorrow there neither will there be any crying or parting of friends but all will be joy and happiness We have traveled about 18 miles and are now in camp in a beautiful place near the river 7 miles from Dayton[23] we passed a herd of camels and dromedarys to day[24] they were feeding on the river bank I have had the most peculiar feeling to day I ever had in my life O so well but I had no Katie to enjoy these good things with me so there was no enjoyment for me as I feel the loss of my darling each and every day how much I have thought of my darling Katie it does seem to me that I must have her back O how can I live without her what is life to me nothing but to drag out a miserable existence I can never enjoy any thing my life to me is cheerless O so dark and desolate the future looks to me and were it not for my little youngsters I wold pray to be taken from this so miserable unhappy world

October 11, 1867 We were up very early this morning had breakfast and were traveling by sun up we were soon in Dayton this is a real pretty little mining town we stoped in front of a large hotel the land lord came out and talked with us a while and soon there was a fruit wagon came along with grapes and apples just from California Mr Duncan was going to by some but the land lord told him to stand back that he wanted to get some first and he bought about a half bushel of splendid apples and 12 or 15 lbs of the finest grapes I most ever saw truly this was kindness but Oh what a cloud of sad feelings this brought these were just what my Katie loved

[23]There is too little information in Elizabeth's diary for us to determine the route they took between the Carson Sink station and this campsite. See ch. 3, n46.

[24]Five other diaries in this collection mention seeing camels. See ch. 14, n21.

October 12, 1867 We left Carson City this morning at 8 O clock Carson is a pretty place with some 6 or 7 thousand inhabitants there is a mint being built there now We camped at one of the prettyest places near the river I feel homesick to night we are now in camp at a tavern called . . .[25] last night I dreamed again of my darling Katie O why do I think of giving her up why was she taken from me when she was so necessary to my happiness.

[25]Duncan does not tell us which route they took from Carson City, but many, if not most, travelers were using the route up the Kings Canyon grade, at this time. If they did take this route, they left the Central Overland Trail when they left the city. (See map 9.)

CHAPTER 26

William Gaines Pennebaker

1868

William Pennebaker, his wife, Louisa, and their five children were part of a twenty-four-member wagon train that left Peoria, Iowa, on April 20, 1868. They arrived in Salt Lake City on June 23.

The editor found the Pennebaker diary on the Pennebaker Family Genealogy website, which was established by Paul E. Pennebaker, a direct descendent of William Pennebaker. While the editor was working on this book, Paul Pennebaker became incapacitated, and permission to publish the diary was granted by his spouse, Sue M. Pennebaker.

June 23, 1868 Started up the summit and crossed it, thence down the canyon 20 miles near the city and camped in the city emigrant corral[1] in Salt Lake City.

June 24, 1868 Lay in city, raining and cool. Funeral service in memory of Mr. Kimball. Health good. Received a letter from John Barnett, John, H. P. & S. Jenison.

June 25, 1868 Still in the city. Raining some. Nothing special. Bought 18 bushels of barley at $2.75. quite sick.

[1]This was probably Emigrant Square. See ch. 14, n1.

JUNE 26, 1868 Started out of the city. Came 21 miles and camped near the Great Salt Lake. Very salty. Quite warm.

JUNE 27, 1868 Passed a little town near the foot of the mountain.[2] Came 12 miles to a mill,[3] six miles to Stockton. Camped three miles below a little lake.[4]

JUNE 28, 1868 Left camp at 7:30 came three miles and crossed a little creek. then to water again 16 miles, 19 miles in all. Camped for noon Rush Valley,[5] afternoon came five miles and camped,[6] went 1 ½ miles for water. Grass good and grasshoppers very bad. 24 miles.

JUNE 29, 1868 Came over the summit to Lookout Station,[7] thence to a creek 10 miles, camped for noon.[8] G. F. very sick with fever. Very warm, good grass. 14 miles.

JUNE 30, 1868 Lay in camp preparing for the desert. G. F. some better. Pleasant day. Mr. Robinson and Butler gone on.

JULY 1, 1868 Started early to cross the desert. Came to Simpson Springs 7 miles,[9] then to Riverbed Station 10 miles and nooned. Started at 4p.m. and came to Black Rock Station 12 miles, then to Dugway 14 miles, then to Fish Spring[10] 10 miles where we arrived at 5 A.M. the second, 53 miles.

JULY 2, 1868 Lay in camp and rested our stock until 2 P.M. and started for Willow Creek[11] where we arrived at 1a.m. the 3rd, having

---

[2]Probably E. T. City. See ch. 9, n4. (See map 2.)

[3]This mill was on Settlement Creek, which at that time flowed through the southern edge of Tooele. See ch. 9, n6.

[4]The lake was Rush Lake, near the town of Stockton. Their camp would have been somewhere near the junction of State Roads 36 and 73.

[5]On Faust Creek, near the old Faust Pony Express and stage station. See ch. 8, n2.

[6]This camp was on the sagebrush flats about halfway between Faust Station and the eastern base of Lookout Pass. (See map 3.)

[7]Point Lookout. See ch. 3, n8.

[8]Government Creek. Although Pennebaker said they had camped for noon, they ended up staying that night and the next.

[9]Pennebaker's party was one of the very few groups after 1862 that went directly to Simpson Springs instead of turning off the stage route and going to Government Spring and Indian Spring. See ch. 7, n6. Pennebaker got his stations out of sequence. He would have passed Dugway Station before reaching Black Rock Station.

[10]See ch. 6, n4.

[11]Pennebaker called this area Willow Creek, but the correct name was Willow Springs. See ch. 7, n9. (See map 4.)

crossed the desert and rested in camp until 2 P.M. Then came four miles west of Canyon Station and camped 39 miles from Fish Spring.[12]

JULY 4, 1868 Came to Deep Creek[13] 10 miles, and lay over to rest our stock.

JULY 5, 1868 Lay in camp until 2 P.M. and came six miles further up and camped for the night.[14]

JULY 6, 1868 marched early. Good roads. Came to Antelope Station[15] 24 miles. There we took the old road, the cutoff. Rough and hilly road but eight miles nearer. Camped two miles west of station.[16]

JULY 7, 1868 Came through the canyon and camped for noon 12 miles in Spring Valley.[17] Pleasant day, all well but mother. Thence over the summit to Lookout Station to camp.[18] 24 miles in all.

JULY 8, 1868 Left camp at one-half past six and crossed the valley and came up Egan Canyon for noon, 16 miles. Rough mountains on either side. Gold and silver mine. Left the canyon at 3 P.M. and came up on the mountain six miles and made a dry camp.[19] Mother and Jane both unwell. 22 miles.

JULY 9, 1868 Left camp at 6 A.M. and came down the mountain 15 miles to a station and watered.[20] Then to a spring 2 ½ miles. Paid $1.40 for water for the train. Then to camp six miles.[21] Jane quite sick, but mother better.

---

[12]The camp was in the pass between the Deep Creek Range and the Ochre Hills.

[13]See ch. 7, n11.

[14]This would have put them near the Eight-Mile stage station.

[15]This station was at Antelope Spring. See ch. 7, n13.

[16]After leaving Antelope Spring, the party began to follow the Rock Springs Pass route, but they only went as far as the mouth of the canyon before stopping for the night.

[17]After passing Rock Springs, they dropped into Spring Valley and stopped for noon near the mouth of Stage Canyon. See ch. 8, n10.

[18]Pennebaker seems to have been confused about the name of this station. It was the Schell Creek station, and the editor is unaware of anyone else ever using the name "Lookout" for this place.

[19]This camp was in the Cherry Creek Mountains, about a half-mile east of where the stage road crossed the summit.

[20]Pennebaker's mileage figures are a little low this day, but the station was probably Mountain Spring station. The Mountain Spring Pony Express station had been located at the mouth of Murry Canyon about two and a half miles to the east, but a stage station was still in operation at the spring.

[21]This camp was probably somewhere near Station Spring in Ruby Valley, but it seems strange that Pennebaker did not comment about the small community that had built up around Fort Ruby. See ch. 6, n8.

JULY 10, 1868 Left the spring and came to a spring on Silver mountain at noon, then over the summit to a valley and Jacob's Wells station to camp. Sick better.

JULY 11, 1868 Left camp at 8 A.M. James Pecks left us at Jacobs Wells and took the Newark road for White Pines district. We crossed Diamond mountain,[22] nooned at Diamond Spring. Quite sick myself. Came to Sulphur Springs 12 miles to camp. 24 miles. Our train all alone. Froze hard last night.

JULY 12, 1868 Came 10 miles to water, 12 to grass and nooned. Then three miles to Roberts Creek to water, then 13 to Grubbs Wells at night. 28 miles. Pleasant. Crossed a nice valley and good roads.

JULY 13, 1868 Left the station at one-half past six for Dry Creek Station where we arrived at 12, 16 miles, good roads and pleasant day over a nice valley. Snow in sight all the time. All well. Camped until morning. Not very good grass.

JULY 14, 1868 Left Dry Creek and passed over the summit and around Cape Horn to the station, thence to Blackbird Canyon and up it seven miles, all in 26 miles.[23]

JULY 15, 1868 Came into Austin[24] four miles, where we visited the Manhattan Quartz Mill and got specimens of silver in the ore. Bought our goods and started for Dayton, 180 miles. Camped on Rees River[25] six miles from town. Warm day, health good.

JULY 16, 1868 Left Rees River in due season and came to station, thence to Big Springs 25 miles and camped.[26] Good water and grass. Lost one horse by guard going to sleep. Indian.

---

[22]They crossed the Diamond Mountains by way of Overland Pass. See ch. 8, n14.

[23]From Dry Creek, the Pennebaker party headed south following the stage road. (See map 6.) After passing the Cape Horn stage station, they crossed Big Smoky Valley and entered Blackbird Canyon, essentially following the route of present-day U.S. 50. The camp would appear to have been just west of Bob Scott Summit, near the turn-off to Grass Valley. From Cape Horn west, this was a new route that the Overland Stage company had begun using in 1865 (Townley, *The Overland Stage*, 251).

[24]See ch. 12, n21.

[25]See ch. 3, n38.

[26]From the Reese River near Jacobsville, Pennebaker headed west and then began to bear north toward Mount Airy and New Pass. This route had been open since 1862 but was used by only one other of our diarists; Martha Logan, who traveled it in September 1864. The editor has been unable to find a "Big Springs" in this area; perhaps it is present-day New Pass Spring. See ch. 21, n27. (See map 7.)

July 17, 1858 Left Big Spring at 9 A.M. Found our horse. Came down New Pass to Tolhouse three miles, then to Smith Creek Station,[27] then to Cool [Cold] Springs and camped on a nice mountain stream. Went three miles to grass, and very poor. 26 miles.

July 18, 1868 left camp at seven for Middle Gate[28] eight miles then West Gate four miles and nooned. Took in water to cross the desert of 34 miles. Came 11 miles and camped at the Englishman's.[29] Paid $2 per barrel for water for our teams.

July 19, 1868 Bought another barrel of water and left camp for Sand Springs 11 miles.[30] Arrived at 11 A.M., watered our stock and came five miles and fed. Then to Salt Wells[31] and camped. Dreadful dusty and sandy. Made 23 miles in good season. Water brackish, grass two miles off, health good.

July 20, 1868 Left Salt Wells and came to bridge on arm of Carson River.[32] Paid $2.50 toll, then across to the main river and nooned at Mr. Toggs. Then to Hills across Old river where we paid $2.50 toll.[33] Camped. Made 23 miles.

July 21, 1869 Left camp for Ragtown four miles, then to Cottonwood six miles, where we paid $4.50 toll. Then to Log Cabin and to the lake five miles west and camped.[34] 23 miles.

July 22, 1868 Wednesday, left camp at 7 A.M. and came to Davis Station on the desert, then to Stockton Station, then to the next

---

[27]Pennebaker was mistaken here. Smith Creek Station was on the old road, about fourteen miles to the southeast. This station was the second Edwards Creek Station, which was located where Edwards Creek crosses present-day U.S. 50.

[28]See ch. 3, n42.

[29]This would have put Pennebaker near the center of Fairview Valley at a place that became known as Frenchman's in the early 1900s. This is the only reference to "the Englishman's" of which the editor is aware. See ch. 9, n35.

[30]See ch. 3, n43.

[31]Today, a place called Salt Wells can be found on U.S. 50, about twelve miles southeast of Fallon. Whether this is the same place as Pennebaker's Salt Wells is uncertain, but it would be in the same general area. (See map 8.)

[32]Because Pennebaker went past Salt Wells, it is quite clear that he was following Simpson's outbound route. His "arm of Carson River" must have been the outlet of Carson Lake.

[33]The location of this bridge is unknown, but Pennebaker's next entry tells us that the camp was four miles east of Ragtown.

[34]Except that they were on or near the Carson River, the locations of Cottonwood and Log Cabin are unknown to the editor.

station, in all 14 miles, and nooned. Then to the next station seven miles, then to Carson River three miles and camped near Dayton. The desert 26 miles long. 27 miles.[35]

JULY 23, 1868 Came to Dayton eight miles, no mail. Bought some barley and beef and came four miles for noon. Quite warm. Came on near Carson City and camped at a stone house and big spring. Quite warm night. Health good 12 miles to Carson.

JULY 24, 1868 Came to Carson and wrote a letter to J. H. Peck. Very nice town, Lively place. Came to Genoa 14 miles, bought barley. This is in Carson Valley, a nice valley. Then came six miles and camped.[36]

---

[35]It appears that Pennebaker followed the route that crossed the Twenty-Six Mile Desert. (See map 9.) However, he got the sequence wrong when he said he went through Dayton and then crossed the desert; the Twenty-Six Mile Desert lies to the east of Dayton, and he would have had to cross it first.

[36]When Pennebaker's party reached Genoa, they had reached the western end of the Central Overland Trail. He was one of only five of our diarists to travel the entire route from Salt Lake City to Genoa.

CHAPTER 27

Mary Hall Jatta

1868

MARY HALL was seventeen years old when her family left Nebraska City and began their trip to California. Mary faithfully kept a diary during the westward journey, but she never did indicate the year during which the trip took place. Mary's granddaughter, Mary Willett, believed that the year was 1865 or 1866, but the editor doubts this could be correct. In the portion of her diary not included here, Mary wrote about seeing railroad tracks in Echo Canyon. This means that the earliest she could have been there was 1868, the year the Union Pacific Railroad laid tracks through this area. Sometime after arriving in California, Mary was married to Joseph Jatta. The Halls began their journey on May 28 and reached Salt Lake City on July 26.

A copy of a transcribed version of Jatta's diary was obtained from the Bancroft Library, which also granted permission to publish it (BANC MSS C-F 138 Mary Hall Jatta journal).

JULY 26, 1868 Traveled all day through Parleys Park Canon reached Salt Lake City about 6 Oclock. The dust has been almost suffocating all day and the City beats anything I ever saw camped in a Corral[1]

[1]This "corral" was probably Emigrant Square. See ch. 14, n1.

July 27, 1868 Visited the city most all day went to the Tabernical it is a Magnificent building It has an organ that is sixty feet high and has two thousand pipes The city is splendidly situated there is a little stream of water running through every street and thickly shaded with large trees Ate Watermelons Apples and Apricots In the evening went to the theatre

July 28, 1868 In the afternoon went up to the Temple on the Dome had a fine view of the city and its surroundings The Turnpile [temple] has a very high wall around it and but one entrance the same around Brigham Young's residence which gives it the appearance of a prison walled in

July 29, 1868 About ten Oclock started out of the city stoped fourteen miles from there for dinner by a salt spring[2] traveled six miles[3]

July 30, 1868 We was here most all day Towards night Captains folks came up and camped with us The boy's went swimming, the Lake water is so salt that a person can not sink they can walk Lie on their backs and fold the arms or on their face and not sink the water is as clear as crystal and as salt as the strongest brine ever was

July 31, 1868 Pa came back The road was quite rough most places We passed through a small town called Toolele a mormon town but quite a pretty place[4] it rained quite hard while there Camped for the night near Stockton a small town

August 1, 1868 Traveled all the forenoon camped for dinner in the Sage Brush went six miles in the afternoon and camped for the night on a small stream in Rush Valley[5] got off the road once it rained very hard for a few minutes

August 2, 1868 Traveled all day come over a very high

---

[2]When the Hall family left Salt Lake City, they traveled in a slightly southwest direction toward the Great Salt Lake. After traveling fourteen miles, they would have reached some springs at the northern tip of the Oquirrh Mountains. An immense pile of mine waste now covers this area. (See map 2.)

[3]Their camp for the night was near the lake's southeastern shore.

[4]See ch. 9, n6.

[5]The stream on which they camped was Faust Creek. They were not far from the Faust stage station. See ch. 8, n2.

hill[6] camped for dinner this side of the sumit at government springs[7] for the night on a small stream nine miles from the desert

AUGUST 3, 1868 Went to Simpsons Springs nine miles[8]

AUGUST 4, 1868 Started about three Oclock went up in the mountains to Indian Springs[9] found excellent water and feed Camped there untill

AUGUST 5, 1868 Four Oclock in the afternoon started across the desert crossed a very high mountain about midnight[10]

AUGUST 6, 1868 reached the opposite side at One Traveled untill at ten Oclock we then came to a great spring called Fish Spring[11] the water salt

AUGUST 7, 1868 Started at three Oclock in the morning traveled over a deserted Country twenty five miles to Willow Springs Valley[12] the water excellent and we took a good rest after a fatiguing two days travel

AUGUST 8, 1868 Traveled up the mountain all forenoon and through a Canon and out into Deep Creek Valley[13] Crossed the Creek about four Oclock quite a little town here went about four miles farther to Thousand Spring Valley and stoped for the night.[14]

AUGUST 9, 1868 Passed an old Station soon after starting[15] had a splendid road over a level country to antelope Springs[16] another Stage

---

6Lookout Pass. (See map 3.)

7See ch. 12, n5.

8According to Jatta, the Hall family left Government Spring and traveled to Simpson Springs. This was unusual. All of the other diarists who wrote about stopping at Government Spring went from there to Indian Spring, crossing the Simpson Mountains to do so. It appears that when the Hall family left Government Spring, they turned back north, getting back onto the stage road and following it around the north end of the mountain to Simpson Springs. See ch. 7, n6.

9The Halls followed the pre-1862 route from Simpson Springs to Indian Spring. See ch. 8, n30.

10Jatta's "high mountain" was Dugway Pass.

11See ch. 6, n4.

12See ch. 7, n9.

13See ch. 7, n11.

14Traveling four miles beyond the settlement would have put them on West Deep Creek, about a mile and a half east of the Utah-Nevada border. The editor is not aware of anyone else who used the name "Thousand Spring Valley" for this area. (See map 4.)

15Mary's "old Station" may have been Spring Station, which had been replaced by Eight-Mile Station, and which was located a mile or two farther to the southwest.

16See ch. 7, n13.

Station where we arrived at four oclock then up the mountain eight miles to the sumit it is called the "Devils cut off"[17] it is the steepest and roughest then went down the mountain about 3 miles and camped for the night about nine Oclock hungry and tired by a splendid spring[18]

AUGUST 10, 1868 Traveled down the mountain to Spring Valley then up through the mountains then down again and stoped for the night on Shell Creek a beautiful stream of water[19]

AUGUST 11, 1868 Came down the mountain into Step Toe Valley crossed into Egan Canon about two miles and stoped for the day here it is quite a mining town are building a large Quartz Mill here

AUGUST 12, 1868 Started from Egan at four Oclock traveled untill seven then stoped to let the horses feed and get our breakfast started on at nine went over the sumit down a long hill into Britts [Butte] Valley camped near Buttes Spring[20] for dinner then up another mountain to Mountain Spring late in the evening[21] camped for the night Distance 30 miles.

AUGUST 13, 1868 Went down to the mountain into Ruby Valley[22] crossed the Valley camped for the day about noon near a Fort by a nice spring Did up the washing

AUGUST 14, 1868 Started about 8 Oclock through Hastings Pass down into the Valley to Jacobs Well then to the mountains again crossed Diamond Hill[23] rough and rugged then down through a canon an old Stage Station and stoped for the night the place is called Diamond Spring[24]

---

[17]This was Rock Springs Pass. Although the name "devils cut off" was not used in any other diaries that the editor has seen, it is a good description of the route over Rock Springs Pass. See ch. 8, n10.

[18]Rock Springs, which is on the western slope of the Antelope Mountains.

[19]The camp was near the Schell Creek Station, later known as Fort Schellbourne and is now Schellbourne Ranch.

[20]Because Jatta mentioned the spring, we can be certain that this camp was near Pony Spring rather than either of the other two Butte Stations. See ch. 8, n12. (See map 5.)

[21]Mountain Spring is in the Maverick Springs Mountains.

[22]See ch. 6, n8.

[23]Jatta's Diamond Hill became known as Overland Pass, but it should not be confused with the Overland Pass at the foot of the Ruby Mountains. See ch. 8, n14.

[24]Most emigrants took two days to travel between Ruby Valley and Diamond Springs, which included the steepest mile of trail on the entire Central Overland route. The Halls made it in one day.

August 15, 1868 Crossed the valley 10 miles then up and down hills all day and finally came to another Station near a splendid well of water[25]

August 16, 1868 stayed over a day to rest the train.

August 17, 1868 Started at noon at Grubs Well's 16 miles and stoped for the night in Smokey Canon.[26]

August 18, 1868 Traveled 25 miles over a barren country road very rough part of the way[27] stoped in the mountains for the night[28]

August 19, 1868 Reached Austin[29] about 10 Oclock traveled 8 miles to the Silver Age House Austin is a very hilly place and a mining town

August 20, 1868 Missed the road went to a Ranch stoped for the day to let the horses rest Good water[30]

August 21, 1868 Went through the meadow for hay found the road crossed a mountain then a valley camped at the foot of canon for the night Distance 28 miles[31]

August 22, 1868 Traveled through the canon nearly all day stoped at noon by a beautiful little Brook[32] came out of the canon about five passed through East Gate[33] then out to White Rock and stoped for the night[34]

August 23, 1868 Passed through Middle Gate[35] then West Gate came to a dessert[36] crossed came over a mountain down

---

[25]On this day, they crossed Diamond Valley, skirted the southern base of Mount Hope, crossed Roberts Creek, and made camp near the Grubb's Well stage station.

[26]This camp was in Dry Creek Canyon. The name "Smokey Canyon" was not used by any of the other Central Overland Trail diarists. It would appear that Jatta got this area confused with Big Smoky Valley, which was on the far side of the Simpson Park Mountains. (See map 6.)

[27]The comment about the road being very rough for part of the way probably indicates that they followed the Eagle Butte route. See ch. 8, n15.

[28]It would appear that they camped somewhere near Emigrant Pass in the Toiyabe Mountains, possibly near present-day Thorpe Spring.

[29]See ch. 12, n21.

[30]They may have been camped somewhere along the Reese River. See ch. 3, n38.

[31]The mountain was Shoshone Mountain, which they would have crossed via Smith Creek Summit. The camp was near the mouth of Smith Creek Canyon.

[32]The brook was Edwards Creek. See ch. 3, n40.

[33]Instead of following the stage road directly to Middlegate, Jatta's party headed almost due south from Cold Springs to Eastgate. See ch. 16, n38.

[34]There is a White Rock Spring about three and a half miles west of Eastgate.

[35]See ch. 3, n42.

[36]See ch. 9, n35.

to Sand Well's[37] the road very dusty with nothing but Alkali and Sage Brush

AUGUST 24, 1868 Crossed Desert all day came to Carson River about 4 Oclock a Ranch and Dairy Distance 25 miles[38]

AUGUST 25, 1868 Traveled all day over sandy road camped at Log Cabin on Carson River[39]

AUGUST 26, 1868 From Log Cabin [to] Deep Well it is 295 feet deep the water is drawn by a horse from there to Gates Ranch.[40]

AUGUST 27, 1868 From Gates we went to Carson City passed through got to Carson afternoon 22 miles

AUGUST 28, 1868 Started out of Carson about noon for Lake Bigler[41]

---

[37]They were at Sand Springs. See ch. 3, n43. (See map 8.)

[38]The Halls' route between Sand Springs and the Carson River is uncertain, but it appears that they probably followed Simpson's outbound trail to the northern end of Carson Lake, and then came to the Carson River about three miles southwest of the center of Fallon. See ch. 3, n44 and 46.

[39]The Hall family apparently spent the day following the Carson River. (See map 9.)

[40]In her next entry, Jatta seems to indicate that it was twenty-two miles from Gates Ranch to Carson City. If this is correct, it places Gates Ranch on the Carson River, about eight miles west of Fort Churchill.

[41]The Halls left the Central Overland Trail at Carson City and took the Kings Canyon Road, heading west into the Sierra Nevada. What she called "Lake Bigler" is now known as Lake Tahoe.

Bibliography

Barton, H. D. "Diary of H. D. Barton 1865." Unpublished diary transcription, California State Library, Sacramento.

Bender, Flora Isabelle. "Notes by the Way: Memoranda of a Journey Across the Plains." *Nevada Historical Society Quarterly* 1, no. 4 (July 1958): 145–173.

Brown, Delia Thompson. "The Diary of Delia Thompson Brown." Unpublished diary transcript, Nevada Historical Society, Reno.

Bushnell, George Edwin. "Trip Across the Plains in 1864." Unpublished diary transcript, Merrill J. Mattes Research Library, National Frontier Trails Museum, Independence, Mo.

Carleton, Phebe Abbot. "Westward Bound by Wagon Train, 1864." Unpublished diary transcript, Washington State Historical Society, Tacoma.

Colwell, Dennis Hand. "Our Overland Trip to California." *Newsletter of the Columbia Gorge Genealogical Society*. July and October 2005.

Colwell, James McNabb. "Journal: A Trip across the United States and Territories by Wagon Train in 1865." Unpublished diary transcript, Alene M. Thille, The Dalles, Ore.

Duncan, Elizabeth "Bettie." "This Far Off Land: The Overland Diary of Elizabeth 'Bettie' Duncan, June–October 1867." Unpublished diary, Kenneth Spencer Research Library, Kansas Collection, University of Kansas, Lawrence.

Egan, Ferol. *Frémont: Explorer for a Restless Nation*. Reno: University of Nevada Press, 1985.

Egan, Howard R. *Pioneering the West*. Salt Lake City: Skelton Publishing Company, 1917.

Epperson, Lucretia. "A Journal of our Trip." In *History of Colusa County, California*. San Francisco: 1880, edited by Will S. Green, 122–132. Reprinted in

Covered Wagon Women: Diaries and Letters from the Western Trails, 1840–1860, edited by Kenneth W. Holmes. Lincoln: University of Nebraska Press, 1999. Vol. 8, 165–198.

Fackler, John G. "Brief Notes of Travels across the Plains to California in 1864." Unpublished diary, Missouri Historical Society, St. Louis.

Fryberger, Wilson. "To California by Covered Wagon." Unpublished diary and diary transcription, Iowa State Historical Society, Iowa City.

Gilbert, Bil. *Westering Man: The Life of Joseph Walker.* Norman: University of Oklahoma Press, 1985.

Greeley, Horace. *An Overland Journey from New York to San Francisco in the Summer of 1859.* Lincoln: University of Nebraska Press, 1999.

Harter, George. *Crossing the Plains: An Account of the George Harter Family's Trip from Cass County, Michigan, to Marysville, California in 1864.* Sacramento, Calif.: Doris Harter Chase, 1957.

Harter, Robert D. *Wagon Tracks: George Harter's 1864 Journey to California.* Tucson: Patrice Press, 2003.

Jatta, Mary Hall. "Journal of a Trip across the Plains." Unpublished diary transcription, Bancroft Library, Berkeley, Calif.

Jones, Darrell E., and W. Randall Dixon. "'It Was Very Warm and Smelt Very Bad': Warm Springs and the First Bath House in Salt Lake City." *Utah Historical Quarterly* 76 (3): 212.

Karchner, Mary. Unpublished diary transcription, California State Library, Sacramento.

Lewis, B. P. Unpublished diary, California State Library, Sacramento.

Logan, Martha. "Diary of Miss Martha Logan Written on Her Trip to California by Wagon Train 1864." Unpublished diary transcription. University of Missouri–Columbia, Western Historical Manuscript Collection.

Mathews, Edward James. *Crossing the Plains: Adventures of Edward James Mathews in '59.* Privately printed booklet. Nevada Historical Society, Reno.

Mattes, Merrill J. *Overland Journal* 10, no. 4 (1992).

Moorman, Donald R., and Gene A. Sessions. *Camp Floyd and the Mormons.* Salt Lake City: University of Utah Press, 1992.

Morgan, Dale L. *Jedediah Smith and the Opening of the West.* Lincoln: University of Nebraska Press, 1953.

———. *Overland in 1846: Diaries and Letters of the California-Oregon Trail.* Lincoln: University of Nebraska Press, 1993.

Nunis, Doyce B., Jr. *The Bidwell-Bartleson Party: 1841 California Emigrant Adventure.* Santa Cruz, Calif.: Western Tanager Press, 1991.

Pennebaker, William Gaines. "William Gaines Pennebaker's 1868 Diary." Unpublished diary transcription. Posted by Paul and Sue Pennebaker on

Pennebaker Family Genealogy website (http://webpages.charter.net/pepbaker/diry1868.htm). Olathe, Kans.

Porter, Lavina Honeyman. *Westward Journeys: Memoirs of Jesse A. Applegate and Lavina Honeyman Porter Who Traveled the Overland Trail.* Chicago: Lakeside Press, 1989.

Ringo, Mary. *The Journal of Mrs. Mary Ringo.* Santa Ana, Calif.: Frank Myrle Cushing, 1956. Reprinted in *Covered Wagon Women, Diaries and Letters from the Western Trails, 1840–1860*, edited by Kenneth W. Holmes. Lincoln: University of Nebraska Press, 1999. Vol. 8, 199–231.

Rogers, Fred B. *Soldiers of the Overland.* San Francisco: Grabhorn Press, 1938.

Scott, Charles A. Unpublished diary on microfilm, Utah Historical Society, Salt Lake City.

Scott, Lumin A. Unpublished diary transcription, Cappy and Diane Cook, Incline Village, Nev.

Simpson, James H. *Wagon Road Routes in Utah Territory.* Senate Executive Document No. 40, 35th Congress, 2nd Session, 1859.

———. *Report of Explorations across the Great Basin in 1859.* Reno: University of Nevada Press, 1983.

Smith, Jedediah. *The Southwest Expedition of Jedediah Smith: His Personal Account of the Journey to California, 1826–1827.* Edited and with an introduction by George R. Brooks. Lincoln: University of Nebraska Press, 1989.

Stott, Clifford L. *Search for Sanctuary: Brigham Young and the White Mountain Expedition.* Salt Lake City: University of Utah Press, 1984.

Townley, John M. *The Overland Stage A History and Guidebook.* Reno: Great Basin Studies Center, 1994.

———. *The Pony Express Guidebook.* Reno: Great Basin Studies Center.

———. "Stalking Horse for the Pony Express The Chorpenning Mail Contracts Between California and Utah, 1851-1860." *Arizona and the West* (1982): 229–252.

Tuttle, Charles M. "California Diary of Charles M. Tuttle 1859." *The Wisconsin Magazine of History* 15 (1931–1932): 69–85, 219–233.

Twain, Mark. *Roughing It.* New York: Simon & Schuster, 2003.

Varley, James F. *Brigham and the Brigadier: General Patrick Connor and His California Volunteers in Utah and Along the Overland Trail.* Tucson: Westernlore Press, 1989.

Warner, Mary. *Diary of Her Journey West.* Unpublished diary transcription, California State Library, Sacramento.

Young, Albert Jefferson. Unpublished diary, Bancroft Library, Berkeley, Calif.

Index